MY WALK WITH CHRIST JESUS

An Autobiography By
Obie Sailors III

Order this book online at www.trafford.com
or email orders@trafford.com

Most Trafford titles are also available at major online book retailers.

Printed in the United States of America.

ISBN: 978-1-4269-3748-4 (sc)
ISBN: 978-1-4269-3749-1 (e)

*Our mission is to efficiently provide the world's finest, most comprehensive
book publishing service, enabling every author to experience success.
To find out how to publish your book, your way, and have it available
worldwide, visit us online at www.trafford.com*

Trafford rev. 09/22/2010

 www.trafford.com

North America & international
toll-free: 1 888 232 4444 (USA & Canada)
phone: 250 383 6864 • fax: 812 355 4082

Acknowledgements:

I give thanks to God my Father, the Lord Jesus Christ, and The Sweet Holy Spirit who is the head of my life, my Master, my Savior, and my Provider.

I would like to recognize my three boys Jonathan, Daniel, and David for being the inspiration of my life. Truly when I wanted to give up I thought about them, and my commitment to give them a better life.

I would like to acknowledge my mother Ms. Jewell Sailors whom I love very much although I don't see or visit her as much as I should.

To a friend Dr. Patricia Mason, who helped me to understand the gifts the Lord God had given to me when I was searching for answers and guidance.

To a friend and daughter Sonya Thornton who stayed with the ministry when everyone else deserted me, do to my inability to be the Pastor I should have been. To my family, friends and acquaintances to all those who have been a part of my life, through my good times, and bad times.

May the Lord God bless all of you.

Dedication:

I dedicate this book to the remembrance of my Dad

Obie sailors Jr. Who departed this life in 1972 at the age of forty two years old. Also to my Granddaddy who left this life at the age of fifty two years old. To my Grand Mother Mary Carter young who passed at the age of 82.

To my sister Gale who passed at the age of 62.

I miss all of you.

Introduction:

Sunday morning August 31, 2003.

This is the last day of the month in which I took my first breath on this earth. I was born August 8, 1946, to Obie & Jewell Sailors. I am the second of three children, the only boy.

My child hood was an enjoyable one, not different from most children who came up during my area. But maybe there were some differences, we will see as we continue on through this story.

The events of this story are true; this is not fiction, but non fiction. I actually lived these events. Some of the things that happened to me may seem as though they came from a science fiction movie, but they really happened to me. I know that I am not the only one on the face of the earth who has lived through these experiences. Maybe my writing this book will help others to come forward and share their stories. I believe what one person goes through, there are many more with the same story, and many more to come. I always say "some one has to suffer so others can be saved. Some one has to have a testimony about how the Lord God brought them through, to let others know they can make it, if they just hold on and keep the faith for the Lord God is faithful and true, and it is He who watches over you. Also some one had to sin so we would know the love and forgiving mercy of the Lord Jesus". The Bible teaches us that the Lord Jesus was the only one who came into this world without sin or from the act of sin. Don't misunderstand what I am saying when I say from the act of sin. The Lord God has established sex for reproduction, and what God has ordained is good. But we know that man has allowed sin to come into those things which God has ordained as good, Misusing that which is pure for the lust of the flesh for man's on pleasure.

My story is one of the calls. From salvation, to sin, and back to salvation. From my child hood (the call to salvation). Through sin (a walk with death, sin). The later years (Salvation) the call being rejected, and later being for filed. There are some people who say "once saved always saved". These people don't really know the Bible, nor have they really studied the Bible. Salvation is a gift from the Lord God to mankind, but this gift can be forfeited through man's constant search for power, lust, and covetousness. Read and study the book of Hebrews for a better incite into this issue, and also study the plight of the Israelites in the Old Testament. God has given man the gift of salvation, but He has left it up to man to accept or reject the gift. To cherish the gift (hold on to the gift), or to throw the gift away. We all know that the Lord God is in control of all things, so this statement will only apply to some people. There are those whom the Lord God has chosen to be saved and they can not alter the gift of salvation. As a reference to this statement read 1kings 19: 18, 1 Corinthians 10:1-13.

Early Childhood (Salvation)

I still remember portions of my child hood, but like so many others there's a lot I have forgotten. Time has a way of doing that to us. We search our minds to remember, but once the hard drive has been erased we can not retrieve the information anymore. Some one may come up to you and say do you remember when you, or I know you, or you use to, and now matter how hard you try the gray matter want kick in, the event is a total blank.

I am very grateful to the Lord God for wiping away some of my memories (cleaning up my hard drive) because there are some things in my pass I don't want to remember anymore. Also there is a lot in my pass I don't want God to remember about me also. If I could stand before Him I would say just throw those pages away. But isn't that what His mercy is all about, forgiving us for our sins, and wiping those pages out of the book of life.

I want to take you back to when I first started having visitors weather wanted or unwanted. You know it would be nice if people would call and say, I'm coming over, or would you like to have company tonight. Wouldn't that be nice? To show some consideration for your feelings, and time. If they would just notify you first you would know how to prepare yourself for them. But there are those visitors who will show up weather you want them or not, and they don't care if you are prepared to receive them, nor the time of day or night they come. Some of those visitors don't want you to be prepared, because if you were they couldn't trick you or tempt you into doing there will. I had unwanted visitors when I was a child. I can't really recall how old I was when the events first started. But I remember them as though they happened yesterday. I do know I was in my last years of elementary school when I started this walk, and what a journey it has been.

We lived in an apartment on Boulevard place in Atlanta, Georgia. My cousin Minnie lived down stairs, and we lived upstairs. I had a room of my own, and my sisters (G&L) had their own room. My room was next to the back steps. I was a quiet child in my adolescent years, not one to get into trouble. People would say "I could be in a room and you would not know I was there". That's how quiet I was, but boy did that change later. I came up doing the times when it was stressed that children should be seen and not heard, and they would implement that stress on your bottom if you were out of place. My family members were Church going people. There was not a Sunday we were not in Church, and I mean all day long. My Granddad was a Minister, and the rest of my family except my Dad, sung in the choir. I thought we owned the Church where we attended. My Granddad was not the Pastor, but the Assistant Pastor, but you could not tell me that.

My Grandmother was not the First Lady. She was in or ran most of the activities of the Church. Everyone on my Mother's side of the family attended that Church. We would have large family dinners on holidays, and the Pastor and his wife would come. The Pastor would bless the food, and get the seat of honor at the dinner table. No one could eat until he was seated and his food was set before him. All of the children were feed in another room away from the adults. The part of the dinners I liked the most was when everyone had eaten my grandmother or uncle would play the piano and everyone would sing. We don't have those dinners anymore, most of the elders have gone on to be with the Lord; I hope. I remember on one occasion Ms. Mattie Murphy, who was the pianist for the quire was playing at my grandparents home, and I went to see what was going on. I loved to hear her play, and see her get happy, I walked in and these ladies were singing. I took a seat and boy I was mesmerized. Inez Mayfield was leading a song, and I fell in love for the first time in my life.

She was a very pretty lady, and her voice was like angels singing. That day made my life. There were others who came to my grandparents home that are well known today, but I remember Inez Mayfield most of all.

No I'm not going to tell you, or have you thing that my family was holier than though, as the expression goes. They had their Church time, and some of them had their partying time also. Sometimes on Saturday nights my cousin Minnie would throw a party and they would get down until Sunday morning. I remember a lot of those parties, because we lived up stairs. I had the opportunity to see both sides of the fence, and not only was I an observer, but I had the opportunity and misfortune to live on both sides of the fence to. (Someone has to sin to know and tell others about the love and forgiving mercy of the lord Jesus).

How many children came up seeing or experiencing both sides of the fence, only to grasp the wrong side in the later years of their lives? I don't care what anyone says, experience can be an awesome teacher. You can read about certain things in life, or hear someone tell you about their experiences, but unless you have been there, gone through what they went through, you can't really appreciate the story. When a child grows up, or is in the environment of certain activities those activities becomes a part of that child's life. Most of us can take a look at our child hood and see the pattern of our lives growing up. There is a pull on a child's life the moment that child begins to comprehend. Are we really a product of our environment? Or is our environment a product of our lives? Do we set the pace? Or do we follow the race? This I will leave up to you to answer. But before you answer take some time out to think about your roll in history. How did you affect the life or lives of others who crossed your path? Were you a leader, or were you a follower? It was this two sidedness in my child hood that I believe permeated some of the events that happened to me as I grew into an adult.

Let's go back to that upstairs room by the steps. One Halloween night I was suddenly waken by the ruffling sound of what seemed to me to be wings fluttering and these wings had an order of leadership about them. I was lying on my stomach and I could not move, nor could I talk. I felt this weight on my back which would not allow me to turn to the right or to the left. I could not even turn my head in any direction. I was completely paralyzed from my head to my feet, although I could sense what was going on in the room. There were these groups of angels there and they were in a confrontation for my life. It wasn't like they were fighting, but like a big debate to see which way I would go in life. The good angels were on my right and the bad ones were on the left, and there was an angel at the foot of the bed. They would flutter back and forth as if talking to each other. Sometimes the fluttering would get intense.

I wanted to cry out but I couldn't make a sound. This went on for sometime; I can not say how many minutes or hours, at that age you are not concerned about minutes or hours anyway. I just wanted them to go, or at lease let me go. They could have the room, bed, and the whole house if they wanted, I didn't care. It was dark in the room, and I was scared. I wanted my parents to come and rescue me. No I did not wet the bed or any thing else thank you. It seemed as though my whole body stopped functioning except my ears, and I was able to understand them. This went on until almost dawn and I understood from the sound that the good angels had won. When day brake came they all left, and I jumped from the bed and began to scream with all I had. I didn't stop until my parents came in rushing to see about me. They thought I was having a night mare and they told me to go back to bed. Who could go back to bed after that experience? Luckily it was daylight and I was not forced to enter my room. Maybe you may say I was having a reaction from all of the Halloween candy. But that will not hold water.

We did not observe Halloween when I was a child, so I didn't have any candy to cause me to have a reaction. I was in about the tenth or eleventh grade when we first started trick or treating. This event took place when I was about nine years old.

The next event took place about spring of the next year. I was all alone in our back yard playing basket ball on a goal I had made out of a vegetable basket. It was early one spring morning. While outside I heard this thunderous voice call my name (**Obie**); the voice was coming from the sky with an awesome bass power. I didn't wait to hear it again, or stop see who it was, or what the person wanted. My feet immediately took flight. I ran up the back steps into the house an immediately began to scream at the top of my voice. I wish today that I did not run from the voice, but stayed there and answered, was this the Lord calling me as He did Samuel? Although I hear His voice today, I long to hear Him as I did when I was a child. Please Lord may your thunderous voice reach out to me again. I can imagine the fear of the Israelites when they stood at the foot of Mount Sinai and the Lord spoke to them. Fear griped their very souls to hear His voice thundering from the mountain. What would you do if you were put in that situation? Imagine a small child alone in a yard hearing such a voice call from the sky. My parents came to see about me again. I can't remember what my parents said to me, but I do know they thought I was hallucinating. A few minutes later I looked out of my bedroom window and I saw my cousin hanging clothes out on the close line in the back yard. Seeing her out there relieved the fear I had of ever going into the back yard again. My family members were concerned about me; they thought I was having night mares.

They didn't know what to do with, or about me. They said I was upsetting my two sisters and they had to do something about me. They took me out of my room and gave the room to my older sister. They did not seek professional help, nor the Church, although I don't believe either one could enlightening them on my situation, the things I was going through. The church at that time was not as enlightened or should I say as knowledgeable as some Churches are today, and I do mean some.

And professionals in the medical field of psychiatry and psychology base their synopsis on Sigmund Freud's theories on the human mind.

The next event took place about the fall of that same year. I t was early in the morning and I was sleeping in the room with my younger sister. The wind was blowing very hard and woke me up from my sleep. There was something strange about the way the wind was blowing, it had a pattern as though someone or something was controlling the way the leaves were moving. I was frightened, I woke my younger sister up and we both looked out the window. It was about daylight but we didn't see anyone. We could hear the ruffling of the leaves, but to our surprise there were no leaves in sight. My sister cried out and ran into the room with my parents. They were angry with me, and said that I was scarring her now with my imagination. They said "what are we going to do with him now? We can't even let him sleep in the room with his sister for fear of him scarring her." They kept me in the room with my little sister until I started high school. Then we moved to the west side of town. They allowed me to have a room by myself after we moved, and the visitations stopped.

What would you do if your child was going through those events? How would you respond or handle the situation? How many parents have faced the same problems with their child not knowing what to do are where to turn for help? Psychiatrists can probably give you all kind of diagnosis for the problem, but are they right? We look to intellectualize things that confront us in life. We have an attendicy to look to society or our social up bringing to find answers to problems that we are confronted with. It is society which is based on the norm, which has its basis founded on the essential principal of our five senses. To see, to hear, to feel, to taste, to smell, if these qualities are not present then by societies standards it must not be real. But how about those things which are out of our norm? Those things which only a few of us are fortunate to experience. Are we having hallucinations? Are we out of or minds? Have our imaginations become a reality to us? Or are their some unknown forces at work in our mist that we are to scared to accept. Do you remember the story of Adam & Eve? They were the catalyst of our standards for society, how they reacted to their surroundings in a new world, how they dealt, or would deal with approaching issues. What they would do when confronted with the laws set down for them by God? Would they remain dormant in their own mental world? Or would they venture out to seek out the mysteries of the world they were placed in? God had given them a format for their society. He had laid out His laws and regulations for them. But because they were engrossed in their own mental effectuation (living according to their senses) they could not see the influences that were and did become a predominant force in their lives, and which are still at work in our lives today.

But there are those who do not rely on their five senses, but on the Lord Jesus Christ for direction and guidance. "Proverbs 3:5-6, 8:32-36, 16:3.

Man seeks the realization of that which he can see, feel, touch, hear, and smell. It is this realization which leads him to seek out the mysteries of outer space. Are we the only terrestrial beings inhabiting this universe? Are their other planets out there which are capable of sub staining life? Flying saucers, aliens, are they real? What is out there? These are questions man as been asking since the beginning of time. But the question I have is why doesn't he seek to know if he lives on this earth alone? Are their un seeable forces at work on this planet? Has our five senses caused us not to venture out beyond our own world of reality? Are we as misguided as Eve, seeking that which can only stimulate our sensibilities? Look at the progress man has made when he chose to venture out beyond the norm. Take for instance the horseless carriage (cars), flying machines (airplanes), walking on the moon (space travel), and then don't forget before theses events took place there was traveling across the ocean to a new land when society had deemed that the world was flat. It was this enthusiasm of a few which changed the world, when there were those who said "are you crazy you can't do that"! When man chooses to venture out in a positive way, then progress is made, better ways of living are formulated. Doesn't God want us to be progressive? Or are we to be stagnant, a people going no where and doing nothing. It is those stagnant minds which have caused us not to seek out the mysteries of this wondrous Earth God has placed us on. What a change could be made if mankind would extend himself out beyond his boundaries. Man looks for ways to understand the human mind. When he should be looking for those things which control the human mind. If we can first conquer those things which control the mind, then maybe we will understand better the workings of the human mind. But I am not concerned about how my mind works, it is not the workings of my mind which gets me into trouble, it is those things which control my mind that destroys or try to destroy me. Water flows down hill. Why should I be so concerned about why water flows down hill? Shouldn't my concern be where is the water going? Or who or what force redirected the flow of the water? My land once was fertile with beautiful grass and flowers and food to nourish my soul, and now because the water has been redirected my land has become a waste land where nothing good can grow. In school we are taught to stretch our minds, to reach out beyond the norm, but they didn't tell us that they have placed limitations on how far they want us to go. Why give me a house and you keep the land? Or give me a car then tell me I can only drive it to the corner store and back. You tell me to reach for the sky, but then you tell me that I can only go as far as the ceiling in my house.

I am not holding anything against my parents or Church for the things I suffered in life. That would be crazy. They gave me a good home and raised me as well as they knew how. As I said before, we live in progressive times. I believe that God has set times when some mysteries about this life will be revealed. Someone has to suffer so others can be saved.

Someone has to sin so we will know the love and mercy of the Lord Jesus Christ. There are things we all have experienced in life, good and bad. It is those things which if used positively can and will better the next generation. And we don't have to wait for the next generation to come, because there are those of us who are living now who would greatly appreciate the stories of your strengths and failings. Tell me everything. I don't want to continue to make mistakes. Mistakes are costly. I don't have to put my hand in the fire to see if it is hot. If you say so that's alright with me. Maybe my telling you about some of my life's experiences will help you with your children, or even to gain understanding about some mysteries in your life.

A child enters this world seeking knowledge. Not knowing the right from the wrong. We as adults are given the responsibility to train the child in the direction the child should go. But what if there are egregious forces on this earth which have sat their mandate on the destruction of our children, or possibly are, trying their best to guide the child into a life of destruction they have chosen. Shouldn't or would you not want to know about these forces? We as parents have been given a great responsibility, to educate, nurture, and to protect our children. How can we fulfill this mandate if we are not equipped to take on this responsibility? What will happen to the child? Where will the education or nurturing come from? There have been great books, lectures and classes held by intellectuals and authoritative people on the subject of raising a child. But how many tell us about those hidden forces out there, how to recognize them, and what to do about them before they become a influencing factor in my child's life. I believe that no child comes into this world with an evil mind or evil tendencies. Look at a baby, you hold it, you feed it, you change it. Does a baby slap you when it does not want to be held by you? Does it curse you out when it wants some food? Will it shoot you if you don't change his or her diaper on time? Where did this desire to do wrong come from? "I lead a Christian life, but why did my child turn out this way"? This question has been asked over and over again. Are we looking in the right direction to be educated on this mystery? And more than that when someone tries to help us, to tell us about the living forces of good and evil which live on this earth with us, do we reject them saying "that's just a bowl of hype". Are we afraid to venture out beyond the norm? To go further than that the limits society has placed on our intellectualism? Until we phantom out beyond our limited minds there can be no hope for a better tomorrow.

My parents loved me, but they were not equipped to handle, the things I was going through, or even to understand. I believe that if they had been equipped (educated) mentally and spiritually my life would have taken on another direction. I would not have made as many mistakes in life as I did. I did not say that I would not have made any mistakes all together, but maybe I would have avoided some of the things, or traps I fell into. Once again some one has to sin so others will know the love and forgiving mercy of the Lord Jesus Christ. I just wish that it wasn't me who had set the example by sinning.

I have counseled many troubled people, adults and children. I find one consistent factor in all of the cases I have been privileged to experience, that is the root of the problem can be traced back to their child hood. Most children I have counseled who turn to drugs, alcohol, run a ways and even some suicides. When you listen to them open up, you find that they were or are looking for love in their families, or family relationship. A number of prostitutes and homosexuals can be traced back to someone in their family and sometimes in their immediate family sexually abusing them. These are not the only causes I have formulated, but I find that these factors provide a higher percentage than others. Once that problem has been permeated into a person's genealogy it becomes a heretical force in that family line. It is like cancer, when doctors ask you if someone in your family line has had cancer. Cancer can destroy a family's genealogy unless someone breaks that genealogical curse.

Adolescent Years: (Sin)

As I told you before the visitations stopped when I started high school. Back then we did not have middle school as they have today. We started high school in the eight grades. I remember my first day of high school. I attended Howard High School in Atlanta, Georgia. I thought I had finally arrived; now I am with the big kids. All of my shyness and quietness were becoming a thing of the past. Girls were starting to look real good to me. Life was taking a change. My first day of school I got into a fight, the guy said that I had stolen his pencil. But it was really about a girl. This girl he liked was looking at me and he got jealous, so his friends coached him into starting a fight with me after school. Neither one of us won the fight because my cousin broke up the fight when the other guy's older friends tried to jump on me to. My cousin was well known around the school; he was on the football team and ran with a gang. He saved me that day. My life was taking on a change and it was not for the good. Remember when I told you that my family was in Church and some of them were in the world to? Well what would make you think that I would be any different? They said I looked pretty handsome when I was a teen, although you wouldn't believe that now. Their objectivity got me into a lot of trouble. On one hand girls became my focal point and that led to many fights with the male persuasion. There was this importing force being brewed in side of me. On one hand I was becoming a lover on the other a fighter. And guess what? I was still going to church. They call this the terrible teenage years. The years of puberty, boy I had it awful. The transformation I was experiencing would rule my life for years to come. If any one needed help I did.

Let me hip you to something. You see I am talking teenage now (hip). Sin can mask it self to where you really have to look close to see it. At home, or when I was with my family I was an angel. But when I was out of sight, that was another story, everything was on. Because I had to fight so much, I became cold and ruthless. I would do what ever it took to win the fight.

People did not want to fight me because they knew if they won they would have to watch their backs. When I was at Howard High not only would my cousin and his boys get you, but I would wait for the opportune moment and hit you in the back of your head with what ever I could find.

People began to leave me alone because they thought I was crazy. I could go anywhere I wanted to go without anything happening to me. I guess I need to explain that statement. You see when I came up there were sections of Atlanta where you were not allowed to go if you did not live in that neighborhood (you know like Harlem in New York). The gangs would protect their areas. Now don't come into their neighborhood talking about seeing one of their girls, you would be signing you death certificate. Thus this did not apply to me, I could go any where, and talk to any one with out anything happening. They would leave me alone.

Now maybe you may think that I was a big fellow, muscular, weighing about two hundred pounds? Well think again. I was short, I would guess about one hundred ten or so pounds. I was not skinny; I guess you could say that I was about an average size for a young teenager. I was brown skinned with black curly hair, and I had hazel eyes. What a combination. People said that I had cat eyes and they would change colors with what ever colors I was wearing. People would always make comments about my eyes. The girls liked me because of them, and the boys disliked me. I was not responsible for the color of my eyes. They came with the package. But boy they would get me into a lot of trouble. You would think I would be coincided, but that was not so. I did not want to be different from anyone else, I wanted to blend in, it would bother me and embarrass me when people would stare at me and make comments about me. I guess this was the catalyst of my emotional problem (my coldness), and the fights. If I could change my eyes I would. I know how some people feel who are not trying to get attention because of their physical appearance. People have a tendency to look on the outside and not see who you are on the inside. Some people like the attention. It makes them feel as though they are somebody. It only caused me trouble. I got tired of fighting, and being talked about. The guys began to call me evil eyes, because I would make this frowning look on my face and they knew that I was ready to get down then. As little as I was I was crazy. They could beat me to a pulp, but I would keep on fighting. The Lord had to be with me. He sends His rain on the just and the unjust.

We moved to the west side of town after my first year of school at Howard. We moved into our first house, before that time we were living in apartments. We moved from the rough side of town, and now we were on the West Side where the aristocrat's lived.

The east side of Atlanta was some what mixed during the time I came up with Blacks and whites. The white people who lived close to me were considered middle classed or lower middle classed, mostly all of the blacks were considered lower middle class. When we lived on Boulevard Place there were white people who lived next door to us on Boulevard. I played with whites and blacks, but the schools I attended were all black because there was no integration at this time. When we moved to the west side there were no whites living close to me, most of the children I played with were black. The upper class blacks lived on the west side of town. These were the Doctors, Lawyers, and School Teachers. All of your white collar workers, business owners, and professional people lived on the West Side of the city. Martin Luther King Jr. for instance lived about a few blocks from my house. If you lived in the area or close to the area I came up in you were supposed to be somebody. This was a fallacy of course, because there were parts of the West Side of town that were just as bad as some of the East Side of the city. Also there were some areas of the East Side where the rich whites lived. And during the time I came up the richest black would probably rank graphically close to the bottom compared to the whites with money. But never the lest if you lived on the West Side especially on the Collier Heights Side of the city, people thought you were somebody, and also most of the people who lived there had this unintelligent opinion of themselves. I had an opportunity to mingle with all sides of society, both white and black rich and poor. Not having any knowledge at this time how this would influence my life later. Please excuse me for using the term white and black when referring to different classes of people, but that was the classifications of society during the time I was a child. Now in today's time those terms are not used as frequently, we have the Americans, Hispanics (Mexicans) and etc.

My life was taking another change now. The children or should I say young adults I associated with were different. I was no longer a conversation piece. I was just one of the students blending into a normal High School environment. In the ninth grade my sister and I were transferred to Turner High School. I was not a stand out student, I guess you might say that I was just average. That suited me just fine. Most of the students that stood out among the others were light skinned with straight hair. They received most of the attention during those times. Most of them came from influential professional families. Because I lived close to a lot of them they accepted me as a member of their circle and that was OK with me, although I was not light skinned nor did I have straight hair. Turner High School was different from Howard High. Most of the students there were regular polished and sociable. Remember I was just an eight grader a Howard High, just entering High school, so my opinion about the students there was through the eyes of a freshman and should be validated as one entering a new society. In other words I am not saying that the students a Howard were ignorant or any thing of that nature. I had some really good friends at Howard who went on to become outstanding people in life. But still things at Howard were different from things at Turner. The students a Turner were very friendly from the freshmen to the upperclassmen. They never let you feel that you were out of your place. There were not many fights or gangs. Although I do remember one gang, but they didn't cause a lot of trouble and they were friendly. Most of the kid's belonged to social groups. I was in one of them we were called the Barniventials. We had our blazers and our own crest. I was becoming a socialite. I was changing from the fighter to the lover. Was this good or bad? Or was I going from one evil to another. Now I was beginning to spend too much time concentrating on girls and not on my school work. I was entering the teenage years, or should I say the life and death years.

A man has a boy child, he's proud, joy fills his heart. He begins to brag to all of his associates, "I have a son". His dreams and thoughts are centered on that child, baseball, football, which sport will he participate in. And more than that he is a man child, so he wants him to be a full man, and that means how many women he will conquer. I have heard men say "I have a real son; all of the young girls are calling him". This makes the dad feel proud; he can stick out his chest around all of his friends. If he's caught with a girl in a sexual act his dad might scold him about protection and babies in his face. But when the dad is with his friends they are laughing and committing on his conquest. That's my boy, he's a real stud. I have even heard of men taking their son's to strip bars when they turn sixteen. One dad told me when his son returned home for his college spring break he took him to a strip bar to teach him about the traps women set up for men by using their bodies. A friend told me about a man who had these young boys look through a window while he was having sex with a woman to teach them the facts of life. This friend was one of the boys. He told me how the woman would look at them through the window and she would make all kinds of sounds and motions for their entertainment. Men want to know they have crated another man. He can carry on my legacy; I can hold my head up high in the company of my associates. What if the child turns and starts liking the same sex? Or what if the child is a girl? Everything changes then. Instead of bragging and boasting he becomes defensive and protective. If he or she starts liking the same sex the dad becomes angry, hurt and threatened, "how could this happen to me"?

"My people are destroyed from the lack of knowledge" Hosea 4:6.

In the eight grades we began to study biology, plants, animals and the construction of the human body. In the ninth grade we continued with biology but more in depth now. We began to study the reproductive stages of plants, animals and humans. We were exposed to sex education in a scientific prospective. It is good to teach a child about a gun, but we are not ful filling our duties if we don't teach him the responsibilities of having a gun. He or she should have knowledge of the full responsibilities of gun ownership. Guns are dangerous when used irresponsibly. They can protect lives, and they can also take lives. So you may ask what a gun has to do with sex. Just as a gun can protect lives, sex when used correctly can protect lives though reproduction of the human race. In Genesis God said "It is not good for man to be alone. I will make a helper suitable for him." Genesis 2:18. Also after the creation of woman he told the man and woman "to be fruitful and increase in number; Fill the earth and subdue it". Genesis 1:28 NIV.

In the first declarative statement "It is not good for man to be alone";

God saw that though He had made all the other creatures on the face of the earth, these creatures could not offer man the companion ship he needed. They were not of his species, so understanding each other would be limited. Also He had placed man in charge of these creatures, and animals. He new that the responsibility would be too great for him to control all of them alone. This would lead to the need of a helper, one who would also share in the responsibilities of leadership. But you may ask "so why didn't He create another man? Wouldn't another man be more suitable to control animals than a woman?" It is a proven fact that women are as capable of controlling animals with respect to man. There are numerous women who work in the field of animal trainers today. Also there would ultimately arise another problem if He created another man. When the animal population increased, there would be too many roaming the face of the earth for to men to contend with. So just as the animals would increase in numbers, man would have to increase in numbers also. Then that called for the need of someone like man in respect to his mentality, commutability, spirituality and physica. Although his and her physica (bodily make up) could not be altogether the same, there had to be some differences for reproduction to take place. There were no adoptions agencies present at this time.

Man could not contact the local human rescores to add to his number. God could have continued to take from the dust of the earth an make more men, but he wanted man to have the responsibility of caring and replenishing the earth. To take dominion of the earth. His words were" Let us make man in our image, in our likeness, and let them rule the fish of the sea and the birds of the air, over the livestock, over all the earth. Genesis 1:26 NIV. Thus there had to be another human being created initially, since God was in the creative mode. So He took from man and created woman. And more men and women were formed from these two through capitulation. Now let's be real, In order for this sexual interlude to continue man and woman had to like what they were doing (the act of sexual intercourse). It had to be pleasing to the man and the woman. If they did not like the act, would they have continued to reproduce? What would have happened if they tried it the first time created one child and said I don't want to do this any more? Would they be fulfilling the command that was given to them to be fruitful and increase and fill the earth? So it would stand to reason that this act would become a part of their lives, and an act that they would take great joy in doing. But let us remember that this was the first instance of a marriage between a man and a woman. Adam said "this is now bone of my bones and flesh of my flesh". Genesis 2:23. Signifying a bond between the man and the woman, a life time bond. What God created for our good, man would eventually turn into a disaster.

The second declaration "I will make a helper suitable for him";

To be suitable to man she had to be made appropriate for him. Meaning that she was made for Adam and Adam alone. She was not to be given to any of her off springs as they grew older (became of age to reproduce). She was made for Adam. Like wise he was not to take any of their off springs and inter into a sexual act also. God took from Adam and made Eve who became one with him in his thinking, actions, responsibilities, care and love. I would say spirituality, but how many people would understand the meaning of the word spirituality. To be one in spirit is a blessing from God, and this is the only way a marriage can coexist and function smoothly. Many have tried to find their soul mate through trial and era. Only to create a disaster in their lives and the lives of others. I am not going to go into that right now, because I would be getting ahead of the story. A child should be given all of the information about sex and reproduction. He or she should know that the act they enter into prematurely can destroy their lives and the life of their partner. We seem to want to leave God out of the conversation when we talk to children about sex. Are His laws different from others on this topic? When I say others I mean what society as deem appropriate. Or do we know what His laws are about sex and marriage. How can we pass on what we do not know? Truly the statement is true, "We Are Destroyed From The Lack Of Knowledge". And not only do we destroy our lives, but others also.

I remember the first time my dad talked to me about sex. I had come home on leave from military service and was getting into the car with some friends heading back to Maryland where we were stationed. I was eighteen at the time. I remember clearly He told me "don't forget to ware some protection". That was the extent of my parental teaching on sex. And boy I wish he had sat me down and taught me more. I needed more than I received in school. Man's laws and God's laws on sex what to do and more importantly what not to do. And what are the ramifications of having a sexual relation ship (intercourse) outside of marriage? Also not to marry some one based on a physical relationship. Maybe I would not have made a lot of the mistakes I made in life. So many parents find it difficult to talk to their children about sex. They leave it up to the school system to educate their children on a topic that can destroy their child for life. You might say destroy is a strong word, but that's your opinion. Countries have gone to war over sex. Many men have lost their lives over sex. Companies have gone into ruin because of sex. In the destruction of human lives I would rate sex together with drugs, alcohol, and diseases. I heard a man say, "I told my son that I would rather you have a drug problem than to get involved in sex before you are married. He went on to say that with drugs and alcohol we can get you some help. But once you start having sex it will dominate your life for the rest of your life. You are hooked for life". Classes are offered on the topic of educating you child about sex. Books are written on the topic. Information can be found on the internet about sex. And still parents find it so hard to educate their children on a very serious topic. When my boys turned twelve years old I sat them down a talked with them about sex. I wanted them to know, I didn't want them to make the same mistakes I had made coming up. There are no guarantees, but a least I can say I have given them the information. And that is not the last conversation we will have on the subject. As they grow older we will continue to talk about sex. I want to be there for them advising them when needed. I will not leave it up to the world to educate my children on this topic. Schools are crying for parental involvement.

They know that they can only give a base on topics, a starting point. To really understand a topic requires study of the topic. Also public schools can only teach according to their guidelines. They are forbidden to teach the religious prospective in educating our children. There is a big problem in this area. Teachers can only teach what the system tells them to. Parents are either to embarrassed or don't have the proper education (knowledge ability) to teach their child fully about sex. People can set their child down and talk to them about drugs and alcohol; you see many infomercials about drugs on television.

We want them to be informed on the topic of drugs and alcohol because they are killers and destroyers of life. But how about sex, can't we see how sex is destroying our lives and our children's lives to when used improperly. So how does a child learn except from trial and error? It is this trial and error which can be destructive. A child experiments with sex (trial and error), and becomes pregnant at fifteen or sixteen. They can no longer participate in activities as a child; they have a permanent responsibility now. Or they relinquish their responsibility to someone else, and for the rest of their lives have to live with the fact that somewhere out there is a child I fathered or gave birth to. Or look at this scenario: Their experimenting results in a disease called aids. Then the result of their action or experimentation results in death. Would you want this to happen to your child? Would you be able to go and brag to your friends now? My child was a stud, but he's no longer with us because he laid down with the wrong one. Or I raised her and now I have to raise her child. Isn't it worth the time and effort to become knowledgeable yourselves and then to pass on what you have learned to your children? Don't let the world destroy your child!

I was off on the wrong track now. Girls and fun time had become more important to me than anything else. I would neglect school work for my pleasures. I had to do my home chores. My parents were strict about that. I had to cut the grass, wash dishes, plant flowers, keep my room clean, wash the car take out the trash, these were my assigned duties. If I did not do these chores I could not go out and play. But what about my school work? I wish they would have been stern with me and made me study harder. I remember one day my homeroom teacher told me "Obie you are smart, but you are lazy concerning your studies". That was very true; I would rather do anything else except study. Although I wanted to, I just wasn't motivated to do well in school. Don't misunderstand what I am saying, I wasn't failing I was doing average work, just enough to get by. In Play time and girl time I was an excellent student. And I regret that today. I needed direction; I needed someone to be stern with me about life. Don't get me wrong, I am not putting the blame on my parents. They raised us as well as they knew how. My dad worked hard, day and night to make sure we had a good life. My mother was a house wife and she cared for our needs. The thing I want you to see is the fact that we can work hard to supply the physical needs of our families, but what about their mental and spiritual needs. A well rounded child must have both or else he or she will fall short in life. You can give a child the world, but if you don't educate him on the responsibilities which are associated with the gift, he and the gift can be destroyed.

How many children from rich families have destroyed their inheritances? Some have turned to drugs, alcohol, and sex. Great minds have been destroyed, great talents have been wasted. And we cry, "I tried to do my best to make sure they had everything they needed. I worked hard and long hours; I worked my fingers to the bone, where did I go wrong"? How many hours a week do you spend talking to you off springs? How many hours a week do you spend at work, watching television, talking to your girl friends or buddies? How many hours a week do you spend researching or studying on the topic of **What My Child Should Know About Life.**

LOVE: the most misused and abused word in the human language. I know because I misused and abused the word. Most young boys and girls use the word to get what they want from their boy friends, girl friends and even their parents. Everyone wants to be loved, and to hear someone say "I love you". Those three words can open hearts, pocket books, and even get sexual favors. Some people tell others they love them because they know that is what they want to hear. We strive to be accepted and loved. And often times it doesn't matter if you really mean it, just tell me you love me that's all I need just to hear you say the word, I love you. I would tell a girl I loved her, and then go down the hall see another girl and tell her the same thing. I used the word to manipulate my way into the life of my pray, to set up my conquest. Oh! Don't be so shocked, you did the same thing to. It was easy to tell someone I love you. You hear it on television with actors; now tell me that they really love every one they say this word to. You hear it in Church; people will tell other Christians I love you and will not lend a helping hand to you when you are in need. Or at the first instant they will gossip and start some rumor concerning you. I have head of a minister telling people in his congregation "I love you" and then on Monday seeing them in the market place and not speaking to them. Some love. Society has used this word in many different forms, so no wander the true meaning of the word has been lost. Could you set your child down and give them the true meaning of the word? Does the word exemplify your life? What do you know about the word? Do you pick and chose those you love? Does your love have a time limit? Do you only love those who love you back? Can you tell someone I love you today and get angry with them tomorrow, and turn your back on them and stop speaking to them? Have you ever told someone I love you just to get what you want out of them, and then after you have gotten it tell them, forget you I was just caught up in the moment? Is this you? Or has someone treated you this way? I could not write about this if I had not been there. I truly was an abuser. I used the word like it was water. I hurt people with the word, and it took me forty years before I got hurt, but I did get hurt. And that wasn't the last. It was the beginning of my pay back for the pain I had inflected on others.

If you live by the sword, you will eventually die by the sword. These words are true. Another truth; what you do to others will be done to you. What they should have said: What you do to others will return to you seven times over or more. Now that's a true statement. I had to find that out the hard way. You talk about **hurt,** when your time comes around there are no words to express the pain you feel. We don't think about the consequence of our actions until it's too late.

Or some people don't care what the ramifications of their actions will be. Hurt you before you hurt me. Hurt me and truly later you will get hurt. And that's for real. But I love you.

Have you been studying my case? Or have you just been reading the story? A Physiatrist can tell you where I went wrong, and the reasons for my actions. Can you?

I pray that you will not only read the story, but study the story. It is my hope that the things I went through, my struggles in life will help you and your children gain understanding about life's struggles. Why does my child act this way? Why so many people do the things they do? Someone has to suffer so others can be saved. Someone has to sin, so others will know the forgiving love and mercy of the Lord God.

Now I am off on the wrong track. It would seem as though sin was dominating my life now. What happened, did the good angels really win in the battle for my life? It doesn't seem like it, does it? Here I am now a teenager, doing all the wrong things. Throwing my life away. Drugs weren't as prevalent in our society among teens as it is today. Maybe that saved me from experimenting in that area. Who was the probabilist in my case? Was I the catalyst of my own actions? Can you blame my parents? My Church? My school teachers? It is my belief that there are no bad children born on this earth. What a child learns has to come from someone, or from something. A child is taught how to walk, talk, and how to sin. And I don't believe you can throw the blame off on any one person or thing. It is the responsibility of all of us to see that we live our lives responsibly, respectfully, and morally, in order for our children to become wholesome benefactors of this life they have been entrusted with. A child patterns his or her life after their surroundings, and teachings. What are you doing to insure the well being of your children? Sometimes you can't escape your surroundings, but you can propagate sound doctrine and morals. Don't we owe that to them?

I was not the baddest child in my school. There were some worst than I was. I didn't smoke, drink, curse, or steal. I had my faults though (my sins), and I am not proud of them. I won't name all of them, but they were there. You may ask "where was Christ in my life at this time? Where was the boy who saw the visions, and heard the voices? I don't know. I did not have visions during my time in high school. I didn't even hear any more voices. I went to Church, but I was just there. Nothing was going on spiritually with me. Was God setting back and letting me do my thing? I don't think so. You will see as the story continues. God has seen our lives before we were born. The Bible tells us in Psalm 139:16; "When I was woven together in the depths of the earth, your eyes saw my unformed body. All the days ordained for me were written in your book before one of them came to be. NIV. Also in Proverbs 20: 24 it says; "A man's steps are directed by the Lord. How then can anyone understand his way? NIV. It is my firm belief that God is in control of our lives, and He directs us in certain directions to bring Him glory.

Does God get glory out of my sinning? No, but when I repent and change from the sin, stop committing the sin. Then God gets the glory.

If I continually drive fifty miles per hour in a thirty five miles per hour speed zone in a residential area someone backing out of their drive way could get hurt. A child playing in the street, or retrieving a ball that rolled into the street could be injured or killed. But if one day I say to my self; I am doing wrong by speeding through this neighborhood, I shall slow down before I hurt someone. Then not only am I respecting the speed limit sign, but also I am giving credit, or praising the one who had the foresightedness to put that sign there. It is the same with God. He will allow us to run wild, and one day He will put in our spirit and brains; that's enough I'd better stop now I'm killing myself and I can or am hurting someone else. He will only allow us to go so far, and then He will put us back on track to fulfill His purpose for our lives. You see we are His people, the sheep of His pasture. Another place He said; "Psalm 33:13-14, NIV. From Heaven the Lord looks down and sees all mankind; From His dwelling place He watches all who live on earth. And then in Psalm 139: 7-13;

1. Where can I go from your Spirit? Where can I flee from your presence?
2. If I go up to the Heavens, you are there; if I make my bed in the depths, you are there.
3. If I rise on the wings of the dawn, if I settle on the far side of the sea.
4. Even there your hand will guide me, you right hand will hold me fast.

5. If I say," Surely the darkness will hide me and the light became night around me,"
6. Even the darkness will not be dark to you; the night will shine like the day, and for darkness is as light to you.
7. For you created my inmost being; you knit me together in my mother's womb. NIV.

It is also written in Romans 9:17; "For the scripture says to Pharaoh": "I have raised you up for this very purpose, that I might display my power in you and that my name might be proclaimed in all the earth. NIV.

No matter who we are the Lord God has assigned a task (job) for everyone on the face of this earth and His will shall be fulfilled.

Could my life have been different? Maybe. I believe we all have to go through something to help others. A man driving down the street, his car runs into a deep hole and destroys his tires. He alerts the authorities that the hole is there, and he warns others not to travel down that street. Wouldn't you want to know if you are driving down a dangerous street? How would you know unless someone went down the street before you and told you not to drive that way? God puts up warning signs, and sometimes those warning signs can come in the form of testimonies from people like you and I. Our experiences, the challenges we face in life, our successes and failures help to shape the lives of others. And through it all guess who gets the glory? God does. I didn't want to go wrong; I didn't set out to sin. I didn't know any better. I needed help and guidance. But how can the blind lead the blind. How can you help me cross the street if you are blind to, then we will both get hit. You may say, "Why would God do this?" How can you tell me that your side of the street is better than my side of the street, if you haven't been on my side of the street? Then you are only guessing. And that want hold water.

Who would you believe someone who has been to the moon, or someone who read about the moon in a book? There are things about this life we do not understand, and maybe we will never understand. Also there are things about the Lord God which are a mystery to us, but He has assured us that all shall be revealed. Matthew 7:7-8; Ask and it will be given to you; seek and you will find; knock and the door will be opened to you. For everyone who asks receives; he who seeks finds; and to him who knocks, the door will be opened. NIV. Things are a mystery only because we don't seek answers. Nothing is hidden that shall not be revealed. There are questions, and there are answers to the questions, Just look in the right direction. **Someone Had To Sin To Tell Others About The Love And Mercy Of The Lord God And Jesus Christ.**

Do you remember Lot and his wife? Lot was a righteous man, but Lot also wanted the things of the world. That is why the Angels had to drag Lot out of Sodom and Gomorrah. His wife was turned into salt for this very reason. Remember I told you about my family, how they would party on Saturday night and go to Church on Sunday? I'm not saying there's any thing wrong with partying. It is where we party, and the way we conduct our selves that cause us to sin. I believe God wants us to have a good time on this earth. That is why Christ said; "I have come that they may have life, and have it to the full. John 10:10. NIV. I hate to see so called Christians with those frowns on their face, trying to look so dignified and holy, deep. Who died? Party people laugh and have joy in them until they get inebriated (drunk). But there are those who can have a good time without drinking, or making a spectacle of themselves. They are the ones who can go to a party on Saturday night, leave and go home at a reasonable hour, wake up Sunday morning refreshed and then go to Church without falling asleep in the pews. I'd rather be around someone who looks like they have life in them, can smile, laugh, and have joy. Those prune faced people run me away. But there is a negative to this also. Some people don't know how to take things in moderation, and become trapped in a party environment or mentality. They began to succumb to the things of the world. Effectuated on worldly pleasures and desires. They are not bad people, yet they don't want to seem that they are withdrawn or unsociable. They want to please and to be pleased. There is a need to live on both sides of the street in them. They become socialites, always wanting not only to have a good time, but to make sure you are having one to. In order to do this they have to join in the interests of those who are living a life of sin. And that's when trouble arises. The Bible tells us to be transformed and not to conform to the things of the world. When we are trying to please people, which is a hard thing to do. You began to give into the things you know are wrong, for the sake of friendship, until your conscience begins to straighten you out. Who knows how long this can take, or how far you will go. Can I have both the world and the Church? No! The world is in conflict with the things of God. God did not create the world. He created the earth.

The world was created by man. The world is our society, how we live, the things we do, our wants and desires. The world is selfish, prideful, deceitful, lustful, and filled with greed. This is not so with the Lord God, He is love, compassionate, merciful, and forgiving. "He causes His sun to rise on the evil and the good, and sends rain on the righteous and the unrighteous." Matthew 5:45. NIV. That should tell you that He is not selfish.

You can have fun without being worldly. I think that is the problem with people, they believe to join and be committed to the church means giving up fun in their lives. I can understand this misconception to look at some people who attend some of these churches. They tell you if you don't walk this chalk line they have set up you are on your way to hell. They set up rules for people that they themselves are not able to keep.

Where was the church when I was growing up? The thing you have to understand is; the church then was not as knowledgably as the church today. Didn't they have the same Bible, you may ask? Yes they did, but they did not have access to the information or should I say theological studies that are available to us today. 2 Timothy 2:15 Study to show thyself approved unto God, a workman that needith not be ashamed, rightly dividing (handling) the word of truth. King James. In order to minister God's word effectively, and correctly, requires a lot of study and research. You cannot set down with the Bible and a dictionary and be proficient in ministering God's word. Reading and researching the meaning of words does not constitute study. When the teacher studies, the student will learn, and the student will in turn study, because it is a requirement set down by the teacher. When this principle is applied we all learn and become knowledgeable. Study means researching the history of the Bible, signs of the times, when and where those events took place, and most importantly how does the stories in the Bible apply to my life today. That you learn, you are egger to pass on with joy and confidence seeing positive affects on the lives of those you come in contact with.

In our church the children set in service with the adults. A child can not understand the topics a minister is preaching on when his message is focused on the older generation. The child becomes bored and will eventually fall asleep. I spent many days and nights sleeping on the pews. Ministers during the time I came up had a style they call hooping. This was done when he was entering his climax. Everyone would get very emotional when the minister started to hoop. But what about the child? How did those sounds help the children? What understanding could they get from them? And to think about it how about the adults also, of what benefit did the hooping do for them? There was nothing left for me to do but go to sleep. Even today I see children in some churches still setting in service with adults. What are they getting out of the message? How does their lives relate to adults? The child becomes not only bored but also confused. We (the Children) had Bible studies in the evenings on Sunday. They called it BYPU. Don't ask me what it means because I have forgotten. Our Bible study consists of the instructor reading us a story, and our remembering Bible verses so we could recite them at Christmas and Easter. We did not have children's church which is so needed. A child needs to learn at a child's age. Adults have things they are confronted with in life and so do children. Each needs to be in a place where they can receive the attention and education that is conducive for their growth. If you don't feed your dog at home he will eat out of your neighbor's garbage can. If the church does not minister to the needs of the children, the world will. And what a tragedy that will be. On the one hand I had the world, on the other I was attending a church that was not reaching out to its children effectively. How could I not go wrong? I thank God that the Lord Jesus was watching over me.

I was eating from both sides of the street. Learning more from the world through trial and error, than from the church. Although still I don't blame them. I am not trying to shift my mistakes off on any one person. I just wish they could have seen the need to instruct the children in the way to live a godly life. I wish they would have read to us, explained the Bible to us, told us how this Bible was the road map for our lives, and listen to us, our needs and our problems. You can not leave it up to a child to grow up on their own. They need help guidance and mostly understanding.

Now here I am in High School running with the big kids. Doing what the big kids do. I did not want to stand out, or call attention to myself. I just wanted to blend in, be average, be accepted as one of the gang, and have fun. This was my focal point now, my motivator, my goal. I was in the middle of things now. High School was exciting. I played in the marching band, joined social groups, partied and I had a good time. Amazingly I didn't get into many fights. I loved (was infatuated with) the women though. We had some of the prettiest girls in the city of Atlanta at Turner High. And I knew them all, and they knew me. I was very friendly and some of the girls took this the wrong way. They began to call me a play boy. One girl I had a crush on all through high school would not talk to me because she said that I was going from girl to girl. I wasn't a play boy, I just liked women. If they would talk to me, then I would intern talk to them. I wasn't stuck up. Maybe sometimes our conversations would get a little extensive, if you know what I mean? But that should not have been representative of the caliber of the name they hung on me. I was just like a good baseball player, playing my position well, (the field). Trying to catch everything that came my way. I was having a good time. Boy was I messed up. I was attracted to older girls. My sister was a year older than I was, and she would have her girl friends over on occasion. They would joke and play with me, and I found older girls more appealing. They had to be my age or older for me to talk to them. If they were younger I had no time for them. There were a few younger girls I attempted to talk to and I hurt their feelings. I remember this one girl I rode home on the bus with, she wanted to be my girl friend and when I told her that I was not interested she began to cry. There was another girl younger that I tried to talk to, she saw me with another girl and she cut my pants leg open with a razor. I decided younger girls and I would not hit it off. You may wonder where I am going with this. Just hold on every thing has a purpose. Older girls were fascinating, they had poise, and they were teachers. You would not believe it but I was shy around girls. If they approached me and showed some interest, then I began to respond. If I liked a girl, she would not ever know it unless she responded to me first. I would not make the first advance toward a kiss, or any thing else. Like I said they were the teachers and I was the student. Now with this I was a good student. I was not aggressive though. To tell you the truth I was not aggressive about anything, schoolwork, house work, games, nothing. I just wanted to be average. I just wanted to blend in. I did not want to be the leader, let someone else lead, and I will follow. I began to concentrate on girls more than anything else. I was dating a girl in my sister's class, they didn't like each other. My sister told her to leave me alone, but she wouldn't, and I wouldn't stop seeing her either. My sister said the girl was fast. If you know what they mean when they say a girl is fast. If you don't ask someone. And she was, fast and frisky, the older folks would say "fast tail", and some other names you can think of.

All I had to do was be there, she was very aggressive. I thought I had it made. But what I didn't know, with my naive self, I was being used. Remember when I told you about those spirits living on the earth with us? Some of them are good and some are bad. Believe it or not those spirits good and bad know your life, and the bad ones want to hinder you in any way they can from becoming successful in fulfilling the call, God is grooming you for. They will use any means, or person to achieve their goals. Their goal is to tempt you and then after you have fallen into their trap they want to accuse you before the Lord Jesus, so God will turn His back on you.

When you are young you aren't concerned about these things. Your focus is on growing up, having a good time, becoming an adult. You aren't worried or concerned about your back, whose waiting in the bushes setting up traps for you. The saying goes; "what you don't know, want hurt you." Another lie someone made up. Wouldn't your life be better if you knew what was around the corner? Would you have made that mistake if you would have known before hand how things would have turned out? Why do people run to people who they believe can foresee the future? Would they go if they had not made some mistakes in their lives, and they do not want to be repeat performers? Or do some go just to get a better prospective on their future so they want make mistakes? No matter what your answer is there must be positives and negatives in our future, and we will do anything we can to escape the negatives. So what you don't know can hurt you. My people are destroyed from lack of knowledge. Hosea 4:6 NIV. I had these two sides in me, one wanted to be accepted, but not stand out. The other was naive, easily led ready to fall into a trap. Boy did the enemy know me. Isn't it amazing, the things you do even when you are a child can shape your future, and the lives of others whom you may never know or meet? Some people will read this segment and the first thing that will enter into their minds is; "we must live our lives by faith." Faith does not stop me from wanting to know about my future. Faith does not stop me from continuing to make mistakes in my life. Faith means I must put all my trust in God acknowledging Him in all my ways so He can direct my pathway. I must trust in a God that I can not see to guide me through a life I can see. If I want to accomplish a task in life, the first thing I do is pray so God will give me direction. If I want to buy something or sell something I seek God in prayer first, He knows what's around the corner I don't.

He knows what traps are set up for me. He knows my future, He wrote the book. If I do this I know, no matter what I face He will bring me through. Proverbs 3:5-6. Trust in the Lord with all your heart and lean not on your own understanding; in all your ways acknowledge Him, and He will make your paths straight. How then shall they call on Him in whom they have not believed? Romans 10:14; To have faith in God, you must first believe that He exists, and that He will supply all of your needs. How do you know this unless you have been there? There must be witnesses to the love and mercy of the Lord Jesus. What does all of this mean to a child a teenager? How do I show him or her the pathway of life? How do I explain faith to them when their only concern is getting through school, and having a good time?

Children, or should I say young adults lives are more complex today than they were when I came up. They have more outlets (distractions) than we had. Advances in technology have advanced the mental fortitude of the younger sect.

They are more questionable, curious and sensitive, than we were. You can't just tell a child no today and get away with it. You have to explain why you said no, and make it sound good. When I came up no meant no, with no explanations, and you had better not seek one. Our curiosity went only as far as we were taught in school and home. We did not venture out into the unknown without someone putting up a wall in our pathway. If you tried to venture out beyond your boundary line you were considered a trouble maker, and you would be dealt with most severely. It is these freedoms which have expounded the sensitiveness of our children today.

They no longer live by faith, they trust in the fact that you are going to be a good parent and do the right things for them. Today they want to help you make the decisions about their lives, and sometimes tell you the direction they are going to take in life, setting their own direction whether you like it or not. They no longer rely on your expertise or experiences in life. Today it is more so, let me try it if it does not work I'll try something else. They do not take into consideration the ramifications of their failures. They do not care who gets hurt as long as it is not them. And if you try to stop them then they rebel, "you don't love me, or you don't understand me, why are you trying to hurt me?" This leads to more youths running away from home, more suicides among the youth, and more teenage pregnancies.

My freedom stops where your boundary line begins. I am as free as I want to be with in the confines of my own space. The problem arises when I try to venture out into your territory. Then my freedom becomes subversive. I am no longer concerned with the problems of my own existence and its perplexities. Taking time to clean up my own back yard, making sure my house is in order. Now I have compounded my life by adding troubles to your life to. How can anyone master where they have not been? I should first master where I am, before I can go forward. Life has dictated if I don't do a good job here, I am sure to fail when I get over there. I need as much help as I can get to understand where I am, only then can I move forward. This is the true pathway of life. When I understand that I can't make it on my own, and I can't make up the rules as I go along, then I am on the right track. Then I can tare down walls, but I'm not tearing them down alone. It is with your help, your knowledge and experiences that caused the walls to fall. A child must understand this in order to become successful in life, and to make a positive influence on the next generation if one is to come. Thinking you have all the answers, or you can get them on your own, only leads to disappointments and disasters. A child needs a knowledgeable leader in order to succeed. The traps in life are many. The older you get, the more there are. Who better to learn from, than someone who has been there? What has been will be again, what has been done will be done again; there is nothing new under the sun. Ecclesiastes 1:9, NIV. Ultimately then you have to have faith in the person whom God has chosen to give you counsel on life's highway.

I had fallen into a trap, and continued to fall deeper. I was being set up, and I didn't know any better. My wife always tells me;" you don't know women, they are devious, they can set you up, get you to do what they want you to do, and you will not know it until it is to late."

She is right; women will smile in your face, talk silky smooth to you, and then have you eating out of their hands. How many parents teach their sons about the traps women set up? A man thinks he has all the answers, but I found out that he only knows what women want him to know. I have found out that you don't try to out think a woman, but try to stay up with them. But there is a problem with that also. While you are on page one, she has gone on to page three. The best remedy to this problem is: Don't try to out think them, and don't even try to keep up with them. Let them travel their road, and you travel yours. Hopefully somewhere down the line you will meet, if only for a little while, and then it's off to the races again.

You know the things you do for one girl, others find out and they want you to do the same for them. Well I had fallen into that scenario. I was kind and generous to my girl friends. My I say to generous for a boy my age. I would buy them nice gifts for their birthdays, and special holidays. I would get a job after school to make some money just to give them a real nice gift. I wanted to be accepted, and to show them that I cared. The word gets out about you around school, and then you don't have a problem getting a girl friend. I don't know but maybe that's why they called me a play boy. I was nice, generous, and friendly and the girls like that, so I had no problem passing me around. But all of this was a trap. And I was falling head first. The Bible teaches us the very thing we run after has become our master. Women had mastered me and I didn't know it. I thought I was in control and all the time I was being controlled I had become a slave. They call this thing the spirit of lust. I told you about those unwanted guest who show up at your door with out an invitation. Well they showed up at my door and I let them in. This does not apply only to boys, because girls go through the same thing. Wanting to be accepted, doing every thing they can to please their boy friends, and the word gets out about them. The boys run after them because everyone calls them easy. The girls don't like them and they call them a slut. The same trap applies to both, only because they want to be accepted and loved by their peers.

I will continue to express this; knowledge, we need knowledge. Not just about world history, the arts, science, mathematics, but also about life, and love. And we need Godly prospective on these topics. Did you know that Godly prospective are moral prospective also? I did not learn about love and women from my parents, at school, or even at church. I learned from trial and error, mistakes and failures the world taught me. Why? Why wasn't there someone available to teach me about the very topics I would need to succeed in life? Maybe if they had taught me about life and love I wouldn't have wasted so much time trying to conquer these topics, I would have focused more of my attention on my school work. I would have been aware of the traps and pitfalls out there. Possibly something's I would have left alone until I became of age.

Someone has to go through to tell others what's on the other side.

I remember a few people during my high school years that could have made a change in my life if they had taken me into their care. I am glad today that they have the big brother programs. A child, especially boys need someone to identify with. Boys need someone to motivate them. And this motivation can even extend into their adult life. The saying goes, "behind every good man there is a **good** woman, or behind every successful man there is a **good** woman." The saying does not imply woman, but a good woman. Nor does it say a complaining, or pushy woman. Better to live on a corner of the roof than to share a house with a quarrelsome wife. Proverbs 21:9 NIV. Better to live in a desert than with a quarrelsome and ill-tempered wife. Proverbs 21:19 NIV. A wife of noble character is her husband's crown, but a disgraceful wife is like decay in his bones. Proverbs 12:4 NIV. A wife of noble character who can find? She is worth far more than rubies. Her husband has full confidence in her and lacks nothing of value. She brings him good, not harm, all the days of her life. Proverbs 31:10-12. NIV. These sayings are good and true, but that was my problem **women**. These sayings could help me later on in my life but what about now in my teenage years. What was I supposed to do get married so I could become a better person? I don't think so. A boy needs a man to identify with, and a girl needs a woman to identify with. Girls have personal issues that can only be expounded upon by older knowledgeable and experienced women. It is the same with boys, there are some things that are embarrassing to boys and girls and they will not feel comfortable talking about these issues with the other sex. So there must be a male for boys and a female for girls in their lives. It is very difficult for a woman to raise a male child, and likewise it is very difficult for a male to raise a woman child. That is one reason why I believe the saying in the Bible Is true, "I hate divorce, says the Lord God of Israel," Malachi 2:16 NIV. Divorce always hurt the children. I have heard people say "it is better for us to go our separate ways, than for the children to see us arguing all of the time." In other words they are saying, they are going to be destroyed (the children) one way or the other, but **I** will be happier without you. Who cares if they get hurt, they will get over it. I have to live my life, and they will have to live theirs." Then the poor child is left without a father figure or a mother figure in their lives and then the world comes in to fill the void left by the missing parent. I think the mentoring programs are a good thing. But they can not replace the personal relationship of a parent. God made them male and female and told them to reproduce and fill the earth. Adam was not told to fill it by himself, nor was Eve. They were two but they were one.

Let's go back to a few people I believe could have made a difference in my life. One was my home room teacher Mr. Butts. He's no longer with us today. I can still hear his words in my ears today, "you can do better, you are just lazy." Mr. Butts was my homeroom teacher a Turner. He was a hard teacher, but a fair teacher. I had a lot of respect for him. He was not only my homeroom teacher; I also took history from him. I have always loved history. I looked up to Mr. Butts. I would have listened to him if he had taken the time to push me. Mr. Butts and my dad had been in school together, I don't know if that was a reason why he wouldn't push me or not.

We transferred to Harper High School in the second half of my junior year, so Mr. Butts was no longer my homeroom teacher. But what about those two years I was at Turner, couldn't he have motivated me then? Today as I look back over my life I regret he didn't push me to do better in school.

Another person was my granddad. I really loved my granddad. He would carry me places. We would go fishing together on Saturdays, and I loved that. I would get very hurt when he would go with his other friends and would not carry me. I went with him and my grand mother when he had to preach at different churches. He was more like my dad than my dad was. My dad worked all the time, so he didn't have time to do things with me. And on Sundays my dad was tired so he didn't attend church. I liked going to church, and I really liked being with my granddad. I remember when he was setting up his own ministry, people came for a while, and I don't know why but the membership fell of. People stopped coming. I remember him carrying me to one of the main deacon's house; they were talking about the problem. There was some confusion going on between the families that attended the church, and this could have been a factor in them not attending. Never the less this didn't stop my granddad, he continued to meet and have service. I remember on one occasion there was only me and his lead deacon. My granddad prayed and lead us in service. He was a good and kind hearted man. I would sometimes get angry with my parents and run away from home. They always knew where I was, because I wouldn't go any father than my grand parent's house. My granddad passed when I was in the tenth grade, and I was really hurt. I remember when I heard the news about my granddad, I ran into the room I would stay in when I was at my grandparents house, I jumped on the bed and began to beat the bed, I was hysterical. I began to beat the walls, crying all the time. My dad came into the room and began to talk to me. That was the first time my dad really had a conversation with me about life, but it was only about life and death. Possibly if my granddad had continued to live my life would have been different, I would not have made some of the mistakes I did in life because he would have been there to guide me.

You know God has a road for you to travel and sometimes you have to travel that road alone. There are lessons God will teach you, and these lessons will come from only Him. He will separate you from family and friends, to fulfill His purpose. This road may not be easy, and there can be hills and valleys along the way, successes and failures, hurt, pain and a lot of tears. But He will be with you until you reach the end of you journey. And you will reach the end, because that is His will for your life. He said, "I will not leave you as orphans; I will come to you. John 14:18 NIV. The Lord said to Abram, "Leave your country, your people and your father's household and go to the land I will show you." Genesis 12:1 NIV. And you know about the Apostle Paul's life, how he was separated from his family and friends, Beaten, imprisoned, went hungry, faced riots and the Bible says that he also faced sleepless nights for the sake of the gospel of Jesus Christ. He had a road to travel, and so do you and you will travel that road. You can read about the Apostle Paul's life in the book of Acts and Second Corinthians.

I am in my junior year now, we have been transferred to a new school to ease the over crowd ness a Turner High School. They separated our junior class. All of the students living north of Hightower road would have to attend the new school. We were hurt and angry. They did not make the seniors go to the new school though because it was their last year. So they separated my sister and I. She remained at Turner and I went to Harper High School. There were other students from other high schools living in the area who were transferred also. New school, new faces, new women. We are the upper class men now. All of the lower grades looked up to us. We have become the leaders of this new school. I was in big trouble. Everything was new, a lot of the teachers and students were new. The remainder of my junior year was lackadaisical. Everyone one was just trying to get to know the school and everyone else.

Harper was a beautiful school. I liked it very much. It wasn't far from where we lived so I could walk to school and back home. My mother or my aunt would pick us up on rainy and cold days, but most of the time we would walk. There were a lot of teenagers in my neighborhood who attended Harper. We walked together everyday, and when school was out, it was play time. By this time there were some students who had cars, and you know it was on now. I did not have a car, but some of my good friends did. We went everywhere. This was the good life. I was not in a hurry to get older. I was having a good time. Although I still wasn't putting to much emphasis on my school work. I would still come home do my chores and then out side I would go. School homework, what was that? Maybe tomorrow, but not today. We would have parties on Friday nights after school, and I loved to get down. I would have to say so; I was not slack in the dancing department. Now this I was good at. You could not go to a party and see people standing around the walls. The floor was full. We came in dancing and went out dancing. There were no fights, just partying. Our parents didn't have to worry about us doing drugs drinking alcohol and getting into a fight that was not our way of things that was not on our agenda. Everybody new everybody and we liked everybody. Even when we played football, basket ball, or any other sport there were no fights. And there were a lot of kids. If someone would get angry, we would cool him or her down. You could not fight in our neighborhood. This was a new life for me because in my old neighborhood I had to fight all of the time. This was like Heaven. But was I learning anything? No, except how to party. A mind is a terrible thing to waste, and I was not doing to good with mine.

I was having a good time, but as the saying goes;" all good things come to an end." I've often wanted to live my high school years over. But not during these times, if I could go back I would want it to be the same as it was when I came up. I would like to see all of the people that have gone home now; I miss a lot of them. These days are stressful, even though we have made progress in the way of health care, technology, and standards of living. All of these advances have come with a price. And it grieves my heart. People have become more distant. Families have grown farther apart. Love and forgiveness are just words spoken, with no real intent. Safety, where are you safe today?

Homosexuality, the very thing God destroyed Sodom and Gomorrah for has become a way of life spoken freely and openly, practice widely.

Crime and lust are driving forces in these new decades. Fear now rules our society. It is no wonder our children are confused and lost, even more than I was when I came up. When I came up there were children that did not share the same experiences that I did. I would say if they took a poll I would be in the minority. But look at the children today, how many of them are struggling with life today, frighten, confused, feeling there is no hope for a better tomorrow. Take a poll and I would venture to say they would be in the majority. Society has gone forward, and still society has left our children behind. Nothing is new under the sun. What has been, is here today, what is here today, will be here tomorrow. When will we stop looking at the physical, and start hearing the spiritual? Souls are crying out for help.

Suicides among youths are more prevalent in this society than they were when I came up. Most of the children when I came up were not talking about taking their lives. We were enjoying life. Families though they did not have the training and knowledge we have today, were close together. Communities shared in watching and rearing children. Everyone knew everyone, if you felt you could go out of your area and do any sort of mischief and it would not get back to your parents, you were mistaken. Someone knew your parents, and you. People would say "I know him that's Obie's son." There wasn't an area in Atlanta where I could go that someone did not know me, or my family. People were interested in our welfare and protection. They were sincerely concerned. I would here adults say "hey, you shouldn't be doing that, I'm going to tell your parents, and don't think I don't know who they are. Maybe you may say that I am contradicting my self from my previous statements when I said that I whish there had been someone there to guide me. Watching out for me and guiding me are two different things. I may be capable of watching you, but not knowledgeable or experienced enough to guide you. There is a big difference. You may tell me to watch your dog, but if I do not have the knowledge to give your dog the proper foods at the proper times your dog will go hungry, and in some instances you dog could die from starvation. Being concerned showed that someone cared. A child wants to know that there is someone out there that cares for them. I have heard parents tell their children after they have grown and became adults that they were sorry for being so hard on them coming up, that they loved them and they were very concerned about their welfare. And the response from the child who is an adult now was "I know you love me and I think you for being hard on me, it kept me out of trouble and made me a better person." But that same adult will say to someone else, "I'm not going to raise my child like I was raised, my parents were hard on me, and I'm not going to be hard on my child." Then we inter into what I call the new morality, what was good for me is not good enough for my child. They also say "I want to be a friend to my child." And the child is looking for and needs a parent instead of a friend. You don't have to threaten your children constantly or beat them to death to be a stern parent. Being concerned about them, where they are going and with whom, setting appropriate times for them to return, and having restricted times for socialization during school nights. Setting up appropriate telephone, and television hours. Making sure they are doing their school work, at school and at home, setting up punishments for breaking household rules.

These things may seem strict to a child coming up, but in the long run will greatly benefit them in their adult lives. And they will thank you for loving them enough to take the time to make sure they do well in life. A child wants to end his or her life because they feel that there is no reason to go on living. No one cares if I live or die. No one loves me or cares about me. My parents are more concerned about them selves than they are about me. I don't have any one to go to talk about my problems that will listen to me and not judge me. These are just a few of the responses I have heard coming from problem children. We as adults have to understand that it does not matter the amount of material gifts we can give our children, the lavishes of life that we pore out on them that will give them everlasting happiness. These things are just temporal, and can not replace love. Material things go out of style, they fade away, they get broken, and they get misplaced and are often forgotten. They can't comfort you when you are lonely, hug you when you are sad, talk to you when you need an encouraging word, nor can they feel your hurt and pain. They can't lift you up when you fall, or guide you in the right direction when your back is against the wall. Material things though they are good at the appropriate time can not replace love and I mean true love. Have you ever been to a party and every one thought that you were having a good time because you were laughing and dancing? Or have you been in a setting with your friends and their families an smiled and talked to those who were there and they said," oh how wonderful you are, and so friendly." No one could see the tears behind you smile, or hear your heart coming apart, no one knew your loneliness, your troubles, and your pain. You could really act the part. And all the time you were crying out for help deep inside. How many have faced these scenarios, children and adults? How many have returned to their homes and wanted to end it all. How many parents have watched their children come and go day after day and not knowing what's hurting them inside. How many parents have been more concerned with their problems and careers and could not see that their children were crying out for help? Though we have made many progresses in technology, we have traveled though outer space, spanned the deepest oceans, we have made advances in medicine, feed the multitudes, traveled to distant lands in a matter of minutes, acquired riches, built lavished houses, bought fine cars, yet we still haven't learned how to see and then repair the broken hearted. How many lives could we save, how many would not find comfort in drugs, alcohol, elicit sex, suicide, homicide if we took the time to see the problem and then have the knowledge and ability to repair the broken hearted? There are always going to be problems in this life. This life has many perplexities. We are a progressive people, and the Lord God wants us to progress. But just as there are problems there are answers.

I believe the reason we don't know the answers are because we do not search for the answers. Someone out there has an answer; there is nothing new under the sun.

I have ministered to a lot of troubled youths. I find the best way to get their attention is to listen to them. Let them talk, they want to poor out their heart. They will tell you everything they are going through if you would just shut up and listen. Don't be to fast to correct them, let them continue to talk until they stop or ask you a question.

Most of the time when they first start talking they are trying to feel you out, at this point you can loose them or gain their respect. If you interrupt too soon they will feel that you are trying to force your authority on them and they will rebel. They may start out with something small or insignificant, but as they continue to talk they will get to the heart of the problem. Another thing don't take notes. They will stop automatically if you take notes. They don't want to feel that you will share any thing they have said with any one else. You have to listen carefully and pray to remember the things they are saying. Children are very smart so don't make up things with them. If you don't know the answer to a problem or have any pertinent advise on the issue, tell them that we need to study this issue together so we will both be able to understand and become better equipped to handle the problem. They can tell when you are lying and you will loose them if you just make up something to appease the moment. And most importantly don't make promises you don't intend to keep. Children will test you to see if you are sincere. They want to know if they can trust you. Once you have forged a relationship with them they will come to you with their problems and confidences because they fill they can trust you to guide them in the right direction without making them feel ignorant. If you don't know how to handle a situation get help, ask questions of someone knowledgeable on this topic, but don't bring the person with you when you are conferring with the youth. They trust you and they will feel threatened by the other person. They will feel that you are trying to gang up on them. They have forged a bond with you and to do any thing to break that bond and trust can destroy the child. One very important thing to remember is; you are an adult, you are not a child, you are their peer, you must advise them correctly no matter if they accept it or not. This is a life you are dealing with. What you say the advice you give can affect them for the rest of their lives, it can save or destroy their lives.

I always say a child has to be a child. Don't try to make your child into an adult. Let them live the life of a child while they can, while they are young. If you don't respect this balance and try to make them grow up to fast they will retrograde when they get older and start to grasp for the life they did not have. In other words an adult will try to become a child. Let them play and have fun. Teach them about life, but only the things that are pertinent to their age group. Expound on them the need for moderation in all things, that there must be a balance in life in order for life to be profitable. Do not with hold the teachings of the Lord Jesus from them. The moral teachings in the Bible can greatly benefit them as they grow older.

Don't wait until it's too late and then say I wish I had, or where did I go wrong. Too many people are saying that today, and what good does your remorse do for the child. Sometimes the mistakes you make with your children are irreversible. Don't be ashamed, or to prideful to seek help. Raising a child can be and is a challenging responsibility. Don't rely on trial and error. Pray for knowledge and wisdom, with these you can succeed. Without them you are doomed to fail.

Now I am a senior in high school, my final years. When you are growing up most teenagers look forward to their final years in high school. Becoming a senior, graduation, having the lower classes look up to you, your final years as a child, becoming an adult, leaving home, going to college, finding a job. These are a few of the things that go through the mind of a senior. During our senior year we had career day, when different professionals would come and tell us about their jobs. Recruiters from the military would come telling us the advantages of joining their branch of military service. These sessions were very interesting. It was during those sessions that I finally began to think about my future. What am I going to do when I graduate? Everyone was talking about going to college, who had received scholarships, what colleges they were going to attend. Some students were even invited to attend recruiting seminars at a few of the local colleges.

Now fear began to set in for me. I began to ask my self, have I passed enough classes to get into college. Have I wasted my time in high school playing and partying and now I won't be able to go to college with my friends. I was beginning to feel dumb. I had to do something. I didn't want to be left behind. I had spent three and a half years trying to be accepted not standing out, just doing enough to get by, and now I'm afraid I didn't do enough. I decided that I would buckle down now and start doing my work. I wanted to begin to study, do well in class. I wanted to change. Have you ever gone on a trip and before you left someone told you; "you need to take a coat it is going to be cold up there?" You left didn't take their advice and when you arrived it was very cold, but it was too late you were to far away from home to do any thing about the problem. Have you ever been there? Well that was where I was. I had wakened up to late. During our senior year we were preparing for graduation, taking pictures, practicing to march, having visitors talk to us, and sometimes only having half days in school, having fun. There were not many classroom assignments. No opportunity to catch up if you had fallen behind. Sure they were concerned about those who were failing when it seemed they would not graduate. The teachers took special interest in them.

They were given extra work to bring their grades up so they could graduate. But what about those of us who only did enough to get by? If there wasn't a teacher who was concerned enough about you getting into college then you didn't receive any special help. It seemed as though the teachers and counselors were only concerned about those who were failing and those with scholarships. Here I was wanting to do better, but to ashamed and embarrassed to cry out for help. I was doing well enough to graduate but not doing well enough to get into college. I sent my application off to the local colleges in the area hoping they would give me a chance to prove myself. I was ready to turn my life around, to try and do better.

I didn't want the other students, my friends to know that I couldn't get into college. I really didn't want my parents to know. I was hoping for a miracle. I knew my grades were low. I knew I wasn't failing though. I thought I had a c average. Only to find out later that I had a c-average which was not good enough to get into college. I waited for the letters to return that I had sent out to the different local colleges. Finally they started to come in the mail. I was rejected, what I was going to do. Pride and embarrassment would not let me talk to anyone about my situation. I didn't want to talk to my parents because I was hurt and afraid. My sister was in her first year at Spellman College and everyone in my family was bragging about her. I felt that they were all waiting to see which college I was going to attend. I didn't want to let them down; moreover I didn't want to hear them talking about me, thinking I was dumb or something. I didn't know what to do at this stage, so I kept my mouth closed and played the part. No one questioned me, so I didn't have to give any answers. Now really, wasn't that sad? Who could look at me and see what I was going through? Where were those who were supposed to be the leaders in my life? If someone had reached out to me would my life have been different? Could I have by passed some of the mistakes I made in life? Would I have been a better person? Someone has to suffer so others can be saved. Someone has to pay the price.

We are taught about pride all of our lives, especially black people. We are taught to take pride in our selves, the way we look, the way we present ourselves, our actions, our race, to have pride in who we are, take pride in what you are and to have pride in our surroundings, our country. We are taught that we are somebody, we can become somebody, we can have, and we can do. I'm black and I am proud, or I'm white and I am right. These are the principals that are ever before us as children. No one can do better than you. No one is better than you. You can have the best that life has to offer. My dad told me that," every man puts his pants on the same way, one leg at a time. So no one can do better than you can." We permeate these characteristics into our children's minds. Is it wrong to do this? No, but we must be careful to instruct our children about the differences in being prideful. I have heard a saying "pride comes before every fall." And this is very true. Pride can build you up, and pride can and will tear you down if not taught the correct way. The American Heritage Dictionary defines pride as; a sense of one's own proper dignity or value; self-respect; pleasure or satisfaction taken in one's work, achievements, or possessions. God says in the Bible; "to fear the Lord is to hate evil; I hate pride and arrogance, evil behavior and perverse speech. Proverbs 8:13 NIV. When pride comes, then comes disgrace, but with humility comes wisdom. Proverbs 11:2 NIV. Pride goes before destruction, a haughty spirit before a fall. Proverbs 16:18 NIV. I will break down your stubborn pride and make the sky above you like iron and the ground beneath you like bronze. Leviticus 26:19 NIV. I will bring the most wicked of the nations to take possession of their houses; I will put an end to the pride of the mighty, and their sanctuaries will be desecrated. Ezekiel 7:24 NIV. There is a pride which God hates and this kind of pride will lead to our destruction. Pride if used the wrong way can lead us to believe we are better than others, causing us to look down on others giving us a feel of superiority this is wrong.

No human should feel that he or she is superior to another human being. If you were to take a rich person and a poor person clean them both up and put them in the same clothing, you will not be able to tell who is rich and who is not. You can even give them both the same paragraph to read, and I will guarantee you, that you still won't be able to tell one from the other. If you take off all of their clothes and stood them side by side you will not know the difference. If you take the skin off a white person and a black person you will not know the difference, who's white or who's black. If I were to take a poor person out of the lowest poverty section of any town or city educate them groom them put them in a mansion.

You will not be able to tell if they were born with wealth or acquired wealth. The problem arises when a person believes they have arrived they are somebody. When I use the word somebody I mean that they feel they are more important than any one else on the face of the earth and that everyone else is subservient to them. They start believing that everyone else should look up to them.

There was a man in the Bible named King Nebuchadnezzar whom the Lord God had used to conquer His people Israel. God gave the children of Israel into his hands. God had even said that He would cause the wild animals to serve Him. King Nebuchadnezzar became so prideful because of his conquest that he thought that he was a god himself, and that he was the cause of his success. His pride angered God and God took his kingdom from him until he repented of his sin. You can read about King Nebuchadnezzar in the book of Daniel. There were others Pharaoh, King Saul, Ahab, Herod, and Jezebel just to name a few. These people were very prideful and they believed that they were somebody, and that all the people of the earth should look up to them. Their pride was their downfall. Pride can cause people to become arrogant, moody, snobs, hateful, abusive and sometimes violent. Prideful people can hurt themselves and those who come in contact with them. Prideful people do not have friends, they only have acquaintances. No one wants to be a true friend to a prideful person because the prideful person when given the chance will turn against their associates. Their concern is only for themselves. Nothing or no one else matters except their will. They are the ones who quote; self preservation is the law of nature. They will do what ever it takes to get their way, no matter who gets hurt in the process. This kind of pride is misplaced and unproductive and will lead to the destruction of the person.

Children's children are a crown to the aged, and parents are the pride of their children. Proverbs 17:6 NIV. The sons of your oppressors will come bowing before you; all who despise you will bow down at your feet and will call you the City of the Lord, Zion of the Holy One of Israel. Although you have been forsaken and hated, with no one traveling through, I will make you the everlasting pride and joy of all generations. Isaiah 60:14-15 NIV. Since, then, we know what it is to fear the Lord, we try to persuade men. What we are is plain to God, and I hope it is also plain to your conscience.

We are not trying to commend ourselves to you again, but are giving you an opportunity to take pride in us, so that you can answer those who take pride in what is seen rather than what is in the heart. 2Corinthians 5:11-12 NIV. As for Titus, he is my partner and fellow worker among you; as for our brothers, they are representatives of the churches and an honor to Christ. Therefore show these men proof of your love and reason for our pride in you, so that the churches can see it. 2Corinthians 8:23-24 NIV. These acts of pride are representatives of humility. They are not rewarding self, but showing respect and admiration to others for their contributions and service. When I look at a person how they dress, look (meaning clean and groomed), walk, talk, their demeanor, how they keep the possessions they have been blessed with. Then I can say this is a person deserving my respect, I can have pride in them.

Although they are the one having respect for themselves and their surroundings because the way they carry themselves, they are not arrogant or boastful not trying to get others to look up to them, or to be seen for their qualities. In humility they give the glory to someone else for their successes. Knowing that they and the qualities they possess are not of their own doing. Pride says I did it myself, respect acknowledges the aid of others for my accomplishments. A prideful person is not a team worker; they will not get in there and as the saying goes get their hands dirty. They are the ones who believe they derived their own successes, and they owe no one for who they are, nor are they owing to any one for their accomplishments in life. In other words though someone else may take pride in me, pride is not a quality I give myself. Everything I do should be done with humility and respect for persons and things, for God's creation. No man is an island, no man stands alone. We all need someone to help us and guide us through this life. Our teachings are not of our own. Our successes are derived from the successes and failures of those who were before us. Inventions are made from wants and needs. If there is no motivating factor (want or need), then there is no need to invent. Inventions are made to simplify the lives of people. And it is the people who make the invention a success or failure. It is the people who supply the want and the need. In order for the inventor to be successful he must appease the people with his invention. It is this coexistence which causes a state of humility on the part of the inventor. I the user take pride in him for his ability to invent something useful for me to simplify my life, and he has humility knowing it took both of us to make his invention successful. Whatever heights we progress to in this life there is someone in the back ground. No one can say I made it own my own. Some one motivated you, or some one pushed you to become successful. You did not do it through your own volition. When I began to believe that I am the author of my own successes then my pride becomes destructive. I may as well go and live on an island by my self. God never intended man to be independent but dependant. An independent person is a prideful person. A dependant person is a person with humility. When the Lord God made the first man Adam. He placed him on the earth with the animals, but God saw that the animals could offer no companion ship for Adam, nor help to Adam, so He made the woman Eve.

Eve was Adams helper, advisor, companion, and motivator. God took pride in Adam because he was a hard worker, caring for His creation, also loving and protecting Eve. Adam knew that all of his help was not self sufficient, he had God and Eve to support him. Thus this made Adam a humble man and not a prideful man. He worked hard in God's garden because he took pride in God's creation. And Adam was proud of the fact that God trusted him enough to place him in charge of all things on earth. Adam knew something that most people don't know or have forgotten. The earth is the Lords and everything in and on it. Be proud of who you are, take pride in what you have though it may be small, most of all take pride and be proud of whose you are, for you belong to the Lord God.

Now my years in high school are coming to an end. Reality is hitting me in the face. I have not excelled as well as I should. I've wasted four years of my life without any thought of the future, or preparing for the future. Who can I blame for my failure? No one but me. Was I capable of doing better? Yes! Did I have the mental capacity to do better? Yes! Then what was my problem? Can you look back into my past and see what went wrong? If you can then hopefully you are learning something about your self or the child you are raising or the children you will raise. I had all the opportunities to do better. I had good and conscientious teachers. There were other students in my classes who were doing well. So I can't blame my teachers for my slowness. I had good parents who loved me cared for me and provided a good life for me. I would be crazy to blame them. I had a problem and that problem was trying to destroy my life. The problem had evolved from shyness through anger and destruction and now to pride. Can you look at a child and see this? The lay person more than likely can't. It takes trained professionals to see evaluate and diagnose these problems. So what about the little person? What do they do? Most of them can't afford to take their child to a trained professional. Most of them can't recognize that there is a problem anyway. What is going to happen to that child? Where will that parent and child receive the help they need? They say the states have set up programs for parents with troubled children. But what if your child does not qualify for this assistance? They are there for extreme cases. Children who are getting into trouble with the law, or so unruly that their parents can't control them. But what about the child who is not getting into trouble with the law, and not causing trouble at home, but just not living up to his or her potentials? Where do they get help? There parent's finances will not allow them to take their child to a physiatrist. The schools have counselors, but there are so many students for them to deal with that my child could slip through the cracks.

I can only recall one time I had to see a counselor when I was in school and that was for fighting. I was expelled for three days and I had to bring my dad to school with me before they would reinstate me. And I didn't start the fight. That was my only trip to see a counselor. So it would seem that they were there for extreme cases only. You may say that times have changed from the time I was in school until now. Well that's true times have changed but the problem still remains the same.

When my boys were in public school I was very active in their education. I was asked to be on the schools parent advisory committee. I knew the principal very well she was a friend of my family. I got to know the counselors very well, and a lot of the teachers. I sat in on the boys classes sometimes. I was very disappointed in most of the classes. I found that the classes were over crowded, and I didn't like the way some of the children were setting in the classroom at the tables with their backs to the teacher. I observed some of the children not paying attention to what was going on because their focus was not toward the teacher. Some talked with each other and some had their heads on the tables sleeping. There were constant disturbances in the classes from children talking, hitting and making all sorts of gestures to other students. The teacher would call on my boys while I was there, but when I wasn't there she would send reports of them not doing well in class. My wife and I tried to keep them in public school for three years and then we said that's enough.

We took them out of public school and my wife began to home school them. I am very concerned about their education. I don't want them to go through the same things I did. They are smart boys, and I will not stand by and watch them destroy their lives. How many parents are concerned about their children's education, but can't afford to take them out of public school and put them into a private school? How many parents can't see the need, or know that their child could do better in school if there were someone there to take a personal interest in them? How many parents are saying well that's the best he or she can do so I'll just have to settle with the fact that my child is slow and will always be behind? Acts 10:34, Romans 2:11, Ephesians 6:9, and Colossians 3:25, these verses tell us that God does not show favoritism. We were all created equal; we all were blessed with a brain. None of us came here smarter than the other. Our brains were trained by someone to comprehend the things we know and do. Where we live (country, nation, state), our parents, schools, churches, and race are a contributing factor in the things we learn in life. And are major factors in our social growth.

God did not create any child born of woman greater that any other child except one, and that was our Savior the Lord Jesus Christ. There fore it is the responsibility of man to nurture and educate the children. For this to become successful the development of the child must begin at birth. Once the brain begins to adapt and comprehend its surroundings the process of learning begins. What you feed the brain at that time will and can determine the path the child will take in life. Then there remains a problem. How can a child progress correctly without the proper guidance? My parents may have the greatest intentions for my life, but if they don't have the knowledge, education and experience to lead and guide me then my life can be filled with trials and errors. My school though they are there to teach me, if they are over crowded, forced to comply with the school board to instruct me in certain subjects at certain time levels and not giving me the time and self help I need to fully understand the subject matter, then my development can and will be hindered.

My church if they do not offer parents classes on parenting which could help them understand God's laws on family and children, how to recognize problems in the family and what to do about those problems, then my growth can and will be hindered. If my church is not spiritual enough to see and act upon the needs of the families which attend those churches then the parents and children suffer. If My country, state government, federal government, society are more intent on the educational standings they have and forget that every child needs special help to become a positive contributor in the future development of society, then a talent, an invention, a voice in helping to construct a better way of life could be lost. Thus it seems that no one person or organization can take responsibility for the mistakes a child goes through in life. Nor can we leave it up to one person or organization to see that our children are fully trained and educated. The growth and education of our children is the responsibility of everyone. No one is exempt. The problem arises when no one will take the time to stand up and say I will help, I will do what ever it takes to see that our children receive the best education available. I will work with them and not force them, allowing them to develop at their level of comprehension.

Then a mind will not become wasted or stagnant. What can one person do to countermand the problem that faces our children today? Nothing! One person can't build and one person can't destroy. It takes the cumulative force of the multitudes to make changes in our society. I can stand on a street corner and warn people all day about a major catastrophe that is about to happen, if no one listens and takes action then I am just a voice blowing in the wind. Take Paul Revere for instance, when he made his famous ride warning the town's people that the British were coming, if no one listened and took action then our history would be changed. Paul Revere could not stop the British on his on, it took the efforts of the towns people coming together to make a difference. We must all stand up to our responsibilities in the growth of a child or children. We are all players in our society, none of us are spectators. What we do or don't do can and will shape history. What are you going to do? I can start the ball rolling, but I need you to help me to keep the ball rolling, I can't do it on my on.

Spring has arrived. Those students who have fulfilled their requirements are preparing to graduate. Classes for seniors have all but ceased now. Graduation day is approaching. Senior day, toddler day, rehearsing to march, baccalaureatus, half days in school are all a part of the last few months of a senior. These are times of enjoyment for the upper classmen. The last few months associated with being a child or teenager. Now we are looking forward to becoming young adults, going out to face the world. Some are looking forward to college to further their education. Others are preparing to inter the job market. Some are puzzled not knowing which direction to take, or what awaits them after high school. Never the least we all are excited having our last big extravaganza in high school. Other students are looking at you with jealousy, wishing they were you, longing for their time in the sun. Wishing their days at school were coming to an end also. Wanting to finish school leave home become an adult be out on their own.

Juniors are happy knowing they are next in line to make this big step. Watching you to see what improvements they can make in their final program when their big day arrives. But it does not matter what others are thinking it's my day now. And boy am I having fun, or so it may seem. I am trying hard to suppress this feeling that's trying to disrupt the mood of the moment. I wanted to enjoy my last days in school but worry was trying to propel its way into the festivities. No matter how hard I tried to suppress this feeling it was constituently trying to apprehend my mind. Though I am partying now having my last fling, what was going to happen to me when the partying ceased? Where am I going from here? I am trying hard not to think about that now, just enjoy the moment be happy let tomorrow worry about itself. I am trying hard, but I can't seem to shake this growing problem. What am I going to tell my friends? They are all talking about the colleges they are going to attend. When they ask me where I am going I make up some sort of excuse, I am waiting for my letters to come back, or I haven't made up my mind yet. Some of the guys that played sports were getting into some of the better colleges, and I knew I was doing better than they were in school. We all talked about them, but that wasn't doing me any good. I was beginning to feel quite embarrassed. What about my family, what was I going to tell them when the question arises? I couldn't make up some superfluous statement to them.

I was in trouble, and the partying couldn't take the place of the insurmountable situation I was in. All of the partying, the good times, my friends, the girls, nothing could keep these thoughts from entering my mind. What am I going to do? I was too embarrassed to seek help, and I didn't know where to get help anyway. I didn't ask, and no one came forward to help me. No one talked to me about my future plans outside of my friends. Did any one care about my future? I only applied to the larger colleges, no one told me that I could or should apply to the smaller colleges and I might have been accepted. I found out later that summer when talking to a relative, she told me that she had been accepted to a smaller college. We had the same grade average. Someone had to advise her. Where were my advisors? And was I the only one who faced this scenario? All I can do now is hope for the best, take one day at a time and see what the future holds. We are thought not to worry about tomorrow, but live for today. For no one can predict what the future holds, but if we just live for today and not make plans for tomorrow when and if tomorrow gets here what will we do? Then we began to live our lives on the spur of the moment. Taking what comes alone at the moment it comes alone. The Bible teaches "Where there is no vision, the people parish. Proverbs 29:18. It is true that we shouldn't worry about tomorrow, but we should plan for tomorrow. There is a difference in worrying and planning. Worrying can cause you not to think clearly, to make wrong assessments about the situation. Worrying can also cause you to overly proliferate the matter. And then there is your health, worrying can and will cause great problems in your health. I always say there are no problems, but solutions. If I get all bogged down on the problem, I will not be able to effectively concentrate and do research on finding the solution.

Worrying can cause me to become unproductive on my job and with my family. I can loose sight of what I am doing at work because of some problem I am worrying about and this could cause me or a coworker to get injured. At home I can make life miserable for my family by worrying about a problem. I will become short tempered, easily offended, argumentative. Worrying can't change things, but worrying surely can cause troubles. Then instead of having one situation to deal with you find there evolves a multitude of problems you are confronted with now. Worrying also shows a lack of faith in the Lord God. Hebrews 10:6, Without faith it is impossible to please God. NIV. Christ Jesus In the sixth chapter of the gospel of Matthew gave a dissertation on the subject of worrying. To worry is a sin, because we are not trusting God to supply our needs and work out our problems for us. A child does not worry about where they will live, sleep or if there is going to be food on the table to eat. They know that daddy and mommy will take care of their needs because they love them, and that they are their children. They know that daddy and mommy are real, alive and they are always there to protect and care for them. It is the same with the Lord God, for He is my father, my maker, my protector, my guide, my helper, and my provider. For me to worry would mean that I don't believe that God exists. Or that He doesn't love me enough to care fore me or my needs, and this would be a travesty in the eyes of God. Worrying is the one thing that is hard for humans to separate themselves from. No matter how hard I try worry seems to always slip in, and then I have to chastise myself for giving into worry.

I know God is real but I am still confronted with worry. I know God loves me, but worry won't leave me alone. How do I over come this perplexing problem. I want to please God. I want to be faithful. I don't want the Lord God to be angry with me. What do I do when problems arise and I began to worry? What helps me is prayer, prayer, and more prayer. We are humans and God knows that. We are weak and God knows that also. We need help at all times and in all circumstances. Sure worry will arise. I'm not going to lie to you and tell you that it won't. But the greatest gift I have is salvation through prayer. I can defeat worry through prayer and faith in Christ Jesus to deliver me. But how do I know this works? I have the testimony of others who are overcomes. Their willingness to help me guides me alone the way. Their witness gives me the strength and power I need to believe. Someone has gone through the same problem that I am confronted with and God delivered them and brought them though. Look for that witness. But you know the all knowing God will send that witness to you without you even looking for them. Someone one day will come up to you and say "you know I had this problem and let me tell you what God did for me." He knows what you need, and when you need it.

The testimony of others helps to strengthen me, enabling me to hold on. And if you take time and look back over your life you can see where God has preformed some miracle in your life also, assuring you He is there and that He loves and cares for you. Then I can become my greatest witness. And who can doubt what they have seen and been delivered from themselves?

Therefore when worry tries to force its way into my life I can rebuke it in the name of Jesus Christ my savior for worry has no hold on me. I can go on because I know that Christ will deliver me from this problem. I am more than a conqueror. I am a child of the true and living Lord God.

To plan – A detailed scheme, program, or method worked out beforehand for the accomplishment of an objective; a proposed or tentative project or goal (The American Heritage Dictionary). Planning should be an essential part of our lives. I know tomorrow is not promised us, but if we don't plan for tomorrow when and if tomorrow comes we will be in a big mess. Then the saying Christ said will become very true "each day has enough troubles of its own." Matthew 6:34 NIV. Why compound you problems by not planning for tomorrow? I have sat down at times and planned out the next day with all intentions of carrying out the tasks and by day's end I have found that there was something I did not have the opportunity to accomplish. But the blessing was I did accomplish some of the things on my list, and I can just roll the others onto the next day. To see my accomplishments made me happy. I came home with a smile on my face knowing I had a good day. And when I arrived home in a good mood I was able to convey my joyous feeling over to my family. Letting them share in my good mood. Then my whole family experience was up lifting. Now supposed I had not planned my day and just took what ever came alone trying to handle each problem without the for knowledge of a plan to expedite the problem. Then that problem became an issue which caused me unwanted stress and worry. This problem produced more problems as the day proceeded. By the day's end I am exasperated, frustrated, stressed out and mad.

Guess what when I get home who's going to get the benefit of my frustration. Then the whole house is in an uproar, no one is happy. I have caused unwanted frustration on my family all because I didn't take the time to plan out my day. To plan out your day means you are taking control, and not being controlled. You plan for problems and you have the opportunity to evaluate and solve those problems before the day begins. Sure things may come up which I didn't plan for, but because I took the time to concentrate, meditate and evaluate my schedule for the day, when an unexpected problem arises I will know how to solve it through meditation, evaluation and communication. This knowledge could only happen because I took the time before hand to formulate a way of handling problems in my daily schedule before the day began. The wise man plans while the fool waits for things to happen. And speaking of plans what better way to plan than to go to the person who knows what's going to happen tomorrow anyway. Proverbs 3:5-6, Trust in the Lord with all your heart and lean not on your own understanding; in all your ways acknowledge Him and He will make you paths straight. NIV. Commit to the Lord whatever you do, and your plans will succeed. Proverbs 16:3, NIV. MY Heavenly Father wrote the book on my life what I have done and what I will do. Who better to go to about my life than the person who knows all about my life?

If I go to Him about the plans I have for tomorrow pray and seek His guidance then I can only succeed. I can succeed because in seeking Him for direction, these are the plans He has laid out about my life anyway. So how can I fail? If I follow His direction, have faith in His leadership. Then my days will be brighter. And when troubles arise, I give those problems back into the hands of the problem fixer. Because I am following His leadership the problems are not mine but His, then I don't have to worry about them being solved. He will supply me with the knowledge, the ability and help I need to overcome all things. That is a part of the salvation process. If the Lord God did not want me to plan for tomorrow He would not have given me visions for tomorrow. Think about that. Visions are pictures Christ Jesus gives us about the past, and pictures and directions He gives us for the future. Don't set around worrying about tomorrow, plan for tomorrow and work today. Seek the Lord God in all things and let Him lead you in the right pass you should take.

I wish someone had taken the time to set me down and talk to me about planning out my life. Helping me to understand the importance of planning for the future. Planning requires study, and study requires meditation and research. When you do these requirements then you have the ability to see which roads to take or not to take. When you take these steps you formulate a direction for you life through association. You can choose which path is right for you and which one is not. No one wants to go down the wrong road. So when you plan you have a better chance to be objective. I wish I had learned this years ago.

Where were my advisors? Where were my counselors? Where were those who could help me on life's journey?

Now graduation is here. The big day has finally arrived. My classmates adorn their caps and gowns, taking their place in line. We march down the isles, singing our last school song, listing to all of the farewell speeches. Hearing our names called, then receiving our diplomas. And then the final farewell march as we depart out of the assembly hall. At this point there are no thoughts for tomorrow. I was just enjoying the day. At the end of the ceremony classmates hugged kissed and said their farewells to the school and to each other. We were all setting out on new pathways in life. Some excited about next fall when they would enter college. Others are wondering what the future will hold for them. This is a bright day for some, a confusing day for others. No matter let's party tonight; we will deal with tomorrow when tomorrow comes.

High school was over now, summer was here. No one talked with me about my future plans. No one made any suggestions. Well I felt I had missed the bullet. No one asked, and I didn't have to make up any answers. I felt relieved for the moment. My cousin Bill asked me to come and work with him. Bill was kind of heavy footed in the truck, so he had lost his license for a while.

He needed me to drive for him, and I needed a job. My uncle had taken me to get my drivers license when I was in the eleventh grade. So when Bill lost his license we did not have to stop working because I could drive us to work and back home. I liked working for Bill. We would go to work early, and we would get off early. I wasn't concerned about the money he was going to pay me.

My thoughts were not on money or the future. I was just happy to be working. And working with someone I cared a lot about. As usual right when I think every thing is alright a thunderstorm is brewing.

I was working with Bill learning everything I could about his trade, having fun. Getting off early, going swimming after work every day. This was the life; I didn't have a care in the world. Then toward the end of the summer my dad called me in to have a talk with me. He told me that by the fall I was going to go to college somewhere. He said he didn't care where, "you'd better go somewhere." When my dad lays down the law, you don't say anything. You just follow through. You know he's serious. I didn't ask what would be the ramifications for not going. I didn't want to know his response. I didn't want to tell him that I had applied to some colleges and was turned down. I was afraid to tell him that, then he would know that I was just playing around in school, and I didn't want to know what his response would be to that. My dad was a hard man, but he was also a fair man. He didn't take anything off anybody. He would tell you about your self, and he didn't care how you took it. That was with adults. With me, I would get mine from his belt. My dad was a construction worker, and he was strong. He was not a tall man, but boy he was strong. You did not want to rub him the wrong way. I worked with him during the summers while coming up. He was very hard on his helpers. He had names he would call them when they messed up, like bonehead and others which would be censored. I was called a bonehead quite often. I was some what afraid of my dad, because I knew he didn't play. So you tell me - I should have told him that I was rejected, and couldn't get into college, no way. I liked life, being alive. I wasn't going to do anything to cut my life short. I had to come up with something. Summer was coming to an end. What was I going to do?

Could I fess up and tell him? No that was not an option. Could I run away? No; where would I go? I'm running out of time, what should I do? I remembered one of the recruiters from the military coming to our school during career day. I said to my self that would be a good way to solve my problems. I'll enlist in the military. The more I thought about it the better it sound to me. So I began to gather information about the different divisions of military service. I talked with the recruiters from the navy, air force, and the marines. They all told me that I would have to enlist for four years. I didn't like that. I wanted to get away, but I didn't want to stay away for four years. I went to the army recruiter and talked to him. He said that their recruitment was three years. Now that sounds good to me. I had to take some test to see what I would be qualified to do. They asked me where I wanted to be stationed when I finished my training. They said I could have my choice.

They showed me a list of jobs they had and they asked me which ones I would be interested in. To my surprise everything I applied for I didn't get. So why ask me if you are going to put me where you want me? I signed up for the army. The next thing I had to do was take a physical, be sworn in, and then it's off to be trained to become a soldier. My troubles were over, I have dodged the bullet, or so I thought. Now I'll go home and tell everyone.

No one knew about my plans to join the military, not even Bill. I kept this to myself as I usually do everything. I was bad about talking to anyone, seeking advice about the directions I take in life. No one asked, and I didn't volunteer to seek help.

I would do things on my own. This was a bad mistake. I didn't know God's word. I didn't really know God. So how could I know to seek Him for directions in my life? As I said before we did not have a children's church, so we did not have anyone to train us and teach us about seeking advice about the directions we should take in life. There wasn't a class in school, and my parents did not set us down and counsel us. So what was I going to do? There wasn't anything left for me but to make my own choices in my life. I should have talked to someone; this was a major event I was beginning to take. Someone should have sat me down and talked to me, questioned me about my future plans. I had not lived this life before, so how would I know what's right for me and what's not. Where were my parents? Where was my school? Where was my church? Were people to involved with their own lives to be concerned about mine? Or did they lack the knowledge to help me? Oh; this happened to me, but how many more children were going through the same scenario I was encountering? How many today are facing this dilemma? I'm pretty sure that not every one is faced with this problem. But how many are? Can their lives be changed with a little help and understanding? How long must a person go down the wrong street before someone asks him? What are you looking for? Where are you trying to go? Shouldn't we be involved in the future plans of our children? Helping them to make good constructive choices? I know they want to make their own decisions. But how long have they been here? How many roads have they traveled? When you enter a new job someone has to train you about your task and responsibilities. They tell you about the safety rules so you want get hurt or hurt someone else. Life is set up the same way. We didn't come into life knowing but seeking. Although some people act like they know it all and they don't need help. They are the very ones making the greatest mistakes.

I know because I have been there and those mistakes can be irreversible. Some mistakes can be changed made new. Some mistakes can never be changed they last a life time. I would like to help someone avoid the pitfalls in life than to stand by and watch them fall into a hole. Oh if I could erase some of the things I did in this life. I thought I knew what I was doing, but I did not ask, I did not seek advice, and because of this I have things in my past which will haunt me the rest of my life. They say when you ask for forgiveness with a sincere heart, you will be forgiven.

They also say that God will not bring those things up to you anymore, that when they come that is the evil one trying to convict you all over again, trying to make you feel guilty about your past. But I tell you that there are something's even though you have been forgiven for them will come up again in some way to remind you of your mistakes and to let you know not to go that way again. There are something's that hurt and you wonder why was I so stupid, how did I make such a bad mistake? Those things are there, you can't erase them, and you can't runaway from them. The only thing you can do is face them, pray about them and move on. There are something's you can't change that happened in your past. Some lives you have hurt, something's broken that can't be repaired. I can't run away from that, that's there. But can I help you? Can I counsel you? Can I share with you? I don't want you to have these same skeletons in you closet. I have been there. I know the pain first hand. Please let me take you by the hand and guide you away from this tentative trouble which is trying to come forth.

I went back home to let everyone know what I had done. No one spoke harshly to me. No one tried to convince me that I had made a bad mistake. No one even asked me why I joined. I don't know if my dad was angry with me or not. We never had a conversation about the topic. When the day came for me to leave, I said my good bys and caught the bus to go to the induction center. I was leaving home for good now. No more running away and coming back tomorrow. This was for real. I had made a three year commitment and I would not be back until the time was up. I am starting my new life. I am leaving family and friends. Going off to a new land. I don't know what's ahead of me, but I'm ready for the challenge. I had no fear for the days ahead. I was excited about the future. I was leaving home not to just get away from my dad and what he would do to me for not being able to get into college. No; there was more to it than that.

When I came up I would always here my parents, grand parents, and other people talk about how you had to have a good job to get ahead in this life. They would always say "work hard get a good job make some good money and then you will be successful." Their focus was on what money could buy, cars, houses, clothes. If you work hard you to can have these things, that was where they were. So when I graduated my focal point was on how I can get these things without going to college. I knew my grandparents had a home and a nice car. I lived in a nice home, and we had a nice car. I wanted the same. My parents did not finish college. My grand parents did not even go to college. My dad attended college for one year. I didn't know anyone who attended or finished college. They all were doing fine to me. They had nice things; I did not hear them complain about bills. We always had food in abundance to eat. We had a new car to ride in. We were doing ok to me. I thought to myself, how can I get a nice house, car, and have money now?

There's no need of thinking about college anymore I have messed that up. Now how can I make these things happen? I knew working with Bill was ok, but I couldn't reach my goals working the way I was at the present time. I needed a plan to succeed. Here I go with that plan, the thing we talked about a little while ago.

I had an itch, and I needed a way to scratch the itch. I remembered the recruiters talking about benefits of being a military person. Right; I can make this happen for me. Three years in the service and I can come out and have the same things my friends are trying to get, and I can get it faster. They will have to go to college four years to get a good job, and then after they get a job they will have to work a while to buy a house. I can do all of this in three years. And when I come out of the service they guarantee me that I will be trained for a good civilian job paying good money. Boy I didn't need college after all. I could get all the things I wanted by just giving Uncle Sam three years of my life. My plan was a good one, I had it all worked out so I thought. I didn't talk to anyone about my plan. I didn't know how to pray and seek God for direction. All I had was my own mental inspirations, and that can be your down fall. Fear will always cause you to run in the wrong direction. Don't misunderstand what I am saying. Military service is not a bad thing. I think the service is a good thing when you enlist for the right motives. I don't believe the service should be used as a way of escape. Then you will not reach your full potential, because you will not put forward your best. There are many people on jobs or serving on committees who are just there, not because it is their calling a place where they really chose to be. It is just a job for them.

They go and do what's required of them and no more. They don't really want to be there so they think to themselves, why should I put forward any effort to excel on this job I'm just here for a pay check. This attitude will stagnate them and the company they are working for. Or if they are serving on a committee they will not put forward their best to help the committee advance and meet it goals. They are just taking up space. I have learned that you can't run from you problems, they will over take you and escalate into larger problems. You must face the situation head on with a positive attitude that you can succeed and demolish the situation. My favorite saying is; "There are no problems, there are only solutions." If you concentrate too much on the problem you will not able to find the answer to solve the situation. Your focal point should be on solving what ever has been thrown your way. Don't run from the wall, but tear it down. And most of all seek guidance. Pray to the Lord Jesus. He is your Savior. He will provide you with the answer so you will become victorious. He will also provide you with the people who will assist you giving you good directions, and will not lead you down the wrong path. I really wanted to go to college. Military service was just a way of escape for me. Though I learned a lot while I was there, my life was heading in a direction which became destructive for me. From this point on I was in a down hill spiral. Did the good Angels win, or was I doomed to be destroyed?

We were loaded onto a bus and off we go to take our training at Fort Jackson in South Carolina. When we arrived we went through all of the scare tactics they put new recruits through. They didn't scare me though; I thought the orientations were funny. After induction and the traditional hair scalping we were assigned to our company and to our barracks. My training sergeant was an Indian. He was tall and slim with long legs. He never laughed in our presence, and he loved to run, so in return we ran a lot. We would wake up a three o clock in the morning an run until revelee at six in the morning.

I liked exercise so this was fun to me. I thrived on the challenge, the physical excursion. Our training sergeant was a master sergeant; we also had a sergeant over our barracks. We were separated into platoons. Each platoon had its sergeant and corporals. I was chosen to be a corporal, the leader of a squad of about ten men. There were some who didn't like the idea that they chose me. Back in those days you didn't select a black to be in charge of whites that was taboo. The funny thing about this was, the sergeant who chose me was white, now wasn't that something. This was the middle sixties and segregation was in force. But there was no segregation in the military at this time. We all trained together and slept in the same barracks and ate together. I guess this was something new for the whites and the blacks. There were some who resented this but they never said anything openly, or acted in anyway to show their feelings. I remember one hand to hand training I was teamed up with this white guy and we were sparing. I thought I new how to fight, but he beat my butt. Later he came to me and apologized, he told me that he used to box in school, and that he was their best boxer. After that we became good friends. I never asked for the position of leadership they chose me, and I didn't want it. In the army you do as you are told without any response. After a while I liked the position and I continued to do my best at the things we were being trained to do. I now can understand why some guys didn't want to go into service at that time. They train you to become cold hearted killers.

All of my training in boot camp was focused on how to survive and take the life of another human being. We were told that we were defending our country and our way of life. Isn't it funny that we must kill others to live in peace? Why can't we talk things out rather than resolving to destruction of life? I did not know the word of God back then, had I know and understand I would have been an objector to. We fight over land which does not belong to us. We fight for our way of life, we say for our freedom. The Bible says "the earth is the Lord's and everything in it, the world, and all who live in it; Psalm 24:1, Man was given stewardship over the earth, but he thinks he owns the earth. Every one has this, my syndrome. This is mine and I will fight you if you try to take it away from me. Nothing belongs to man. Man doesn't even own himself. So why is he so possessive? In the beginning of creation when The Lord God made Adam and told him that he was giving him the birds, the seed – bearing plants, every tree that has seed in it, everything that has the breath of life in it (Genesis 1:28-31). To this date man has misinterpreted this statement. God was putting Adam in charge of His creation. Telling Adam and Eve to love and take care of it. Not to abuse and misuse His creation. Nor to become possessive. God formed the earth and filled it before He created mankind. After everything was put upon the earth then God made man.

Man did not have to do anything but enjoy the work someone else had labored to create. Man was given the job of naming everything on the face of the earth. Calling them whatever he chose. Man had no need to be possessive. God would give him everything he needed to carry out his mission. God watched over man visited him to see how he was doing. He never left man alone. Though man could not see Him all the time, He could see man. The Lord God was always there watching, surveying, caring, and loving man and His creation.

The Lord God never gave up His kingship over His creation. Everyone wants to tell his neighbor how to live, but who's to say that I am living correctly or incorrectly? If you have what I want and you do not give it to me, then I'll take it from you by force or I will steal it from you. We call others barbaric, but are we any different? We send our son's and daughters of to war to die for our way of life, while we remain in our comfort zone far away from the fighting. Man was given the job to take care of the earth and everything on the earth, land and sea. How would you rate man's efficiency in fulfilling his job?

Basic training was exciting to me. They worked us very hard. We were up at 3: AM in the morning running up and down hills until 6: AM. Revelee was at 6: AM then we had breakfast. After breakfast we trained all day long even into the night. They push and pulled us mentally and physically. If we could not take it they wanted to know it now, not when someone's life would depend on us and the decisions we would make in the heat of trouble. They wanted to know if we could follow orders without question. If we would stand fast under pressure, keeping our heads when the situation seems hopeless. They wanted to prepare us for every situation we might face with hopes that nothing will be a surprise to us.

Isn't that how God prepares us for life? We have His book of instructions to help us in every situation we may encounter. Our days are supposed to start with Him, seeking Him for our instructions for the day.

Praying to God for help to meet the day's challenges at home, at work, at school, wherever life carries us this day. Life has many challenges, many mysteries. We must be prepared to meet the challenges each day will bring, and I said each day will bring.

I don't care who you are, or what level of life you may be on, where you live, how much money you may have, if you are sick or healthy, every day has it's challenges. If we are not trained to meet these unknown challenges what a disaster the day can bring. God trains us for service to Him. Just as I had to go through military training, God also sends us through Christian training. Sometimes the training can be easy, and sometimes the training can be hard. I have learned in my life that the easy lessons we sometimes forget, but no one forgets the hard lessons, they stay with us no matter how old we may get, or how many years may pass. Sometimes God's training (lessons) seems as though we have reached our limitations, we have attained our breaking point. Yet God carries us a little further, further than we though we could go. He knows how much we can bear, we don't know our limitations. Sometimes we give up when our help is right around the corner. Our limited faith blinded us from reaching our goal. We have to be pushed, stretched refined, and polished in order to meet the challenges of life.

With some of us the training (test) is harder. My training in the military was not as hard as the front line soldier (infantry), and the front line soldiers (infantry) training was not as hard as those in special service. We had different levels of training for each level of service.

This was based on the crucial ness of your mission. It is the same with our service to God. There are those who God has set aside for special service, and their training can be awesome, stretching them to the limits He has set for them. God knows His creation; He knows how much we can bear, and He will never put on us more than we can bear. Some of us are chosen to stand at the gates of hell, as Christ did, but He was there to set the captives free, we are there to stop people from entering by helping them to know the word of God, and to know God Himself, His love and mercy. Those He has set aside for this special service are faced with situations which seem unbearable. I know you have heard people who have gone through things in life, and you have said boy I could not have gone through that. Those with greater testimonies go through great test and challenges. They must endure these test and challenges for our sake and salvation. Their testimonies help us to see the actual workings of God, His love, mercy, faithfulness, blessings, and even His wrath. Through their testimonies we can see the Bible take life, become a reality.

I made it through basic training, graduated, and know it was time to go to my next training station. I was headed further north now. I left Fort Jackson South Carolina headed to Aberdeen Proving Grounds Maryland. I had never been this far north before in my life. It was the beginning of November now the snow had not started yet. Aberdeen was a very pretty post. I was excited seeing the beauty of this facility. They had all of the heavy armament positioned around the Post. Armament I had only seen on television, now I am seeing this heave artillery in person. I was mesmerized. I was taken by the size and veracity of these huge weapons of destruction. There ability to fire projectiles miles away with accuracy was awesome. They were sending me here to be trained to keep these machines in operation. Although that was not the job I signed up for.

I signed up to be a truck mechanic, but I found out that it does not matter what you signed up for they were going to use you where they needed you according to their discretion. I found out a lot of things I asked for in my induction never materialized, but being in school was interesting. There were a lot of new recruits there and also veteran soldiers. A lot of the veteran soldiers were there to change their job classification. I became friends with some of the older soldiers. They would take me into the surrounding cities on our off duty time. I got to see Washington, Baltimore, New York and Philly. I was being trained and seeing the Northern United States at the same time. This was very exciting to me. To get trained paid and travel was OK. And the training wasn't hard. All you had to do was look listen do what you were told then you could make it. We worked in groups helping each other out, boy this was a breeze. The instructors were not like they were in basic training, hollering at you pushing you; they showed us what to do then they allowed us to perform the task. If we made a mistake they did not jump all over us, they just comely corrected us. I could appreciate this. This was easier than being in high school. I was in hog heaven now.

Our barracks was next to the women barracks. They were there being trained for nursing and office duty. During this area there were not any women fighting with the men.

Their barracks was strictly off limits for us, but that didn't stop us from associating with them. I didn't get the opportunity to make my move. They were only interested in the older soldiers with rank. They didn't have time for us raw recruits. That was ok with me; I met a lot of young ladies when I went into the cities. The Wacks could be stuck up all they wanted to, I didn't care.

Christmas was approaching, and they let us go home for Christmas if we wanted. One of my friends had a car and he was going home. He lived in South Georgia, I don't remember where. Four of us piled into his car and headed home for the holidays. This would be my first time going home since I left. All of my family and friends were excited to see me, and I was excited to see them also. I wore my military uniform to Church; the Pastor had me stand up in front of the people. I felt special. After Church service every body had to hug me kiss me pat me on the back and wish me well. They really made me fill good. I had a wonderful time those few weeks I was at home. Now back to duty.

It is the first of March now and we are completing our training. I really enjoyed my time here. I got to see some of the cities in the north, and how the people lived. I got to see more snow than I had ever seen in my life. I had never experienced snow up to my waist. The snow was dry and not as cold as the snow at home in Atlanta. When we have snow at home it is cold and wet followed by ice. The snow in the north was different; I enjoyed walking in this snow. Now it is March we are ready to graduate. They didn't hold any graduation ceremony. They just told us that we had passed our course. There were no diplomas, or certificates just you've passed, that was all. They told us to get our barracks in order and then fall out in formation.

The Company Commander congratulated us on our completion of our classes and told us that from there we would be heading out to our permanent duty stations. There were ½ ton trucks parked next to the driveway where we were in formation. We all noticed them as we were standing there. I thought those trucks would carry us to our next destination, or to some other mode of transportation. The Company Commander said "as I call out your names I want you to step forward. He called my name and two others, we stepped forward and he told us that we would be going to Germany. He told us to go back to the barracks and wait until some one comes to get us when the bus arrives. He told the other soldiers standing there to go back into the barracks grab you duffle bags and load up on the trucks you are going to Vietnam. There were about seventy five soldiers headed to Viet Name from our Company.

I was not happy about going to Germany. When I enlisted they asked my where I would like to be stationed? I told them in Hawaii. Now instead of going south, I was headed farther north. Why ask me what job I want to have? And where I want to be stationed? And then give me the job, and duty station you want me to have.

It seems to me all the questioning was a lie. You lead me to believe one thing when I enlisted and then gave me something totally different. It was to late now what could I do about it. You are in the army now. Keep your mouths closed and take orders that's the army way. I was tough that in basic training. You belong to Uncle Sam now; you no longer have a life of your own. The Army is you mother, father, sister and brother. Complaining means you are a trouble maker. I did not like what happened, but I wanted to be a good soldier.

When I was in the Military we were taught to obey the orders given to us without question. That was the sign of a good soldier. No matter how you felt about the orders given to you, you had to obey those orders. If you did not obey there were disciplinary actions that were imposed on you. The punishment could be severe to the extent of a court martial with time in the stockade or it could extend to a dishonorable discharge (dismissal from service). They were very serious about you doing what they told you. Your obedience or disobedience could result in the saving of lives, or the lost of life. There were officers over us who had beforehand planned a course of action we should take. Our mission had been carefully planned before the orders came down to us. Our job was to obey those orders without compromising the mission. To change or alleviate anything in those orders could affect the out come of the mission.

When I think about it, God has established a set mission for our lives and we are to seek Him for direction and guidance to accomplish the mission. Proverbs 3:5-6 NIV: Trust in the Lord with all you heart and lean not to **your own understanding**;

In all your ways acknowledge Him and he will make you paths straight. The King James Version say: And He will direct your path. We were not born on the earth by mistake, or to fulfill our own selfish desires. In the Book of Ephesians 2:10: For we are God's workmanship, created in Christ Jesus to do good works, which God prepared in advance for us to do. In advance means God prepared a job for us before we were born. The job or assignment came first, and then we came on the scene. His plan for our lives is to bring Him praise and honor through His son Christ Jesus. We are to look to Him for direction and guidance in all areas of our lives. Our obedience to God can bring others closer to Him. When we disobey it could be detrimental to the lives of others. We may not always understand the assignment God has given us to do, but

God knows why and when we are to fulfill a particular job. I remember a story I heard a Minister tell one Sunday, he said "He was asleep early one morning about midnight when God woke him up and told him to go out to the bridge and holler "the Lord loves you". He said he thought he was just dreaming and didn't really believe that was the Lord talking to him, so he fell asleep again. As he was asleep the Lord woke him up again and told him to go out to the bridge and holler "the Lord loves you".

Once again he said that he knew that wasn't the Lord because it was dark and cold outside about one o'clock in the morning, and why would the Lord tell him to go out to the bridge and holler the "Lord loves you". Instead of falling back to sleep this time he lay there for a few minutes and he heard the voice say again "go out to the bridge and say the Lord loves you". This time he got up put on his coat drove to the bridge got out of his car and hollered the Lord loves you. He then got back into his car drove back home and went back to sleep. He said the next Sunday a man got up in Church an said " that he was under the bridge last night about to jump and take his life when he heard this voice from heaven say the Lord loves you and he stopped and did not jump off the bridge. It is not for us to understand the orders that God gives us, or even to question Him about his orders. Our job is just to obey God.

If you remember in the book of Genesis 1-2, before God made man he created the heavens earth, light, expanse in the sky, land, seas, plants, trees, vegetation, sun and moon, living creatures in the seas, birds to fly in the air, living creatures to move along the land, and wild animals.

It wasn't until after God had created all these things then He created man. Then after he created man he told him to give names to His creation. God put man in charge of his creation. He did not give man supremacy over His creation. God will not give His supremacy to any man. Man was given the task of taking care of God's creation. Man was to be a care giver, a watchman. Not the supreme authority, the master. Also man was not supposed to change God's creation. After God made everything He said that His creation was good, finished. He did not ask man to recreate what he had made. Being fruitful and replenishing the earth does not mean to recreate.

After God had given man his duties then he created woman (Eve). Woman was the last to be created. Woman's (Eve) job was to help man (Adam) take care of God's creation. Woman was made to help man. Man was not her master, nor was woman man's master. They were to work together in harmony caring for God's creation.

God had prepared everything for the arrival of man. Everything was laid out for man before man came on the scene. Man's assignment had already been planed, but through the disobedience to God's orders to man the world took on a drastic change. Death became man's master. Because man did not follow God's orders precisely, man gave himself over to sin and death. Many people would suffer and die because man did not follow God's orders. God told man (Adam) not to eat of the tree of the knowledge of good and evil. Man (Adam) and his mate woman (Eve) chose to disobey God. The Bible does not tell us that God sat man down and told him the full ramifications if he disobeyed God's orders. God did tell man if you eat of the tree of the knowledge of good and evil you will die. For some of us that would be good enough. But for some folk they would have to test God to find out if they would surely die. We call these people Eve's. God did not tell Adam that if he disobeyed not only would he die, but every one born after him (Adam) would die.

Some people have to know the whole story before they commit to a task. Don't get me wrong, sometimes we need to have the whole picture revealed to us, it depends on the messenger, and the message they are carrying.

If I know you are a liar, deceiver, and a person with low morals. Give me the whole story, and repeat it to me more than one time. A liar can't tell a lie the same way twice, they will turn the story around, or they will subtract or add to the lie. Adam was not dealing with a liar, this was God his creator. It wasn't like he didn't know who God was, because God visited him in the garden occasionally. Adam saw God face to face, talked with God, saw Him ascend into heaven, and descend to the earth. So what excuse could he (Adam) give for his disobedience? Oh the woman you took from my rib, she made me do it. And when God confronted the woman (Eve), she said Oh the snake made me do it. The fact is both of them were wrong and guilty of disobedience. Both of them were responsible for their actions. Both of them could not follow orders. Both of them caused the world to fall into sin. God did not punish Adam alone, He punished Eve also. He punished both of them. Woman get of the man's back, and man get off the woman's back. Adam and Eve were wrong.

Obedience was crucial. The world would fall into darkness because of the disobedience of Adam and Eve. Their disobedience not only affected their lives but it migrated into our lives today. We are at war with our selves because Adam and Eve could not follow one simple order, "don't eat the fruit". Because of their sin we have this inner war within us taunting us to be disobedient to God's orders (Commandments). The Apostle Paul describes it this way; "for I have the desire to do what is good, but I cannot carry it out. For what I do is not the good I want to do; no, the evil I do not want to do this I keep on doing, Now if I do what I do not want to do, it is no longer I who do it, but it is sin living in me that does it. So I find this law at work: when I want to do good, evil is right there with me. For in my inner being I delight in God's law; but I see another law at work in the members of my body, waging war against the law of my mind and making me a prisoner of the law of sin at work within my members. What a wretched man I am! Who will rescue me from this body of death? Thanks be to God through Jesus Christ our lord. Romans 7:18-25

Orders are commands given to us by those who have been place in authority over us. In the military we did not have the right or authority to disobey those orders. When you work for someone you still don't have the right to disobey their orders or they will fire you. Take a lesson from Moses when he was on Mount Sinai with God. Exodus 32:1-14; the Israelites and those who left Egypt with them were camped at the foot of Mount Sinai. Moses went up on Mountain Sinai to be instructed By God. Moses had been up on the Mountain for a long time. The people though that Moses had died up on the mountain because it took him so long to return. They told Aaron, Moses brother to make them a golden calf so they can worship it. God knew what they were doing. Now listen to what God told Moses, and what Moses said to God.

Then the Lord said to Moses, "Go down, because your people, whom you brought up out of Egypt, have become corrupt. They have been quick to turn away from what I have commanded them and have made themselves an idol cast in the form of a calf. They have bowed to it and sacrificed to it and have said, "These are you gods, O Israel, who brought you up out of Egypt". "I have seen these people. "The Lord said to Moses." And they are a stiffed neck people.

Now leave me alone so that my anger my burn against them, and that I may destroy them. Then I will make you into a great nation." But Moses sought the favor of the Lord his God. "O Lord," he said "why should you anger burn against your people, who you brought out of Egypt with great power and a mighty hand? Why should the Egyptians say, "it was with evil intent that he brought them out, to kill them in the mountains and to wipe them off the face of the earth." Turn from your fierce anger, relent and do not bring disaster on your people. Remember your servants Abraham, Isaac and Israel, to whom you swore by your own self: "I will make your descendants as numerous as the stars in the sky and I will give your descendants all this land, I promised them, and it will be their inheritance for ever." Then the Lord relented and did not bring on His people the disaster He had threatened.

Though you may not agree with your employer about the orders he has given you, you can take a lesson from Moses. Moses used diplomacy when questioning God; maybe we need to relook at the orders you are giving me. Maybe we should rethink this situation. May I offer some suggestions which might be helpful and arrive at the same conclusion you are attaining to achieve. Diplomacy is always the best avenue to take when you know the orders you have been give can be harmful to safety and life. Diplomacy can work most of the time, but diplomacy can not help you when you are wrong. Only mercy can save you then. Adam and eve were wrong for disobeying God. Instead of throwing the blame off on someone else they should have appealed to God's mercy, accepted their guilt, and took what ever punishment God would institute on them, and then maybe we would not be fighting this fight with sin today.

We do not need to know all the answers to follow orders. We were not given all the answers when I was in the military, and we don't need to know all the answers in the Lords army either. We are a questioning people. We have to know the whys. Why does the sun rise in the east? Why is there air? Why do salmons swim up stream? Why am I told to do a job I don't understand? Why is Obie writing this book? If we don't know the whys we become uncomfortable. Our search to find the answers can sometimes lead us into disobedience. Our disobedience leads to God's anger and punishment. God's punishment could lead to our eternal death. Every action has a reaction weather good or bad. We teach our children to obey without questioning us. We want them to do as they are told. It is our belief that we have the years of experience (knowledge) to guide them in the right direction. But when it comes to us we have to know why. Does God our Creator not have the ability, expertise and experience to guide us in the right direction? Can we trust Him that if He tells us to do something that he has already seen the out come? Has the book of life already been written? Or is God still writing the book adding pages as events unfold? Think about this for a minute: You are in an accident. The officer arrives on the scene. You are bleeding profusely, the car is all mangled up, and you are suffering. The officer approaches you, are you hurt he asks you? Then he proceeds: what happened? Where is the other vehicle? Remember you are loosing blood while he proceeds to ask these questions. And he continues: May I see you drivers license and proof of insurance? Then after all these questions he calls for the ambulance. After about forty minutes the ambulance arrives, they put you into the ambulance rushes you to the hospital, upon arriving at the hospital you expire (die). And guess what the hospital was only five miles away. If the officer had not been so questioning you life could have been saved.

Now I am going to throw you a curve. I am not in the military any more where I can't ask questions. I do believe there are times when it is permissible for me to ask questions. I do believe that there are times when God will allow me to ask him a question. But in all things we must have wisdom, knowing when it is permissible to ask, and when we are to go forth without questioning. Remember Job? In the Book of Job, Job questioned God about the things he was going through. Job wanted to know why he was suffering so badly. Job wanted God to come down hold court and let him plead his case. If you haven't read the story of Job check it out. Mostly every one when they are going through something refers back to the story of Job. I do it, and I know you have done it to. I believe it is ok to ask God why I am going through this situation. If I have done anything wrong please let me know so I can repent and not do whatever I did again. Why did my mother, dad, brother, sister, etc, have to die? Why didn't I get the job I asked you for? I believe God wants us sometimes to ask Him why. There are times we need to know. There are times when we need to know the answers. We can not grow if we don't seek answers. But we must use wisdom. We must know when it is permissible as in the case of Moses and Job, and when it is not permissible and can lead to sin. This knowledge can only be attained through prayer and reading and knowing the word of God. A close relation ship with God will let you know when not to step on his feet. Be careful. It's on you.

The bus came to pick us up, and we were off to meet our ship. I had finished basic training. I had finished my MOS (specialist) training. And now I was off to my permanent duty station. When the Army says permanent, they mean until we need you somewhere else. We arrived in New York, and began to board the ship. I had never been on a ship before. The ship was a personal carrier, it was huge. Standing out side looking up at the massive structure it looked like a large building. There were a lot of soldiers boarding the ship. As we walked up the ramp we were meet by officers and master sergeants who assigned us to our births (sleeping quarters). In our barracks were these bunks like hammocks. The only difference was they were solid and able to hinge up out of the way of the aisles. We were in this large room with no portals (windows).

I did not know it but our birth was below the water line. The ship had many levels. The Navy had the first level. The army officers had the second level. The NCOs (Noncommissioned officers) had the third level. All of the other soldiers occupied the remaining levels. It was good to have someone there that I knew. This kind of helped me with my anxiety. I had boarded this massive hunk of steal preparing to cross this large ocean. That was kind of unsettling. Well we are off headed to Germany.

As we left port the ride through the harbor was very smooth. I thought to my self that this was going to be a piece of cake. Yea right! I wanted to be able to look out side as we left, but we were not allowed up on the deck. All we could hear was the roar of the engines and the motion of the ship moving. This was not a cruse ship. When we got settled in they came around to give us our duties on the ship. We were not there to lie around and take it easy. We had to work. All of us were assigned duties. We were not allowed to go above deck, or to go on any other level unless we were assigned some duty. I was assigned kitchen (galley) duty along with the other two guys that left my last duty station. We had to report to the kitchen at 3: AM in the mornings. We worked there until 2: PM in the evenings. We pilled a lot of potatoes. Every day all we did was pill potatoes. For eight days all we did was pill potatoes. They had this huge mixing machine, the bowl was about four feet tall, and about two feet wide. We would wash the potatoes and put them into this large mixer, and the mixer would mash and whip the potatoes. As we finished pilling a large pot of potatoes we would drop them into the mixing bowl.

I didn't mind kitchen (galley) duty it wasn't hard. The cooks on ship were civilians. They called them merchant marines. There regular jobs were on this ship, and where ever this ship would go they went also. They were very friendly. They took care of us. If it were not for them the trip could have been very tough for me. They helped me make the trip across the ocean. I had never been on a ship before, but I had been on a boat. My Dad had this boat he had gotten from doing a job for someone. I remember the first and last time he took the boat out. My Dad, myself and Mike a friend of mine was at Lake Altoona. MY dad was sitting on the side of the boat at the driver's position. We were coming out of a cove, my Dad speeded the boat up and as we reached the open water the boat began to lean one side and almost turning over. Mike and I were on the back, it scared us so bad all we could do was laugh. That was our first and last time on that boat.

This was the ocean now, the water was calm, and the ship was running very smooth. All the first day every thing was fine. While we were in the kitchen there were portals (windows). I would go and look out the portals at the ocean. All I could see was water. I wasn't afraid, nor sea sick. The boat was running very smooth.

The second day out we hit a storm. The boat began to be tossed around. The boat would go up and down; it would roll from side to side. When you would eat you had to hold your plate or it would slide to the next person or off the table. You didn't want you plate to slide to the next person because it might come back with more in it than it left you with. Mostly all the soldiers were getting sea sick. I was ok the first two days, but seeing the other guys and the smell of them getting sick was getting to me. They gave us sea sick polls, but the pills weren't helping me. I would look out the portal in the kitchen, when the boat would rise; you could see the top of the ocean, when the boat would roll or go down you could see the portal go under water. I began to get sick. The cooks saw my condition and took me to their birth. They pulled out a bottle of rum and told me to drink some.

I had a few drinks and forgot all about my sea sickness. I began to roll with the boat. Everyone else was getting sick, but I was going around singing songs. Every day from that time on I would go to their birth before work and after work. If it wasn't for them I would have been in bad shape. I was in bad shape though not from sea sickness.

We remained in rough water for six out of eight days at sea. Can you imagine being tossed back and forth rolling from side to side for six days? Watching guys heave up their guts. That was awful. By the seventh day the storm had subsided and they allowed us to go up on deck to get some fresh air. This was the first time I got to see out over the ocean without looking through the portal in the galley. The site was breath taking. The ocean was gray as far as you could see. The ocean looked like mountains that rise and fall. The ship seamed as though it would go up this mountain and then go over the other side down into this valley then back up again. It was awesome watching from the deck. I could not see another ship out there with us. It was as though we were alone out on this large body of water. As far as you could see out in any direction it looked as though the water would meet the sky. I began to think about how awesome God is to create something this beautiful yet so awesome. This ship was like a rowboat in this massive water. How could a person even want to attempt to cross this ocean in a small craft? You would have to be crazy. They allowed us to stay up on deck all day, and then it was back down in the hole. That night as they were taking head count we were told that one of the soldiers was missing. They believed he had fallen overboard. They searched the ship from top to bottom, but they could not find him. They did not turn around to go back to find him because they said if he fell over board he couldn't survive more than a few minutes in the cold water. I did not know the soldier, but that did not stop me from filling sorry for him.

By the seventh day we were getting close to land. They allowed us to go up on the deck. As we approached land you cold see these high white peaks in the distance. The Captain of the ship came over the intercom and told us that we were nearing the White Cliffs of Dover. Form a distance they looked like clouds with clouds all around them, but having very distinctive shapes. Everyone was standing there in awe.

The closer we got, the more my mouth fell open. The mountains were white from the bottom where they touched the water to the very top. These were not white snow capped mountains, they were all white. You could not hear a word on the ship. Everyone was memorized at the sight. I had seen the ocean with its grayness and the waves forming mountains, and then now this, these massive white mountains of land white as snow. How fortunate I was to behold sights which a lot of people only read about in books, or see on television. Only God can make such and awesome vision of beauty. I was getting a first hand look at only a fraction of God's creation, of His power and might. Could science explain what I was seeing? I know they would try to make up explanations, but why. Why not believe in a supreme being that could create all these things and put them in their prospective places. God had laid out the earth, everything has a place, and everything has a purpose. Why can't we just enjoy what He has created for us, why do we have to explain it (creation), and try to destroy it (creation)?

Boy I was really enjoying this, and by the way I was sober. We were going through the straights the water was very calm. There were no more mountains of water. The water had turned from gray to blue. It was very peaceful and beautiful. I did not want to leave that area. But no matter what I wanted the ship sailed on.

On the eight day we reached Bremarhavin Germany. It was time to disembark. I said my good bys to the cooks, had a final goodbye drink with them, and headed for the truck they sent to pick us up. At first glance Germany looks like any other state I had been to. It wasn't until we left the docks that I began to see the difference. They drive on the wrong side of the street. Their street signs have graphics on them instead of words. They speak this foreign language. And I didn't see any black people as we went through the towns. Their land was beautiful. They land scraped even the sides of the hills. The land was beautiful. Here I go again, I was mesmerized, and I had never seen anything like this in my short life. The towns were clean and beautiful. The majority of them rode bicycles. There were Volkswagens every where. They use Mercedes Benzes for taxicabs. What kind of people are these?

We arrived at our post early morning. The members of my company were at work. The barracks looked like an old stone warehouse from the outside. There were two buildings which stood next to each other. As you entered the first building there was steps that went up and down. It reminded me of our building when I was in High school. I was taken in to meet the Company Commander and the first Sergeant. Their office was on the left at the top of the first set of steps. Our first Sergeant was a Hawaiian. He was about my height and very friendly. He introduced us to our Company commander. The Company Commander welcomed us and then told the first Sergeant to get us signed in and settled. After we had filled out our paper work the first Sergeant turned us over to another sergeant who was an Indian. He was not like my Sergeant in basic. He was fat and not as stern. He was real nice, we got along very well.

I was not assigned a job the first two days I was there. The other two guys who came with me were. I was given small details around the barracks. All the soldiers under E-5 (Sergeants) slept in rooms of about ten men. There were two Sergeants per room. Our Company was small, probably about one hundred men. Our job was to support the infantry, repairing their trucks, jeeps, and tanks. We had a supply office for our company and a major supply office for our Brigade. We had shops across the motor pool where we worked. The room I was assigned to was on the third floor, I could see the motor pool and the shops from my room. The Building maintenance was preformed by Germans. After eight o'clock at night you had no hot water, so if you were going to take a bath you'd better get it done before eight o'clock. In the military you were going to take a bath every day. If you did not the guys would get together and give you one. They called them GI baths, and they used hard brushes. I saw them give one guy a bath, and it was not nice. They would tell you up front you need to take a bath, you have not taken one in a couple of days and you stink.

That was the last warning you would get. I only saw this happen one time with one guy. They didn't have to tell him again, he beat everyone in the showers after work. We were a close family, and we looked out for each other.

I was put in a squad of three guys, four with myself. It was our job to work on the small arms, mortars and the armament on the tanks. We had our own bay we worked out of our own truck with an office in the back. We did nothing. Most of the day we sat around reading comics and listening to music. I was the only black person in my squad. We got along very well. We slept in the same room one on one side of me and another across the room from me. Our squad leader had gotten promoted to E-5 (Sergeant) so his bunk was not with us. On occasion we would go out and pull maintenance on the tanks. That was exciting. I got to ride in the tanks and on occasion they would let me drive. That was the extent of our job. They did not mind us setting around, that was the Army way. When you had something to do, do it, when you don't have any thing to do wait until you do. I thought it was a lazy system, but I was a good soldier and a good soldier does not buck the system. Not all of the guys in my company had it that easy though. The mechanics who worked on the trucks and jeeps always had something to do. The guys who worked in the supply depot always had something to do. My squad was probably the laziest one in my company.

You could not tell that segregation existed in our company while we were on post. No one acted better than anyone else. We all got alone very well. We worked from 7: Am in the morning until 4: o clock in the evening, and we were off on the week ends. There were not racial slurs written or spoken in our company. If anyone had any thing in their heart they kept it to themselves. We had Blacks, Whites and Hawaiians in our company.

We slept in the same rooms, used the same showers, ate in the same mess hall and worked together in harmony. This was the sixties and we could do in the Army what we could not do at home.

But segregation still crept in. When we were off duty and left the post the Whites went their way and blacks went theirs. Though I worked with the whites we never went out together. The Hawaiians partied with the Blacks. It was like being in Church, we go to church set together, pray together, sing together, shout together, cry together, but when we leave the church we are no better than those whites who didn't want to socialize with the blacks off post. Just as they had their own social groups who they chose to socialize with, church folk are the same way. And that is from the choir stand through the pulpit and into the pews. It's bad we are segregated in God's house. The quire members have their little group they socialize with, the Pastor has his group, and some in the pews have their group. If you are quiet or new you get left out. Unless you are a person of promonice, then everyone wants you to join his or her group. How hypocritical. My Bible tells me that God does not show favoritism. Aren't we supposed to immolate Him?

There were these two guys named Scott and Jackson who took me in and showed me around. Scott was heavy set an a little taller than me, and Jackson was tall and lanky. They were the first to take me off post in to town. We were stationed in the rural part of Mannheim Germany. You had to have a car or take a taxicab to town where the stores and clubs were. Scott, Jackson and I would take a taxi to town, but every time we arrived Jackson would leave us and go off on his own. We would not see Jackson until the next day at camp. I enjoyed being with Scott, until I learned the ropes he never left me alone. There was this beer in Germany called Hell, and they named it appropriately. It came in large quart flip top bottles. One bottle would have you spinning. I thought I was a pretty good beer drinker when I got to Germany, but this beer was totally different than any beer I had ever consumed. Scott warned me not to try and drank a whole bottle. You know I didn't listen. The beer was good and cold and before I knew it I had consumed the whole bottle. I was floating. I wasn't like most people when I got inebriated (drunk). I would get very silly. I was young about eighteen; all I wanted to do was have some fun. So when I would consume too much I would laugh uncontrollably, sing and make up jokes. I didn't bother anybody though, but if you were with me you would have to shut me up. The only way to shut me up was to give some more to drink and then I became very quiet, and

I wouldn't say a word. Scott had to carry me back to the Compound a few times until I built up a tolerance to the beer, then it was own. I graduated to two or three flit tops before I had my fill. Hell was the strongest beer they had, so when I would drink beer in regular bottles they would not bother me at all.

Drinking beer was like drinking water to the Germans. They drank beer all the time, for breakfast, lunch and dinner. It was nothing to see the workers at lunch flip the top on a bottle of beer. Everyone drank beer, even the children. It was not illegal to walk the streets drinking beer. When they were out at night they would drink beer and chase it with snoops. Snoops was a liquor like gin, but stronger, boy did it burn and take your breath going down.

Most Germans were very friendly; if you sat next to them at the bar they would always buy you a drink. They would buy you some snoops and a beer chaser.

I couldn't drink too many of them. I didn't like snoops anyway, so I would just drink beer. The Germans were very sneaky. They would buy you drinks laugh at you and speak German to you, knowing that you didn't know what they were saying. I would just laugh back with them. I didn't care what they were saying they were buying me beer. I would sit at the bar when Scott was with a lady friend. I didn't want to interfere. I sat there and drank with the Germans. By the time I new my way around Scott would leave me and go off with one of his lady friends. I felt fine I watched my intake and there was always someone from my company I would run into anyway. One day Scott and Jackson were telling me to watch out for the Germans, they would buy you drinks, laugh in your face and talk about you at the same time. That made me want to learn the German language. So I began to try and learn as much as I could. When I learned to speak German I still accepted drinks from them, laughed with them, and when I had my fill I would speak German back to them letting them know I understood everything they were saying.

Some would get very apologetic, and some didn't care. I didn't care either I was spending their money. As long as they did not put their hands on me we were ok. I had a Hawaiian friend who would go out with me that they could not do that and get away with it. He would fight at the drop of a hat, before you knew it he would hit them in the mouth and get up and walk away. The next time they saw him they would leave him alone.

I was indoctrinated to my surroundings after a few months in Germany, so I was ready to make my move on the ladies. You really didn't have to make your move on them; they approached you before you could approach them. Don't get me wrong, that was just the ones who frequented the bars. Most of the German women outside of the ones who came to the bars wouldn't speak to soldiers anyway. And the German women who were around the white soldiers would turn their head or cross the street if they saw a black soldier coming. I wandered about that. The first time I was with a German woman she wanted me to take her home before twelve o clock midnight. I wasn't ready to go, she became insistent, so after a few more drinks we left. While we were at her place she began to rush me. I wondered what was going on. So I asked? She told me that we had to finish before 12 o'clock midnight. I asked why? She said that's when your tail would come out. I got mad and asked her who told her that blacks had tails. She said that all the white soldiers were telling the people that blacks had tails and that they would come out after 12 o clock midnight. I assured her that that was a lie and stayed around until midnight had passed to let her see the truth. The next day at post I asked Scott and Jackson about that at breakfast, they laughed and asked me was that the first time I had heard that. I had been in Germany for about four months now and I had never heard that before. It was a big laugh a breakfast, even the white guy's laughed. When I went to work the white guys I work with told me that the guys in the infantry would tell the women that to get them to leave the black guys alone while they were in the field. The infantry stayed in the field six months out of a year. They didn't want anyone to move in on them while they were gone.

I found out that that rumor spread not only to the girls who frequented the bars but also to the surrounding country sides.

Most Germans believed Blacks had tails like animals. This bothered me every time a German would look at me in a disconcerting way. Maybe I became paranoid.

As I was telling you before Scott and Jackson and I would go out together, and when we would arrive in town Jackson would always leave. One day we were looking for Jackson at breakfast, we thought he had gone AWOL (absent without leave). We wondered what had happened to him. We found out later that Jackson had been arrested for murder. We were told that when we went into the city Jackson would go and meet homosexual males and murder them. They caught him when he took a taxicab driver's car beat him up and ran over him. We knew about the homosexual murders they were all over the news, but we never thought that Jackson was the person committing the murders. At no time when we would go out did we have any idea that Jackson was committing these crimes. Scott and I were puzzled.

They had Jackson's trial and sentenced him to Levinworth back in the States. Scott was assigned to escort him back. Later we heard that Jackson had gotten into a fight with a guard and killed him. I don't know what happened to him after that. I was very careful about the people I went out with after that. Although Jackson was never mean to me or anyone else in our company. I guess he just had a thing about homosexuals.

This was the beginning of my fourth month, and after breakfast there was an alert called. Alerts were readiness exercises we had in Germany to test our preparedness to see if we would be ready if we were attacked by Russia. We had one every month. They were always called in the mornings before breakfast. We had to go to the supply room get our weapons, proceed to the motor pool load up on our assigned trucks and wait until we got the all clear, or orders to move out. We got the orders to move out only once while I was there. We went into the field and set up for a day, then returned back to post. Most of the time we would just set in our trucks in front of the shop until we got orders to stand down. Sometimes we would set there for an hour or two. They were boring. We called the alerts hurry up and wait exercises.

This time was different. They waited to call an alert after breakfast. They also told us to fall out with our duffle bags, our personal items and this time we were issued live ammunition. They had never done that before while I was there, and from the conversations the guys were having that was the first time any of them knew of our having to fall out with all of our gear and being issued live ammo. We proceeded out the barracks but the trucks were already out side in front of our building, and they were not our trucks. We knew something was up. Maybe we are under attack by Russia was the general conciseness. We were called to formation in front of the barracks by the first sergeant. Our Company Commander came out along with the other lieutenants in our company. We all were wondering what was going on. The company Commander said, "all the names that the first sergeant calls out were to take a step forward." I began to remember what took place when I was in school in Maryland.

This was happening all over again. Our first sergeant began to call out our names. He called my name. I said to myself, well I missed going to Viet Nam once but now it's my turn. The Company said all the names that were called go back inside secure your weapons and secure your gear. The rest of you load up on the trucks, you are on your way to Viet Nam. I felt a sie of relief, but I felt sorry for my friends. Or company was cut in half that day. We heard later that some of the guys were killed as they disembarked from the airplane when they arrived in Viet Nam. We were really touched upon hearing the news.

We never had that many people leave going to Viet Nam at one time after that, but we did have people leave on occasion. We also had people come to our company that had survived their duty in Viet Nam. They would tell us about the situation over there. When they started coming to our camp some of them brought marijuana with them. That was the first time I saw someone with marijuana.

I never tried the drug, nor did any of my close friends, we stuck with beer and alcohol. I did not like smoking. I watched my mother and dad smoke regular cigarettes and I thought it was crazy to inhale smoke. I wanted no part in that. Smoking marijuana was crazy to me. The guys who came to our camp told us about all the money they were making in the black market in Viet Nam. They were not front line soldiers, they were mechanics and they stayed in the rear. Their stories were very impressive. They showed the fighting in Viet Nam on television in Germany. We were able to see guys getting shot, arms and legs being blown off. The German news media was reporting the war.

They said they could not show these graphic scenes in the United States because family members may see their son's being killed. It was something to see the guys being shot and hollering. I wanted no part of the war. But when the guys came to our company and told us that was only happening to the front line soldiers, and how much money they were making I had to rethink my position on the matter.

I started making rank fast in Germany. My Company Commander and My First Sergeant liked me. Within my third month there I received my first stripe. By the end of my first year I was promoted to Sp4 E-4 (specialist fourth class). I was moving up in this man's army. Right after I received my promotion I was told to report to the Company Commander. I liked our Company Commander, his name was Captain Swartz. We got along very well. I had to report to him, when I went into his office he was looking out the window. I stood there in attention for a while before he spoke. Then he turned around and told me to stand at east. He proceeded to tell me that I had come down on orders to go to Viet Name, but he rejected my orders. He had a smile on his face and told me to get out of his office. I had mixed emotions in a way I wanted to go because of the money I heard they were making, but I did not want to die, I was having too much fun in Germany. I had dodged the bullet again.

Was someone watching over me? I was not going to church, I was really sinning, but this was the third time I came close to going to war.

Things were quiet for a while; no one was coming from Viet Nam nor was anyone leaving headed to the war. I had this good friend who was a cook. He would always look out for me. He would save me seconds in the foods I liked. You sometimes had to rush to get seconds. He always looked out for me. He was white kind of fat lets say stocky, he wasn't obese. They didn't allow obesity in the military. I would in tern look out for him when he was on duty and wanted me to purchase something for him. One day he came down on orders to go to Viet Nam. He left and later I was told that he got shot and died when he was getting of the plane. It took me a while to get over that. It was something to be with you friends one day to see their smiles, to hear their voices and then to hear about them being killed.

I was getting home sick about my second year in Germany. There was so much going on and I didn't know when my time would come so I made arrangements to go home for Christmas. I paid for my ticket and headed home.

When I arrived home everything appeared different to me. I couldn't remember some of the streets. I found myself getting lost. I had been gone two years and things had changed. My sister would get mad at me when I would ask her for directions. She would say you haven't been gone that long. But I was serious. Maybe I had consummated too much alcohol and it was robbing me of my memory. Yea Right!

Everyone was happy to see me. The whole family got together. I was the center of attraction. I brought gifts home for everyone from Germany. I bought my girlfriend a record player in Germany and on Christmas day presented it to her. I borrowed my dads car went to pick up my girl friend and headed back home to my house. On the way we stopped in the school parking lot did a little kissing, nothing else, and after a while went on to my parent's house. I really enjoyed my visit at home. I was there for thirty days. I hated when it was my time to return, but I had to go back. My girlfriend and I spent a lot of time together before she had to go back to college. She had to leave before I did. During our time together we never did anything but kiss. I respected her to much to put a move on her. I really liked her. Well its time to go back to Germany, so off I go again.

It started snowing early in Germany. Snow would start about October, and continue until the last of April. I do not know when it starts now because of global worming.

I remember it was about the middle of March, I was in my room looking out the windows. We had windows that went from one end of the room to the other. The room was about twenty feet long and about fifteen feet wide. The windows were about four feet tall, and four feet wide. There were bunks under the windows. I was looking out the windows at all the snow on the ground and on the vehicles. I remember saying to myself that one day this will only be a dream to me.

Every time I go through something I remember looking out that window and saying that one day this will only be a dream to me. That has really helped me through some tough times. When we are in the mist of a trial or test it helps to be able to look back over our life and see how God brought us through that situation. Knowing that He did not leave me in that valley for long, but He came to deliver me from my troubles. Knowing that He delivered me before, I have a reassurance that He will deliver me again.

As long as I have that testimony I can wait patiently for I know my help is around the corner. Isaiah 30:5, Weeping may remain for a night, but rejoicing comes in the morning. King James version, Joy will come in the morning time. Psalm 18:2-6, The Lord is my rock, my fortress and my deliver; my God is my rock, in whom I take refuge: HE is my shield and the horn of my salvation, my stronghold. I call to the Lord, who is worthy of praise, and I am saved from my enemies. The cords of death entangled me; the torrents of destruction overwhelmed me. The cords of the grave coiled around me. Psalm 18:2-6. To listen to someone give their testimony about how the Lord Jesus

Christ brought them through a situation, but boy when you can testify your self, when you can look back over your own life and say how I made it over. OH! What a blessed filling.

It was entering spring now around the first of April. The snow was melting, and you know how you feel dead during the winter? Well life was returning to me, until! A lot of guys were getting what we call dear johns from their girl friends back home. Dear Johns were letters saying we are finished, I am with someone else now. I would see how the letters would hurt them. I said to myself that I don't ever want to go through that. I kept a picture of my girl friend in my wall locker during the day while we were at work, and I would putt the picture on my foot locker when we returned to our barracks. We wrote each other at least twice a month, sometimes more.

I knew my situation was secure, so I thought. The whole month of May I did not get a letter from her. It was the middle of June now and no letter. I wrote my sister and asked her to give my girlfriend a call to find out what was going, and why I haven't heard from her. My sister wrote me back and told me that my girl friend was going to write. That was all she would say. One day I received the letter, I was excited, but I had this feeling something was wrong. I opened the letter and began to read. I was setting down on my foot locker reading the letter. I got so mad and hurt that I got up and began to walk around the room. She told me that she was with someone else now. That didn't really hurt, because I wasn't faithful to her, so how could I ask her to be faithful to me, and we were so far apart. I believed that no matter who we were seeing while we apart, we would get back together when I returned home. So the part about her seeing someone else wasn't the kicker. No! But when she told me that she was pregnant and she blame me for her pregnancy, then that burned me up. She said that when I was home I didn't attempt to make love to her, so when she went back to school she met this guy and one thing lead to another, and now she was going to have his baby. Why put the blame on me? She did what she wanted to do. I was in Germany I had nothing to do with her decisions. All the time I was with her I respected her. Not one time did I try to approach her in a sexual way. So why blame me for you mistakes, if it was a mistake. She also said that she loved me and she wished the baby was mine. Yea Right! If you want someone else, ok. If you get pregnant by someone else, ok. But don't put the blame on me because I didn't lay down with you. I was angrier (madder) than hurt. That event changed me.

Now you can tell from some of the things I was doing that I wasn't a good boy. I was walking with the devil. I wasn't holy and fire baptized. Although I was in the fire. I was self destructing, and I could not blame anyone but me. Though I was doing all sort of things unbecoming a Christian, God was still watching over me. A few weeks after I received the letter from home, I was called into my Company Commanders office again. I walked in, this time he was setting at his desk looking at some papers. He looked up at me and said well you are on orders to go to Viet Nam again, and I am going to revoke them again. I said that I will go this time. He said, did you hear what I said, I have revoked the orders now go back to work. I saluted turned and walked out the door murmuring. I had changed I did not laugh and sing as much as I use to. I consumed about the same amount of alcohol, but I wasn't the same jovial person.

I wanted to go to Viet Nam; my mind was on the money now, and how I can get it. I had taken a different prospective on life. I had become cold inside. But no matter how I had become the Lord still saved me from going to Viet Nam. This is not a reflection on the guys who went and gave their lives for their country. A lot of my friends died in that war. If they had sent me I don't know what would have been the out come. Maybe I would have came back home alive, and not hurt, some guys did. Or maybe I could have killed someone, taken a life that I did not give. Do you remember what the Lord God said to King David when David wanted to build the Lord's house? The Lord told David that he had too much blood on his hands to build his house. God was saving me for his purpose and not mine. His purpose for my life would be for filled no mater what. I had to go through some things, I had to suffer, and I had to reject God's laws (sin) to see the love and mercy of the Lord God. What was written about my life would be for filled. Although I wanted to go, it was not God's will that I should go.

It was approaching the end of the summer. All of the guys in my platoon had returned to the states. I was the only one left in my platoon. My Company Commander called me in and told me that they were going to dismantle my job assignment. He said that they were going to put me in shop supply. The sergeant who was over shop supply was getting ready to leave and they needed someone to take his place. I was going to get my own office. I was moving up in the world. I had my own office, my own jeep and my own desk. I was living in hog heaven. My job allowed me to travel around the country procuring parts for the vehicles in the repair shop. I loved that. When something was needed they told me to go and find the part.

I always returned with what I was sent after. Sometimes I would hear them bragging on me when they thought I was not in my office. I just wanted to do a good job. I felt that, that was all I had now.

My office was next to the shop office. You could walk through a door from the shop office to my office. We had a Sergeant E-7, a warrant officer and two clerks who worked in the shop office. Every time we would have an inspection by Battalion they would take my office and send me off somewhere.

I always made sure I had a bottle of liquor in one of my desk drawers. When I returned it would be empty, or less than half full. I knew how to keep the bosses happy.

We were getting ready to move to another barracks because our company had lost a lot of men rotating back home. They were going to let the infantry have our building. One day while we were getting everything ready to move my Company Commander had me to report to is office. I didn't think anything about it because I would go in on occasion when he wanted to send me of on some mission. I reported to him, he was burning some papers. I stood there for awhile, when he finished he turned to me and showed me the board on the wall where he kept a break down on our company with each position, who was in that position and their job classification. I wondered why he was showing me that. He said that I had come down on orders again to go to Viet Nam, but that was the last time.

He said that he was going to promote me to Sergeant Specialist E-5, and that he was going to put me in a job classification that was critical in Germany. I thanked him, and left very happy this time. I was going to be promoted to E-5. I was making rank faster than the other guys in my company. I had been in my company only two years and now I was going to be a Sergeant. I had my own office, my own jeep, I had bought a little green Volkswagen and now I am going to become a Sergeant. Someone was watching out for me. I no longer wanted to go to Viet Nam. I had everything I wanted right here in Germany. I was having a ball.

We moved into a different location closer to our division headquarters. We were in a one story building now, and the shops were a distance away. We were right out side of a small town. All of the Officers clubs and NCO (None Commissioned Officers) clubs were on this post. The Post was very clean and well kept. Because I was a sergeant now I was allowed to have an apartment of Post. I enjoyed living with the Germans. I would go to work and get off at 4 o clock; it was just like having a civilian job. I still partied with the guys, but this was a different set of guys now. The ones that I started with were gone by now, some returned home and some went off to Viet Nam. The new group I hung out with was different from my first group. We enjoyed going up into the mountains or in to the small villages rather than going into the city. The mountains were not as crowded and the people were friendlier than those in the city. Also you hardly saw any military personal.

I enjoyed these guys because they wanted to see the country. I traveled as much as I could. I went to Berlin. At that time the wall was there which separated North (Communist) Germany from South Germany. If you rode the train you would have to be careful because the train would go into the Communist side. If they caught you on the communist side they could hold you as a spy. You had better know what you were doing before you got on the train. Berlin was like being in the States. A lot of the people in Berlin spoke English. You could see American cars every where. The restaurants and night life was just like being home. I would go to Berlin as much as I could; it was my home away from home. I traveled so much that when it was time for me to rotate out I owed the military money because I went over my leave time.

It was getting close to my time to rotate out (return to the States). I had about three months to go in Germany. I had extended my time in Germany, so my tour was three years. My Company Commander Captain Schwartz was leaving before me, but he was headed to Viet Nam. Isn't that something the man who stopped me from going to Viet Nam all those times was now headed to Viet Nam? We all hated to see him go. He was a good commanding officer. He saved me a lot of times from making some dumb mistakes. Although I made one which I wish he had stopped me from making. That mistake really affected my life for many years after I left Germany. I'm not going to tell you everything I did while I was in service, nor in

Germany because there are something's I want to forget, some mistakes I made that I don't want to recall.

It was time for me to leave Germany now. I remember when I signing out my first Sergeants words to me was "you aren't going back home and get involved in all those riots are you"? I ignored his statement. I thought he was trying to be funny. I was returning to the states during the times of the marches and sit-ins. We would see some of the things that were happing in the States on German television. They did not show a lot I guess they did not want the soldiers to watch and start taking sides. No one talked about the marches; it was as though they weren't happening. There was more talk about Viet Nam than anything. The only person I heard say anything, and that was when I was headed to the airport was my First Sergeant.

I am off to the States now. I was sent to Texas because I had four months left on my enlistment. They sent me to an armored tank unit in Fort Hood Texas. When I arrived they put me in charge of their motor pool. I had come from a cool climate in Germany to a very hot climate in Texas, and I mean hot. During the days the temperature would get into the hundreds. They would stop all work and tell us to go somewhere and stay out of the sun. The days were hot and the nights were mild. I really had to make some adjustments. I didn't care because I wouldn't be there long anyway. Do my four months and go home.

When I arrived at my company they were preparing to go out on riot control. They were sending these young soldiers black and white out to handle the unrest that was going on because of the sit-ins. They were sending them out with full combat equipment. Their weapons were loaded with real ammunition and the rifles were equipped with bayonets. It was bad enough to send them out with real ammunition, but to also equip the rifles with bayonets? To equip a soldier in this fashion was not only to control the crowds, but to also take lives if needed. The ammunition we used back then when fired could go through two or three people when standing close together. The bayonets were razor sharp. You didn't have to fire a round at a person, just lunge at him or her with your bayonet that would be enough to kill them. I had missed going to war in Viet Nam only to return to a war at home in the States. That to me was pitiful.

They would ask for volunteers to go on riot control. They did not ask me, and even if they had asked I would not have volunteered to go. I did not come back home to fight against my own people, black or white. Some of the soldiers asked me why wasn't I going? They said it was a good way to get out of work. They looked at the situation as some sort of game. They didn't understand that they could be asked to hurt one of their family members or even a neighbor. Not only to hurt someone but possibly kill someone. They told us that we were going to protect lives and property. But if all we were supposed to do was protect lives and property then why equip the soldiers to kill, to take lives? These were black and white soldiers. I know we were trained not to take sides, but I saw the hidden effects of racialism when I was in Germany. On Post the whites and blacks were together, but that was a different story when they left the Compound. What was going to alter the situation now? I heard the black soldiers say that a white person had better not spit or throw something at them or they would retaliate. I know if the black soldiers were saying that wouldn't the white soldier harbor the same feelings in their heart?

What would stop them from taking sides? Oh! I did not mean to kill him or her, but it's to late now. I can not restore a taken life. When someone hits you with an object and it hurts your first instinct is to retaliate. When you retaliate in anger someone is going to get hurt. We were trained to take lives. That was our goal, to take your life before you could take mine. Why put a Rock wilder in the pen with a poodle? You know what the out come will be. I told the other soldiers that going out on crowd control was not for me. I thought that the job could be better enforced by the local police and the National Guard. A lot of regular soldiers had returned from Viet Nam, what would stop them from having relapses and hurting someone?

I gather because of my sentiment on the issue that is why my first Sergeant never asked me to go? I was not quiet about the way I felt. So what did my opinions change things? I don't think so.

They divided up my company about a week after I was stationed there. They sent some of us out into the field. Guess who they sent? There was this out post away from the main post. It was close to an abandon airfield. I spent the remainder of my service time there. I did not know why they sent us out there. There was nothing there. The barracks the office, mess hall, motor pool were all in tents. We did not do anything but set around all day. I lived off Post, so that broke up some of the monotony.

I had the weekends off, so the only time I had to report was Monday through Friday. When I was at work I spent most of my time alone since I was the only one in the motor pool. Sometimes I would take a jeep out to explore the areas around the post. Many times I would see rattler snakes as long as the jeep. I would not run over them because I thought that if I were to run over one his head could possibly bounce up and come into the jeep and bite me. I just left them alone and watched from a distance as they crossed the road. I would leave them alone, and I wanted them to leave me alone. We had a mutual understanding.

The time came for me to be discharged. We had to get all of our paper work processed, and the final thing was to be signed out by our Company Commander. Our regular Company Commander was back on the regular Post. We had a First Lieutenant who was in charge of us in the field. He didn't like me to well. I don't know why, we hardly talked. I was never called into his office, and he never came into the motor pool. I had a friend who was a cook. I always made friends with the people who handled the food. My friend told me that they were giving out reenlistment bonuses. He said that our acting Company Commander asked him if he wanted to reenlist? He said, "He told him that they were offering five to ten thousand dollars to reenlist". My friend said no thanks. When it was my time to go in my acting Company looked me straight in the face and told me "It is good that you are getting out before I bust you. I looked at him, laughed and said good by. I told my friend what happened, and we both had a good laugh.

Well I made it, my military time was over. I learned a lot while I was in the military. I had grown up fast. I was not the quiet naive boy who left home four years ago. I was a man now, so I thought.

My focus was self sufficient now, what I can have, what I can buy, and what I can do. I had the I's now. I was on the road to heartaches suffering and self destructing. Though I had a good time when I was in service, my life was on a down hill course. I left God at home and started flirting with the devil. I was in big trouble now. You know the bad thing about it was that I did not know it. I had put God on the sidelines, now all I wanted was good times and things. That was first in my life. My focus was on impressing my friends and having money. I was committed to that goal.

I was back home now, I stayed with my family for a couple of months until my dad told me that I need to get my own place. I used my Veteran eligibility and bought my first house. It wasn't what I wanted, but I was happy to have it. I was the first one in my high school group to buy a house. I thought I was something. Wrong! I would apply for jobs and every job I applied for I got it.

I would work a job until I heard that another job was paying more money, and then off I would go. I had some good jobs. If you were a veteran at that time and applied for a job the companies had to consider you first for the position. I not only worked one job, I got a part time job to. I thought I was on a roll. I worked and when I was off I had my fun. My dad was proud of me, I had bought a house of my own. I was twenty two years old and had my own house. My dad was impressed. He would come over and we would have some drinks together. I would barbecue sometimes, and because I worked on the evening shift I quit my part time job at Richs and worked with him in the mornings before I went to my regular job. My dad and I had gotten real close. We had never been that close before. I really enjoyed my time with him. I began to understand my dad. Things were going pretty good. So I thought. When the water is real calm watch out for the storm. There was a big mistake I made in Germany which changed my life, and it would try to destroy me. And it almost did. When you are flirting with the devil, God will stand by and watch, allowing you to make your own decisions until He is ready for you to go on the journey He has set for you. The whole thing is a journey to me, from hell to Heaven. Someone has to go through Hell to help others not to go that way.

It is bad to think about, but someone had to sin so God would show His love and mercy through His Son Christ Jesus who would come and save the world. If there was no sin, and I wish there wasn't, Christ would not have to make that sacrifice for us. It hurts me to think about Him hanging on a cross because I rejected Him, and all he wanted to do was help me, to save me, not only from the Evil one, but also from myself.

Everything was going pretty good. My sister and some of my friends would come over on Saturdays sometimes and they would ask me to go partying with them. I could not go with them because I had to cut grass and take care of the house. They would laugh at me and tell me that I was always working and that I never had any fun. I began to think about that. Then I began to neglect my responsibilities and start partying with them. They lived a few miles away from me in some apartments. They would start partying on Friday evening all the way through Sunday, most of the time all night long. This was a trap I fell into. I left my house.

Partying meant more to me than my house and my responsibilities. My dad tried to find me, but I hid pretty go from him. One day he found out where I was living in some apartments. I saw him coming and I told a lady to tell him that I didn't live there and that she didn't know me. I knew he would try to make me go back to my house, but I did not want to. So I hid and he did not know that I was looking at him all the time. I loved my dad, but I feared him to. He was shorter than I was, but he was muscular than I was and I did not want to get into any confrontations with him. The Army taught me how to take care of myself, but I would never raise my hand to my dad no matter how much I knew. I loved and respected him to much.

And you know I might not have won anyway. I was off on a wild trip. A trip that would eventually lead to a dead end, and I could not see around the corner. I was destroying myself, and I did not know any better. I did not need Satin to destroy me, He only provided the temptations. It was my self indulgent my lusts that was destroying me. Alcohol, women and money were my lovers. I was trapped and I could not get out.

I was living with this girl and her mother in their apartment. We broke up when I found out that she was cheating on me. I left her and moved into the apartment complex where my sister and my high school friends were staying. I had an apartment on the grown floor at the end of the building. My sister and her husband were living on the top floor at the other end. I was in the mist of the partying now. I would go to work Monday through Friday and party Saturday through Sunday. I thought I was living the good life. Boy was I wrong.

One day my mother told me that my dad was in the hospital sick. I went to see him. He was kind of delirious. He kept asking me to take him home. He kept saying "I want to go home, take me home". They said he had double pneumonia. After work I would go straight to the hospital, I was there whenever I was not working. The only time I left was to go home and get some sleep, or go to work. One day they moved my dad to the intensive care units. When I arrived at the hospital they told me they moved him because he was getting worse, and they wanted to monitor him closely.

That Sunday my family was together in the intensive care waiting area, my mother had gone to my grandmother's house to get some rest. My grandmother did not live to far from the hospital. We were taking turns going to set with my dad. I was on my way back to see him when the nurses and doctors rushed pass me with a lot of equipment. I wondered what was going on. I was close to my dad's room when a nurse stopped me from going in. There was a glass window where they could monitor the patients. They closed the window and I knew they were working on my dad. The nurse set me down in a chair beneath the window. She was talking to me but I did not hear a word she was saying. My whole concentration was focused on them in the room. I heard them trying to resituate my dad. After a while they quit, and the nurses came out crying. I heard my dad take his last breath. I was too shocked to cry. The nurse held me and tried to console me.

I pushed away from her ran out the building went to my car and headed to my grandmothers house. I do not know how fast I was going, and I did not care. When I got in the car I cried all the way to my grandmother's house. I tried to keep my composure when I entered the house. My mother and grandmother were sitting in the living room, when I walked in I did not say a word. Just as I turned the corner into the room my mother cried out "brother no! No brother! I did not have to say a word we all began to cry. I live that moment over and over again even today for a long time. Every time I relive that incident I began to cry.

It is not every day you are there listing to you dad take his last breath. It is a pain you can never forget. My dad was forty two years old when he was taken away from me. We had just begun to get close to each other, and then he was gone. I felt robed. My granddad passed when he was fifty two, and my dad passed when he was forty two. I needed them in my life, but now they were gone. You would think I would straighten up after that, but I did not.

It was business as usual. I stopped going to church. I felt that there was nothing there for me anyway. In my church the pastor just hoped and hollered, and talked about people. I needed to know the Bible, God's word not what was going on in the streets. I was out there I knew what was going on in the streets. I needed salvation, I needed

Christ Jesus. Maybe if my granddad and dad were around I would not have made some of the mistakes I made.

When I think about setting there listing to my dad as he takes his last breath. I reflect back to the gospels when Christ Jesus was nailed to the cross and those standing there watching. Some were mocking Him, insulting Him, shaking their heads at Him. But I know there were some there whom He had chased demons out of, and some He had healed watching with tears in their eyes. I can see and feel the pain of His mother Mary as she stood there watching her one and only son hanging on a cross numb not hearing not seeing anything around her. Her heart being torn open as she watched her child. Blood running from His side where they pierced Him, and blood running from his head where they placed a crown of thorns on Him. Looking at the bruises they had inflected on Him. I can hear her crying out Dear God save my son, hoping with all her heart that what she was seeing was only a dream, and soon she would wake up and this terrible event was not happening.

I can feel the Lord God's pain having to turn His back on His only son hanging there for nothing He had done wrong. Although God could not watch, He couldn't close His ears. He heard the insults, the mocking, and He also heard the cries the tears. What a moment for a Father and a mother to go through. Imagine if it were your child the one you nursed from birth carried in your arms, felt their pain when they were sick or in pain. The child you watched grow from a child to a man, and now they want to kill him for just trying to help us. Think about the pain you would feel, and then you would know the pain God and Mary felt. It is not an easy thing to be there when a loved one takes their last breath. The pain is unimaginable. Yet it was God's will that He should suffer that we may be saved. How awesome is the God we serve, and His Son Jesus.

They thought they took His life but He gave it up willingly. He knew what He had to go through, the rejection, the suffering and the pain. But that did not help Mary as she felt this emptiness inside of her. Why did you give me a child and then take him away this way. The hurt and the pain is real, but just as Mary later had joy, we to one day will have that same joy.

God had taken the two most influential people in my life away from me. I would have to face the rest of my life on my own. I would not have anyone to go to that would talk to me openly, scolding me when I need scolding, having compassion when I need compassion. Not giving into my will, but helping me by telling me what's right and wrong. You can't replace a dad or a granddad. You can bring in substitutes, but a real loving caring dad and granddad can never be replaced. There have been stories or broken homes where a child grows up and searches for the missing parent. There is a part of them missing and they will do what ever it takes to find the missing part so they can be complete. But what if the missing part has gone home to be with the Lord?

Then the person is left with this emptiness for the rest of their lives. Only those who have experienced this pain can comprehend the magnitude of this experience. I had to go through this tunnel. At the time I did not know how the lost of my dad and granddad would impact my life.

I thought I was alone now. Little did I know I was never alone. Christ Jesus was always there watching over me, even though I did not acknowledge His presence or serve Him. He was just being patient with me waiting for me to come in out off the cold.

I quit my job and took over my dads business. My mother gave me my dad's truck and some of his tools. I finished up the job he was working on, and gave the money to my mother. My dad had trained me to do the work so when I took over I had no problems with doing the job. The only problem I had was holding on to the money. I made a lot of money and I spent a lot of money. I don't have to tell you on what, you already know, partying and women. I loved both, and the devil would use both to try and destroy me. Like a rat looking for cheese I was falling into his trap. I was so dumb that he did not have to try very hard. I thank God for His Son Jesus Christ for I know without Him I would not be here today. I was committing slow suicide. God would let me go so far, but when I reached a point He would step in and stop me.

I wish to this day that He had stepped in sooner. But where would my witness be, my testimony about His love, mercy and saving grace. Boy some of those testimonies really hurt.

I met this young lady who was having some problems. She was a high school friend. We started dating doing this and that. You know what I mean, having sex. She got sick and her doctor told me not to leave her alone. So I moved in with her. Back then you don't stay with someone without getting married. So I took the step. I really did not want to get married, but I wanted to do what was right.

After two years we started having problems. I left her, I thought I would be better of by myself than to go through some of the things I had to go through.

I wish the Minister that married us would have counseled us completely then we would have known that the marriage was not going to work. I do not blame him or her for my mistake. I blame myself for not being honest and just saying that I don't want to get married. Divorce is hard on both parties and all parties involved. Ours was extremely hard. I am very sorry for what I did.

I got into relationships knowing they were not going to work, and every time I had to pay the cost of a failed relationship, and it hurt. I even had a young lady tell me that she was trying to find a way to poison me without it being detected. When she told me that I said I quit no more relationships for me. But did I stop? No. I told you before women were my weaknesses, and the devil was using them to destroy me. He was exploiting my weakness. He's good at what he does. I am not glorifying him, but I want you to know that you have to stay close to Christ Jesus or you can and will fall into his trap. Just ask Eve. And you don't have to go back that far. Just ask me. He will use the things you love the most to try and destroy you, and that includes people. Just ask Job. Job's wife told him to just curse God and die. Now that was heavy coming from the woman you live with, love and had children with. Just curse God and die. Die so I can get someone else to come in here and take care or me. You are washed up, and God is after you.

I met a young lady who was about ten years younger than me. Boy my eyes, ears, mouth, nose and heart was wide open. It did not have to rain hard and I would have drowned. I really loved this girl. I said I know this is the one. I would follow her to the moon if she asked me. Just command me and I'll do. I was like a dog after a bone. Oh boy was I stepping into trouble, I mean troubles. I had never experienced real love. I was forty years old now, and I did not know what it meant to love someone. All the relationships I had before were just that, relationships. I don't know if I was afraid to get close to someone, or allow them to get close to me because of the lose of my dad and my granddad. I really loved them and when they were taken from me that could have had an effect on my relationship with others in my life. I would be a good prospect for a psychiatrist, ok. It was nothing for me to say I love you and not really mean it. I thought it was what I was supposed to do to get what I wanted. I thought that was what the young ladies wanted to hear, so that is what I said.

I did not understand at the time I was playing with the emotions of another human being, nor did I care. I was just playing the game. I found out first hand that what goes around comes back twice, sometimes thrice, or even more.

Before I meet the young lady I was in church. Don't misunderstand what I am saying. I said I was in church, and not that the church was in me. There is a difference. I sang in the quire, was one of the lead singers. Everyone would complement me on my gift. I tried to be as humble as I could. But I liked the praise. One time we had a choir musical. You could have said that I was the feature singer.

I was in about every solo and trio on the program. I even had the solo in the final selection. My pianist liked me and I loved to sing. Although I never thought I sound that well. There are some people out there who are half good that could blow me away. But I was very happy with my little spotlight in the sun. Don't give me the mike, it's own.

I had season tickets to the Atlanta Falcons home games. We would be in the quire stand singing and after we finished, before the Pastor would get up to preach I would sneak out of the quire stand go down to the stadium change my clothes in my van, and set up for the tailgate party. I had packed my van the night before the game, so all I had to do was put the cooler and meat on ice and off to church then to the game. I we would be in the parking lot drinking dancing and partying. Don't forget I had just left church singing; now I am out in the street drinking and partying. Some of my friends said at least he went to church. But they didn't know I was not in any better shape than they were for not going to church. Truthfully I was worse. At least they weren't pretending to be someone they weren't. I was in church but the church was not in me. I'm not saying it is wrong to go to a sporting event on Sunday.

But to sneak out of church with a Bible in you hand, and go out to the game party, and with the same hand hold a liquor bottle or beer bottle, there is a problem. And I did not even stay long enough to hear the message. Why did I go? Was it just to show off my talent? I had to take a good look at myself, but that was later, not now I was having too much fun, so I thought.

When I started dating the young lady I fell in love with, I would take her to the games. I furnished everything. All she had to do was be ready when I arrived at her place to pick her up. I have to admit she was pretty, and I had my chest stuck out and my head held high when she was with me. I thought I had it made. When I told her I love her I really meant it. For the first time in my life I was experiencing love. The Lord God has a way of getting your attention and you don't even know what is going on. I was slipping, I had slipped. I had let my guard down. I was open now, let it all hang out. Let's get it on.

I remember one Sunday the New Orleans Saints were here playing the Falcons. One of the Saints fans would bet with me on who would score first. We wagered beers. If I won he would by me a beer, and if he won I would buy him a beer. I won the first beer. Then we started betting on who would make first downs, score field goals, and make catches.

I was winning all the time, and he was trying everything to win. I began to get sick, not drunk. I could drink beer all day and not feel the effects. I was filling sick and I did not want any more beer. I was finished. I never drank another beer in my life after that. Beer was off my list. When anything would make me sick I was finished with it. You would never see me with that thing or person again. I was a person who would drink at least a case of beer a week. I liked the expensive beer. My dad always told me if you are going to drink, drink the best then you won't get sick. I did not care after that if the beer was cheep or expensive I was finished.

I did not realize at the time that God was cleaning me up, and He was getting ready to work on me. I was getting ready to take a trip from which I would never return. My whole life was getting ready to change, and I did not know it. I had no idea what was getting ready to happen to me.

I really loved the young lady and I would have married her in a minute. I did not ask her to marry me, I was afraid to. I did not want to mess up what I had going. I said I am going to take this slow. I had never tried to kiss her, and we had been seeing each other for about four or five months. That was not like me. If I had not kissed you after the first date I did not come back anymore. Three dates and we were supposed to be going all the way. That was my limit. This was different; I wanted this to last, so why rush. I had all the time in the world. Don't move to fast and loose the fish. I wanted this fish, and I was going to be patient. I would let her make the first move, and then I would jump right in. Patience, be patient.

I rented a house and I told her about the house. She wanted to see the house, so I invited her over. She like the house and said the she wanted to move in. She said she wanted the spare bed room. The house was small with two bedrooms and two full baths. I was surprised she said that, but boy was I happy. The love of my life was coming to live with me. I was happy even though she was going to be in the spare bed room. I did not care just to have her under the same roof with me. Boy I must be doing something right. Let's get it on! I was as happy as a fox in the hen house. She moved into the spare bedroom, it was like sharing a house with a friend. We did not act like we had a relationship, because we did not. From my military training I was a neat freak. I would clean and cook. She helped cook sometimes. She only had her bedroom and bathroom to clean. One day I was cooking and she came to where I was and started crying. She said "I don't know why I am here, you do everything". I thought she was happy that I was taking most of the responsibilities of the house. All she had to do was tell me, I was just trying to be impressive. After that we shared the tasks. Then we even shared the same bedroom. I liked that very much.

She was younger than I was. She liked to go out a lot. I was forty now and I was slowing down. I did not care about going out as much as I use to. I liked to go to church now. I was changing. Being in clubs with all the smoke and lies was not my thing any more. The smoke starting bothering me, it was time to give up my club life. She would come home after work change clothes and off in the streets she would go.

We were spending less and less time together. Monday through Sunday the same thing, come home change clothes out the door. The only time she would stay home was once a month when she was sick, about two days out of the month. When she was better off she went again. I began to get jealous and angry. I asked her to stay home sometimes and spend some time with me. She told me that she worked from nine to five and after that she partied, and that's her life. She said that was the price an older man had to pay to be with a younger girl. I had mellowed out by now.

I did not say a word, but turned and walked away. She said why don't you get some friends to hang out with. She told me that I need to get a life. Get a life, I thought I had a life; I was not dead so I thought. I would get angry, but I kept my anger inside. I loved her and the love I had was choking me. I had never taken this kind of treatment of anyone in my life. I was the giver and not the recipient. This was a new roll for me. I did not quite know how to handle this new position I am in. She told me that while she was out with her friends guys would buy her drinks, she would dance with them and then she would come home to me. I guess that was supposed to make me happy. When she started going out she would be back by 2: AM in the morning. After a while she returned by 4or 5: AM in the morning. I could not sleep well while she was out. This thing call love is hard.

We moved to a larger house that I was trying to buy. When I could not purchase the house she told me to move out and let her and one of her girlfriends stay there. I was crazy but not that crazy. We moved after that she got an apartment, and I moved in with a friend until I got and apartment.

We continued to see each other occasionally. I was still in love with her. I had stopped going to church, I was hurting inside. I left the church, the church where I was singing, when she started staying out late. I did not feel like singing anymore. My heart was not in it anymore. Love hurts, and I was hurting all over again. This was a pain that I thought I would not have to face anymore. I had dropped my shield, and now I was paying for it. Later I started going to a church which had more life in it than the church I was attending. I liked going there. I would attend the Sunday morning services and then back for the Wednesday night services. I did not miss a Sunday or a Wednesday. One day she called me and told me she was pregnant. She said all she wanted was the baby and for me to take care of it. She said that she was not going to marry me, and that I was going to take care of the baby or she would cause big trouble for me in my life. I was hurt and angry. What have I gotten myself into? My heart was broken. I was crying inside. I would go to work come home and set in the living room in the dark listing to music. The only time I would leave the apartment was to go to work and or church. I did not want to be bothered by anyone. When I was in church I sat quietly during service, and when the service was over I went home hurting. No one knew what I was going through. I was hurting, grieving inside. People were jumping up and down all around me in church, but no could tell that I was dieing inside. They were to busy getting their shouts on, concerned about themselves to even ask me "are you alright, how are you today? Or brother I feel your pain, what's going in your life". No one even asked me my name. My pain was bubbling over.

One night I was grieving so bad that I wanted to die. I got into my bed and cried myself to sleep. During the night I feel into this deep sleep. It was not like a dream at all. I was actually in my parent's house in the basement, or so I thought. I was walking up the steps from the basement. I reached out my hand and opened the door. This very bright light was before me. I saw all these people walking around in the light.

It was very peaceful, like nothing I had ever experienced before. I was drawn to the light. I was stepping in when my dad hit me in the chest, and he said "it is not your time yet". I fell back down the steps. I woke up gasping for air. I knew that I had grieved so hard that I had a heart attack. I lay there for a long time thinking about the experience. Everything was so vivid, so real. God had let me see life on the other side. Everything in me changed that night. I no longer felt grief or pain. I was not even hurting inside anymore. I felt a great relief had come over me. I was free, I was free. All I could do was thank God for setting me free.

I began to pray thanking God. I also said Lord I don't want my child to come into the world this way. If I am to have a child I want to be with the mother and the child as a family. I already have one child not living with me, and it hurts. I don't want to go through that again. Please save me from her wrath. One day later she called me and told me that she was in the hospital, and that she had a miscarriage. I went to see her in the hospital. She smiled and was very causal. She said that the doctor told her that she should not give up that she could still get pregnant and have a baby. She said that we can try again. While she was talking the telephone rang. I heard the voice on the other end ask why I was there? She said that I was the baby's dad and that I needed to be there.

When she hung up I looked her straight in the eyes and told her that I was not going to bring a baby in to this world unless I am married to the mother. I turned around said good by and walked out the door. I was free and I was not going to step back into that trap again. I felt no pain, no sadness, and no love for her. The only thing I felt was pity for her. I was free, thank the Lord Jesus I was free.

I was happy now; a big burden had been lifted from me. I was attending church regularly. I had not joined; I just wanted to be there. I did not want to get involved, just go and return home. Though the Lord Jesus had saved me I still wasn't ready yet. It takes a while to give up your old habits. You don't just stop over night. Though I loved going to church I still had this desire for women. But I said that I will be more cautious this time. I would set behind these young ladies every Sunday. They looked very spiritual. They would sing, stand up and clap their hands. They were very friendly. We would speak and smile at each other. That was alright OK. One Sunday one of the young ladies asked me to come and set with her. The pew was already crowded, but I squeezed in anyway. We began to set together on Sundays, and the next thing I knew we were dating. She was younger than I was also. There was no sex involved.

We probable kissed once or twice. I had started building houses now, and I had bought a house about twenty miles from where she lived. She would have to be at work about five o clock in the morning, she did not have a car. I would get up early in the morning go to her house take her to work then go back and pick her up in the evenings. She was in beauty school. I would even carry her to school and return when she got out and take her home. This went on for a while. I did not mind but I was being cautious.

This went on for about two months. One day I was visiting her at her apartment when she told me that we had to stop seeing each other. She said that she had a boy friend and that she was just using me. I was not even hurt when she said that, because I did not open the door to get hurt. I said ok and walked out the door. I did not even care; I said to myself that I could save some gas and sleep now. I thought to my self even those in church you have to watch out for. Some of them are just like I was when I used to sing, doing something to be seen. In church but the church is not in you. I guess by now you would think that I would quit. Wrong! I met another young lady in church at a church dinner. We were setting next to each other. While setting next to the young lady we started talking. I called her a few times, and then we started seeing each other. She lived in some apartments on the other side of town. I invited her over to my house a few times. She started talking about how her furniture would look in my house. She would call me all the time. There was not a day that went by that she did not call at least three or four times. I shared an office with my partner he would tell me "she called you and said call her. He said she's not giving you any space is she. This began to bother me. What was there to talk about three or four times a day? She wanted to get married and move her and her children into my house. I wasn't thinking about marriage, and there was no way I was going to move them into my house. I told her that this is not going to work. After that neither she nor her daughter would speak to me any more. I would see them in church and they would turn their heads the other way so they would not look at me. I would laugh and ignore them.

There has to be an end to this madness right? Well it happened. I was invited to a yard party a friend of mine was having. The young lady that I fell in love with was there. We did not say a word to each other. I did not care, I was over that situation. I was having fun with the rest of the guest. By this time the only ting I would drink was wine, and it had to be good wine. But while I was out I did not drink at all. The only time I would have some wine was when I was at home with dinner. Boy had I changed. The hostess introduced me to a young lady there and said that she wanted to move to the area. She was from New Jersey. We talked and I said that I have a house with three bedrooms and maybe I can help. I was falling into a big trap again. She asked me to fly up to New Jersey to help her move. I consented, dumb me. When I got there she had her things ready to go. I asked her where is the truck. She told me that we have to pick it up. When we went to pick up the truck she told me that I would have to pay for it. That took me by surprise. I rented the truck loaded up her things and drove all the way from New Jersey to Atlanta. I moved her things into my house. She said that she was going to get a job. That was part of our agreement. I would go to work and return home to find her in her night clothes. I asked her about her job hunting. She said that she was looking.

This went on for about a month. I told her that she would have to get a job or find another place to stay. She told me that she wasn't going anywhere and that I was going to take care of her. She said that she worked for a lawyer in New Jersey and she knew how to mess me up. By this time I did not care. I put her out of my house. She went next door and called the police on me. They came and locked me up.

I told them that the house was mine and that I did not want her there. They told her that she had to leave. They let me go the next day. When I got out I said I am finished,

I quit. I don't want another mother's daughter in my life. I will live the rest of my life alone. I am hanging up my shoes, I am finished and I mean it.

I was doing well. I would go to work put in long hours go to church twice a week, I was happy. Then soft hearted me fell for the bait again. Another friend wanted to move to Atlanta. She said that she had this couple who wanted to move also. I consented to let them stay with me until they could find a place of their own. I even offered to give the husband a job. The young lady was just a good friend. I had gone to Saint-Louis to do some work for her. There was no hanky panky going on. I said that I was finished, and I meant that. Everything was going well. I enjoyed having them with me. They went to church with me; I showed them around the city. Everything was going ok. Then my friend said that she had to go back home and decide if she was going to come back. I enjoyed having them there, they were company for me. One day the husband's wife called and said that the lady from New Jersey was there and she wanted to get her things. I said that her things were in the garage, and do not let her in the house. I felt uneasy in my spirit. We continued to work that day. We did not get another phone call, but I felt that something was wrong. When we got home the young lady not only took her things, but she stole some of my thing also. I asked the young mans wife why she let them in the house? She said that the woman said that she had some things in the house. I said why didn't you call me back? She did not give me an answer. I was mad, not angry but mad. They stayed with me a little while longer. After that I said that's it no more, finished, that's the last time I will try to help someone out. I have learned my lesson.

Almost two years had passed, and I had put the entire pass behind me. I was content with my life as it was until one day while I was setting in church I looked around at all the people there. I asked the Lord God, Lord why am I here? Why did you make me? Why was I born? I know you did not just bring me into this world to make money, and buy things. I would like to know why I am here? I look around this church at the families here sitting together; I would like to have a family to. Was I meant to be alone? Every time I try to get involved with someone bad things happen to me. I am tired of trying now. Please show me why I was born? Why I am on this earth. I have a good job. I have nothing to cry about like some of the people I see here, but I feel empty inside, I am missing something. Please show me my purpose for being.

This stayed on my heart. I had purchased a Bible and I read it from Genesis 1:1 to revelations 22:21. After reading the whole Bible once, I read it again.

I decided to join the church. One Sunday I made that step. I joined but I did not want to get involved in any committee. I just wanted to go enjoy the services and go home. I had to attend their new member's classes. I did not like the classes. I thought they were shallow. Their focus was on everyday things. I wanted to learn more about the Bible.

I had this thirst, a yearning to know God, to know His word and to know my purpose. I wanted more than they were giving me. I did not blame them; their program was set up for new converts. I was not new to Christianity. I was not where I was supposed to be, and I was seeking direction. They were on page one, and I was one page fifty one. I would set quietly though until I heard something wrong, then something inside me would not let me be at peace until I would speak out. I knew every story in the Bible. I could close my eyes and the spirit of God would put a picture before me. If you said something wrong I knew it. I was not argumentative, but I would make my point. I had one class with the Pastors secretary. She was very pretty. I did not know at the time that she was the Pastors secretary. I did not say anything out of the way, though she was pretty. I was finished with that part of life and I was serious. I just looked at her as one of God's beautiful creations, nothing else. They had a booklet that we were supposed to be using in our classes. I studied the booklet and there were things that I did not agree with. When we had class with the Pastors secretary she started reading from the book, and she went to the portions that I did not agree with. I spoke up, and the whole class joined in on the debate. We took over her class. Later I apologized; she laughed and said that was Ok.

One day I was at work, I had taken a job to remodel an apartment in a condominium down town. I was on the first floor talking to the door man when my Pastor came off the elevator. He recognized me and asked me what I was doing there. I told him that I was there working on one of the units. He asked me to come by the church that they have some things that needed attention. I told him that I would. I thought to my self, here I go again. I had become well known at the church where I left. Not only did I sing in the quire, I also remodeled the church inside and out. I got to see and hear a lot of the things that go on behind closed doors. Things that would make you leave the church. I did not want to go through that again. I came up listing to my parents talk about things that were going on in the church. The gossip can run you away from the church, even if some of it is true. All churches have their problems, large and small. They are made up of people, and people have problems, but they also cause problems. My focus was selfish right now. I was seeking God with all my heart, and I did not want any distractions. There were things I wanted to know about my life, my walk. I did not want to go back there behind closed doors. I thought well I must be obedient if they need help and I am capable of assisting them in any way I have to help. I'll just stay clear of any gossip or idle talk. That sounds good and right doesn't it? But the fact is once you go behind those doors people will run you down carrying some mess. When you walk into an office someone is talking about someone else. If you are there you can not help hearing gossip. That is bad that goes on even in the house of God. You can bring people into the church, but it is hard to put the church into people.

I was obedient and started working on the church. I even brought some of my sub contractors to help me. Everyone was very pleased with the work we were doing. We had a number of projects we did for the church. I stayed away from rumors and gossip, and they were there. I would hear, but I would not respond. It was not my business anyway. My opinion could not change a thing. It could only hurt by carrying things that I did not know any thing about. My job was to do the work I was contracted to do. Any thing else was out of my job assignment. I was like the three monkeys, see nothing, hear nothing, and say nothing. You could never go to anyone and say Obie said. Don't you wish everyone was like that? Wouldn't things be better if people would mind their own business? I have a saying: Stop trying to sweep around my door, when there is so much dirt around you door. You can sweep around your door, and two minutes after you have swept, you can go back and still find some dirt. They don't make a vacuum cleaner that can get all of the dirt out of your house. So leave my house alone. Sounds good? Then practice it.

While I was working on the church I would have to communicate with the Pastors secretary. One day she was going up the back steps of the church. We spoke and smiled at each other. She had the most beautiful smile. She was about half way up the steps when out of my mouth I asked her to have dinner with me sometime. She looked back down the steps at me, smiled and said OK. I was shocked that I had asked her. I just opened my mouth and the words came out. Later I thought to my self, OH LORD WHAT HAVE I DONE? Fear gripped me; I did not know what to do. I wanted to back out, but that would not be the Christian thing to do. I began to wrestle with this in my spirit until the day we went out to dinner. We went out to dinner and it was not like any thing I could have imagined. I really enjoyed being with her. She was different from all the women I had been with. We talked about the Bible and God. The subject I was most interested in. I told about some of my experiences and dreams, and she helped me to see those things scripturally. She was a big help to me. She told me that she wanted me to meet Sister Pat. Sister Pat was a counselor for the church. She had the gift of discernment. She was also one of the ministers at the church. I thought to my self God has sent this young lady into my life to help me with the answers I am seeking. I was really excited about the journey I was on. I looked forward to my session with Sister Pat.

The day came when I was to meet Sister Pat. I thought we would meet at the church, but she invited us to her house for dinner. She was very friendly. A pretty lady also. I could tell she was sizing me up by our conversation. I did not care, I had nothing to hide. If pouring it all out would help me, let's get it on. I was ready and open to hear. I could tell if someone was lying to me. I would not say anything to the individual, but to my self I would say: lie, lie, lie. I did not under stand me, my purpose for being, or the things I see and hear, and I wanted help. We talked for a while, she prepared some food for us, we ate, and all the time I felt her reaching in to my mind. Have you ever talked to someone and you could feel like something was pulling on you inside you head.

That's the way I felt, especially when she looked at me. She was very jovial; she made me feel real comfortable. I guess that was her way of getting you to open up to her.

After we had eaten she asked me to talk about my self. Before I began she told me that God had given me these special gifts and I had to learn how to use them. I was still puzzled, and her remarks did not make the matter better. I did not tell her about my childhood. I only told her about my recent experiences. After I started attending the church things started happening to me that mystified me. I was working one day on a window. I was installing the locking mechanism to the window. I reached down to pick up my screw driver and the locking mechanism. I saw the screw driver but the window lock was not there. I looked all over the floor for it, but I did not see it I could not find it. I knew I had brought it into the house and laid it next to the screw driver. It was not there. I was puzzled. I looked at the window sash and there it was with a screw in it ready to be installed. I knew that I did not put it there, nor was anyone else in the apartment but me. Things like that began to happen to me. I would see images of people walking, but when I would go to where I saw them no one was there. I would listen to the radio and tell the song they were going to play before they played the song. I new things about people before they told me anything about them selves. I was puzzled what was going on with me. I looked at her and she looked at me. I felt this urge to tell her something about herself. I opened my mouth and the words seem to roll of my tong. I could not help myself. This was happening to me lately and I could not stop the words from coming out. I would get this urge to speak and I had to. The funny thing about it was I did not know what I was going to say. It was like something or someone was controlling me. She listen and her eyes never left me not once. Then after a while she began to tell me what was going on with me. She said that I was a prophet of God's, and that I needed training in the word of God. She recommended that I go to school and learn about God and His word. I thanked her. She prayed for us before we left. When we left I felt like a heavy burden had been lifted off my shoulders. But now I was left with another question. What is this gift and what am I supposed to do with it. More questions that needed answering. I thanked the young lady for taking me there. We talked about the event all the way home. I was excited and puzzled what next?

It is my belief that God has already manifested the gifts we are going to use for His glory in us before we were even conceived in our mothers womb. In Ephesians 2:10, for we are God's workmanship, created in Christ Jesus to do good works, **which God prepared in advance for us to do.** Psalm 139:15-16, my frame was not hidden from you when I was made in the secret place. When I was woven together in the secret place. When I was woven together in the depths of the earth, you saw my unformed body. All the days ordained for me were written down in your book before one of them came to be. I believe that sometimes the gift can remain dormant until God's chosen time for the gift to be used. Some gifts require a time of suffering so when the gift is manifested through us we will not get the big head and thank we are the ones performing the task, robbing God of His glory and praise. The greater the suffering, the greater the gift, or the greater the gift the greater the suffering.

The gift is there but we must be prepared (formed) to be able to use the gift. Job 14:15, you will call and I will answer you will long for the creature your hands have made.

It is no telling how long the gift may remain dead in us until God breaths life in the gift and calls it forward. It is to His good will and purpose. In 1 Corinthians 12:1-30, the Apostle Paul gives us a discord about spiritual gifts. I will refer back to this book and chapter later in my writings to look at some issues in some churches which are causing burdens on the body of Christ. Right now I want to mention one thing that is found in verse 31, "Eagerly desire the greater gift". It is ok to want to sing like Shirley Caesar or Marvin Sapp, but if you have not been blessed with the gift don't get up and embarrass yourself. It is ok to want to preach like DR. Charles Stanley or Bishop T.D. Jakes, but if God has not blessed you with the gift leave it a lone. You will only be a clamoring cymbal, a lot of noise but no anointing. It is ok to desire spiritual gifts another person has. To say I wish I could sing like, pray like, and preach like; there is nothing wrong with that. It shows admiration for the blessing God has placed on the individual. But if the gift has not been given to you leave it alone. Don't let your desire become covertness. Thank God for giving them their gift for service and eagerly seek the gift God has prepared for you. God has a purpose for all gifts of service, and that is the formation of the body of Christ. To nurture and grow His church. If we all have the same gift where would the church be? Each gift has a place in the church of Christ. If one gift is left out then the church can not function. It is not a church, but a social gathering. No mater how small you think your gift is, it is valuable in the sight of the Lord God and Jesus Christ our savior the head of His Church. I never desired the gifts God blessed me with; they were there inside of me when I was born. We are born with our gifts. God did not leave it up to us to choose the gifts we want. Hebrews 2:4, God also testified to it by signs, wonders and various miracles, and gifts of the Holy Spirit distributed according to His will. Ephesians 4:7, but to each one of us grace has been given as Christ appointed it, this is why it says: "When he ascended on high, He led captives in His train and gave gifts to men". I remember one time I was watching Benny Hin on television and he said "there is someone out there God wants to give the gift of healing as I have. He said raise your hands and I will pray for you. I raised my hands and asked God for the gift of healing. Like a dummy I did not remember that God had already used me to heal some people. I was praying for a gift I already possessed. I should have been praying that God would use me in according to His will, and thank Him for the gift. We can get caught up sometimes when we hear people speak. But the Bible teaches us to keep our heads when others are loosing theirs. I remember when I was in ministerial training our Instructor said "he (Obie) is a prophet of God's, but he will never tell you that he is." I do not believe in wearing your gift on your chest. I have a problem when people want to justify themselves by calling themselves prophet, or prophetess. I believe in letting the Lord God show who you are through signs, miracles and wonders. If I justify myself then my word is worthless. But if God justifies me then the power of the Holy Spirit will flow through me and both I and the recipient will be blessed. I don't have to ware a sign to let you know who I am, or the gift I have been blessed with. The gift will manifest it self at the proper time. We run people away with our titles. Christ was the King of the Jews, but he would not let it be known until He was preparing to leave this life.

I have found that the lost will talk more comfortable to me if I don't introduce myself using titles, or surnames. I had a lot on my mind after the session with Sister Pat. You would think I would be bubbling over with joy finding out things about myself. I was not, this only added more questions. Now I know I have these gifts, why me? What am I supposed to do with the gifts? What does God expect of me? So many questions, my mind was becoming perplexed. I needed more answers now. I was never a patient person. If I wanted something I wanted it right now. I wanted answers right now. Who do I talk to, where do I go to get the answers I am seeking? It seems when we get in a hurry, God slows down. Our rushing does not excite the Lord Jesus. He will reveal to us the things we ask in His time and in His way. So you might as well be patient and wait on Him. I was not ready yet. I still did not have the church in me. I was getting there, but I had not arrived yet. I had not surrendered my life yet. I was still holding on to my way. My way says give it to me now, not tomorrow or next week, but right now. I have got to have it right now. Tomorrow is not promised to me. Lord please help me. He was helping me, but I was to dumb to realize it. Slow down be cool, you will get there. Easley said isn't it. Yea right!

The young lady and I started dating a lot. I was happy just being in her company. She did not pressure me with a lot of phone calls. And neither did I call her a lot. She was a devoted church worker. And I was devoted to my job. So we did not get into each others hair. My partner had a cabin in the mountains and we went up there one weekend. Then we got closer. You know what I mean. There were a few other times when we were close. Then one day she told me that she was an evangelist, and we had to stop doing what we were doing. She said that we could still date and be friends, but we had to stop getting close. Although I did not want to stop, I knew her way was right. We continued to go out to dinner, and we still talked, and that was all.

One day after Wednesday night service, I was on my way home and I walked her to her car. We were talking and I told her that I heard the Lord say something to me. She said what did you hear? I opened my mouth and hear comes the words again. I said He told me that you are my wife. She looked at me and laughed, and put her arm around my neck, and I don't remember what happened after that. I was out of it, everything went blank. Here I go.

We started making preparations for our wedding. I moved her things into my house. Our friends were helping with all the preparations. We were going to have a house wedding. She was staying with a friend not to far from my house. I was getting cold feet. I started thinking about the troubles I had been involved in with women, and I did not want to go through that any more. I kept saying to my self that she was different, and I did hear the Lord say that she is my wife. That was you Lord wasn't it? I kept dealing with this all the way up to the day of the ceremony. It was like my body was proceeding, but my mind was out to lunch. Here I am should I go through with this, or should I back out? We were standing before the Minister now, well it is too late. Hope for the best. Maybe this will work. I married Geraldine A. Sailors November 22, 1998.

The ceremony was fine; we made it through this part. Two months gone by everything's fine. This can be alright. Third month, she told me that she was leaving me. She said that I work too much and that I was not showing her enough attention. I did not put up a fight, and said ok if that is the way you fell I understand. I worked long hours. I would leave home about 6: AM in the morning, and return about 10: PM at night. I worked Monday through Saturday. I did not work as long on Saturdays, probably to about six in the evening. I never worked on Sundays. I was a workaholic. I had been by myself for a while and I did not consider the fact that I needed to change my work habit. I knew that she spent a lot of time at church, so I thought that I would not be missed. I guess I was wrong. She left, and I continued to work. I loved her, but I was not hurt because she left. I guess by this time I had become impervious to pain. I was not going to force anyone to do something they did not want to do. I had been through so much, I was just going to right this off as another chapter in my life. What can I say?

We still talked when I would go to church. I would still go to the office and see her. Everyone started looking at me funny. One day sister Pat walked up to me and said "you should be ashamed of yourself. I thought to my self what did I do? I did not leave her, she left me. I should be ashamed why? What has she been saying about me around the church? More questions I can add to my époque. Well I guess I should be ashamed. But I am not, I did not do anything. What ever.

She stayed gone for three months. One day I called and asked could I come over? She said yes. I arrived at her apartment and told her that I did not want to live like this with my wife being in one place and I am in another. I said that I was going to file for a divorce. She told me to wait, and give her some time. She said that she was going through some counseling and that she had some issues she was trying to work out. I said ok. I really wanted this to work, but I was not going to force her. I was not going to plead, cry or get on my knees. She would have to make up her own mind to come back that's the only way it was going to work. If I pleaded, cried, or got on my knees begging she might feel sorry for me and come back only to leave again sometime later. I did not want that. If she made up her own mind to come back of her own volition then she would be happy, and hopefully we could put this behind us. The next week she came back, and I bought a dog. I did not want her to be alone anymore while I was at work so we picked out a dog and brought him home. Do you know that worked. I even started coming home earlier. The dog was a blessing.

Everything was going fine between us. She would walk the dog in the evenings and I walked him in the mornings before I went to work. We even carried the dog to the beach with us. I was happy, and she seemed happy. Life was beautiful. I was not concerned as much about the things I had been asking God about. I was waiting patiently. I could concentrate on my life with my wife and my dog. I even joined the quire at church. I did not lead any songs that was alright with me, I did not want to lead anyway.

I loved to play tennis, so I asked the pastor about starting a tennis tournament to raise funds for the church. He consented. We set out on the task of forming a committee and putting our program in place. I had to make the announcements for the program. I was getting another opportunity to get up in front of the congregation, this time instead of singing I was talking. God can prime you for a position and you don't even know what's going on. I had to make my announcements informative and humorous to attract attention to our program so people would support us. This was my first attempt at public speaking. I was comfortable being in front of people this came from my experience in leading songs. The difference was I was not singing a song where the words are already provided. I had to come up with the words to say. Make it short, lively, humorous and get your point across. This was a challenge. I was learning, being trained for my walk with Christ. Little did I know where I was headed.

Out tournament was a success. We had a large crowd come out every Saturday. We grilled and had fun. We raised a large amount of money for our church. We had a play off and purchased trophies for the winners. Our Pastor would come out on occasion to support us. Everything was beautiful. The Sunday when we were to present the trophies our Pastor had me to come up front with Him. He handed me the mike. Don't give me the mike, it's on now. I told how it was supposed to rain the last Saturday of the tournament and we prayed and God heard our prayers and not a drop of rain fell where we were. This was my first experience witnessing about the power of Prayer. It felt real good. Everyone was in awe when I spoke. I did not realize what I was doing, or what God was doing through me. I was mesmerized. I just opened my mouth and the words just flowed out. What was happening to me? Christ Jesus was drawing me closer, there was nothing I could do but submit to His will. Our Pastor was happy, we were happy, the congregation was happy, the event was a success.

We had such a big success that our Pastor wanted to have another tournament the next year. Other churches had heard about our tournament and wanted to compete against us. Some wanted to imitate our program. Our Pastor even told us that while he was in Washington D.C. visiting one of our Senators, the Senator had asked him about our tournament. I guess this made him proud that our tennis tournament was heard about all the way in Washington D.C... There was no way that I was going to get out of heading a tournament the next year.

The next year came and we were preparing to plan the tournament. We started planning early. During our planning stage my wife Gere got pregnant. O boy I went through something. I was not expecting this. I was forty four years old and thinking about buying myself a Porsche, taking a lot of trips, retirement and having a nice bank roll. I saw all my dreams go up in smoke. I said **NO**! How could you do this to me? I am too old to have a child, why me. She looked at me and did not say a word. I said well with one child I probably still can have my dreams. I did not know that my plans for my life were not God's plans for my life. One day she had to go to the doctor to have her check up, and when I came home she said that I have a surprise for you.

The doctor said that they believe we are going to have twins. I wanted to faint. I said no way you are lying. I said I'm not going to believe you. She said that is the truth. I could not say a word. I was out of it. Every dream I had was going out the window. I am forty four years old and starting a family. Why me Lord? Why me? I was taking it hard, but I did not want her to know. I smiled as much as

I could. I was down cast until we went to church and she told everyone that we were going to have twins. The word got around and everyone started patting me on the back and saying "boy you sure are potent, you did not produce one but two". I started getting the big head then. This old man can produce twins, I'm not dead yet. Everyone would look at me and smile. I said to my self this might not be so bad. I really wanted them now. The more accolades I received the larger my head got. I probably could have toppled over. I began to get excited about her pregnancy. I would call all the time to see how she was doing. I had so much joy that I could not control myself. Boy was I happy. I had forgotten about all the things I had gone through. I was a new creation. I was beginning a new life in Christ. I was beginning to allow the church to come into me. I was so happy and so thankful, but I did not know nor could I see the troubles that lay ahead. It is a shamed that you always have to be on you guard. When you feel that everything is going fine, and the Lord gives you peace, rest and happiness, then here comes the enemy.

We were doing fine, and she was growing. I told her she looked like a little round butterball. She was only five feet one or two, and carrying twins. In her fourth month she looked like a round ball. What did I say that for, she got angry with me; mad would be a better word. I was just making a joke and she took it hard. Other people could talk about her size and she would smile and laugh. Boy I could not crack a joke at all. I was learning about the emotions of women, through trial and error. I made some mistakes and boy did I pay, but I learned what to say and what not to say. I would let other people make the jokes, and I would laugh with them not to hard though. This was a new experience for me, and for me to get through it would take a lot of prayer and wisdom. Her emotions were very high. I had to walk very softly around her. I did not want to do anything that would upset her and cause any complications. I was being taught patience, compassion and love. Qualities which were not in me, so I thought. A person does not know what is inside of them until the occasion arises, and they have to reach a new level of action, compassion and understanding.

She was growing so fast that our doctor told her that she would have to stop work. The doctor put her on bed rest. One of the members of the church came to live with us to care for her. She was a real nice lady. She cooked and cleaned for us, and prepared meals for my wife. I thanked God for her being there. We had a lot of talks about the Bible. I was still learning. Everything was going fine until one day Gere called and said that she was having complications and the doctor said to get her to the hospital. I rushed all the way home as fast as the van could go. When I arrived we headed for the hospital. We arrived and they carried her to a room. I remained outside the room waiting and praying that everything was ok. Later they came and told me that she had gone into false labor, but she was ok now. I breathed a sigh of relief.

They said that they were going to keep her in the hospital to monitor her. It was her fifth month. I was concerned, but I was not worried I knew that she was in good hands and they would care for her. I stayed with her in the hospital every night. I went to work In the daytime and at night I was back in the hospital. All of her nurses new me. They were real nice to us. I hated sleeping on those hard carts, but I put up with it to be close to her. I did not like hospital food though. I would go out and buy my food and go back to the hospital. The only time I would leave her was to go to work and get some food.

One day I got a call and they told me to rush to the hospital. I arrived and they told me that she had gone into false labor again, and that they were trying to stabilize her. The nurses were monitoring her trying to stop her from going into labor. I sat there watching, and praying. Eventually they got her stabilized. One of the nurses told me that she had gotten a telephone call and that the call had upset her sending her into false labor. I asked Sister Mary what had happened? She told me that one of the members of the church had called and told Gere that a good friend of ours had died. I was very angry. Why would they do that? They new Gere was in the hospital because she was having complications. How could you be so dumb and call her. The lady who called was supposed to be an evangelist, she should know better. The young man that died worked with Gere. He was a real good friend. Why call her, what could she do? She could not leave the hospital to attend the services, so why call? I was very angry with the young lady. I wanted to call her back, but they stopped me. I did call the church and told them what had happened. I told them to ask people not to call her anymore with bad news.

Later I received another call to come to the hospital she was going into labor again. I rushed to the hospital again wondering what was wrong this time. When I arrived the nurses told me that one of the doctors had upset Gere and sent her into false labor. When I talked to Gere she told me that the doctor said that we would have to loose one of the babies so the other baby could survive. She said that we needed to make a decision soon. I told Gere not to worry that they were not going to take one of the babies from us. I asked who the doctor was? She said that the doctor was not one of our regular doctors. I asked the nurse attending Gere about the doctor? The nurse said that the doctor was assigned to come in as a fill-in, and that she should not have said what she said to Gere. I told her that I would handle the problem.

I immediately went to the hospital office and asked to see the head of the hospital. They referred me to the person in charge of the hospital staff. He told me that they were not responsible for the attending physicians. He said that I would have to contact our doctor about their staff. I called our doctor and told him the problem I was having. I told him that I did not want that doctor in my wife's room anymore. He said that he wanted me to talk to the doctor that maybe there was some misunderstanding. I consented to talk to the doctor, but I insisted that I did not want that doctor to attend my wife anymore. The next day I meet with the doctor I was as cordial as I could be. I had already prayed before our meeting. I met with the doctor I allowed her to talk first. She said that we would have to make a decision about the boys.

She said that they were concerned about their growth. She also said that the smaller one was taking nourishments from the larger one, and in order for one to be born they needed to take one of them out. She also said that we need to make a quick decision. I looked her straight in her face and said as comely as I could that I have made a decision and this is it. Neither of my boys are going to be aborted, and if she goes back into the room with my wife I was going to sue her and the hospital and anyone else involved. She asked me what if something happens when she is on duty. I told her that she had better find someone else to attend my wife, because I am very serious about what I said. I told her that I had already spoken to the hospital and made them aware of my decision, also I had talked to the head of their doctors, and my lawyer. Without saying another word I got up and left the room with her setting there. The next day the nurses were complementing me, and they said that people were talking about me all over the hospital. We had already prayed, and we were standing on our faith in God. Who were we going to believe God or the doctors? We stood firm in our faith. I guess she got the message that I was serious because she never came into the room again.

They assigned another doctor to come in and check on my wife. He tried to explain to me what they were seeing as a problem. I listened to him and I said just care for her and leave the rest up to God. He looked at me and said well if that is you decision then ok. Everything went pretty well after that. She had a few minor alerts, but they were able to stop them. Then one day I got another call to rush to the hospital. She was in her Seventh month now. When I arrived her head doctor was there in the room with her and the nurses were there to. The doctor looked at me and said well Obie we can't stop them from coming now. We have to get her into the delivery room. They got her ready and off we go to the delivery room. When we arrived on the lower floor they put us in a room across from the delivery room. Her doctor said that they were getting the room ready and it would be a few minutes before we go in. She told the doctor that she wanted her tubes tied. He said that we needed to think about that, because if any thing goes wrong we can still try again. I told him to grant her request these boys will be born. He said I know that you have faith, but I want you to take a minute and think about it. I said we have already prayed and that we were standing on our faith in God.

Off we go into the delivery room. They rolled her in to the delivery room. I had put on my robe, hat, shoes and mask. They had me set behind her at her head. They would not let me stand, or be in front of her. They had a nurse with me I guess in case if I were to pass out if something went wrong. The nurse sat there holding my hand. There was a cabinet next to where we were, they did not know that I could see every thing off the reflection of the cabinet, and I wasn't going to say anything. I sat there watching as they cut her open and parted her skin on both sides. I saw as they took out the first child and the doctor spanked him and he cried. Then came the next one and the doctor spanked him and he started crying also. It seemed as though the whole room breathe a sigh of relief. I was so happy my boys were born; my father had heard our prayers and granted our request. God showed out that day. He showed how having faith in Him really works. These people were trained physicians.

Skilled in their jobs, but God is still Lord of all the earth when we have faith, true faith he will come through for us. This we can be assured of. What an awesome God we serve. I was not surprised at the miracles of the Lord God. I was filled with joy and happiness because He showed man that He is still in control. The next day when I returned to Gere's room, she told me that the doctor had been to see her and he was praising God for the miracle. I smiled and said thank you Lord.

The boys were born premature. Daniel was first, then David. They were very small. They had to be kept in incubators. There was a different doctor over them while they were in the intensive care unit. The doctor said that they were very healthy, and they would have to stay in the intensive care unit until they weighed enough to go home. He also said that the doctors were so concerned because they were so small and that one weighed less than the other. I said they wanted us to abort my child because one weighed one ounce less than the other? When have you seen twins come into the world weighing the same? I thought that was totally ridiculous. I told Gere what the doctor told me. I also said how many families have aborted their babies taking their advice? It is not up to them to say who should come into this world or not. Mankind does not have the right to say who should live, or who should die. Man can not give life. I have never seen a man reach down into the earth make a man, and then breathe life into him. Man wants to destroy that he can not restore. Even if God allowed man to clone another human being, and I hope with all my heart that will never happen. But even if God allowed it to happen man has to take living cells from another living human being to make a clone. Mankind can not reach into the air and take nothing and make something. He can only try to copy what God has already made. So again I say who gave man the right to destroy what he can not create?

I wish there were no wars. We send our sons and daughters of to fight in wars, to give their lives for our way of life, our security, to protect us from tyranny. They go off and some of them never return, or some return in a pine box. We say they gave their lives for their country. We call them heroes, patriots. We honor them, thank them, and then we bury them never to see them again. But a mother and a dad only have a picture to remind them of the child they raised from birth.

Every night for the rest of their lives as they lay on their beds dreams of their child will filter in. And at mornings light they awake hopping to hear their child's voice, but there's only silence. They awake from a dream only to hurt again. The holidays seem empty for them. They remember when they all gather together for that special dinner. But now my child is no more, who can replace my child? Why did my child have to die? Why are their wars? Why can't we all live together? I read in the Bible where it says; yet I will show love to the house of Judah; and I will save them – not by bow, sword or battle, or by horses and horsemen, but by the Lord their God. Hoses 1:7. I also read in 2 Kings 7:1-20, how God had made the Amerians flee from attacking the Israelites because the Amerians thought they heard the sound of chariots and horses and a great army.

I also read in 1 Samuel 17: 47, David said "All those gathered here will now know that it is not by sword, or spear that the Lord saves; for the battle is the Lord's, and he will give all of you into our hands." Why does man chose to destroy that which he can not restore? We have laws to protect endangered species, plants, animals and the environment. But can't we see how mankind is becoming extent. Why do we need to have wars? Is there on God in the land that we can call on to fight our battles? Are there any warring angels He has to protect us from harm? Why did my child have to die? But I realize that life is like a small snow ball at the top of a tall mountain, when that snow ball starts coming down that mountain who can stop it? That snow ball turns into a destructive avalanche.

And every time they look at a picture of their child their heart is torn apart. That smile, that cry, bruised knee, laughter, will never be heard again. Why Lord did my child have to die before me? I should have been first to go. Why do we have wars? Why can't we all live together, at peace with each other?

We were told about a twin support group that was part of the hospital. We went to a meeting and we were shocked at the things we heard some of the parents say. We were not the only ones that went through the situations we encountered in the hospital. There were others who experienced worst things than we had. My heart went out to them. They were meeting to see if there was a way to put an end to this kind of treatment. I hope they succeed in their fight.

Well you would think we had been through enough. Not so. Before the boys came home we had to move. I lost the house we were living in. I worked hard every day except Sundays. I had two partners when I first started building houses. One was a real estate broker and the other worked for the federal aviation association. I was the working partner. It was my job to hire and supervise the subcontractors, do the material list for the houses, coordinate all inspections, order all the materials etc. I did all the field work. I was the builder. The real estate partner handled the payrolls and the clients. The FAA partner did not do anything because he did not know anything. He was our money person. We built three houses and they told me that when they sold we did not make any money. They said that after they paid the FAA guy back there was nothing left. The FAA guy got money, the real estate guy made money for selling the houses, but I got nothing.

I told them that I had put in all my time on these projects and now you are telling me this? I was in the process of losing my house. I did not want to hear that. We parted company after that. I started building with another partner. He was a trip. He was very scary. He did help me out though when I lost my house. We were able to get another house, but I made a dumb deal which cost me later. When you have your back against the wall you can do some dumb things without really thinking things through. I needed a place to bring my family home. The boys were growing and they would be coming home soon. We found a house that I could get on a loan assumption.

The people were asking for five thousand dollars to assume their loan. I found a lender who would give me twenty five hundred and I had to put up the rest. My partner let me have the twenty five hundred and we went to closing. At the closing I found out that the lender was charging me three times the amount to borrow the money. And though the house was in our name we had to make payments to the lender then the lender would in turn pay the mortgage. I thought I could our smart him by paying him for six months and then have the house refinanced getting rid of him and cutting him out of all the money he was trying to collect. My plan sound good at the time. So I went through with the deal. I stepped into another trap.

We moved in time for the boys to come home. I had provided a house for my family. I was happy. Gere would take care of one of the boys, and I would take care of the other one. We had our routine down pat. They were good babies. They did not cry that much and they slept through the night. They were so good that I thought something was wrong with them. I would constantly check on them. I was very proud of them. Before they came home David the smallest had a hernia. They had to operate on him to remove the hernia. That made me very sad. Then they said he had a thyroid problem. We would have to carry him to the pediatrician to get shots. I was always the one who would go in the back with him to get his shot, while Gere kept Daniel in the waiting area. I had to hold him while the pediatrician gave him the shot. He would look up at me and cry when she stuck him with the needle, as if to say daddy why are you letting them do this to me. I wanted to cry with him. We had carried him three times and than I said I have had enough. I began to cry out to the Lord God to heal my Baby. I did not want him to continue to suffer like this anymore.

I laid my hand on him, and Gere and I prayed. When we carried him back to the doctor they sent him to be tested. The test came back negative; they said he was alright and that he would not need anymore shots. We were very happy and began to thank and praise Christ Jesus for saving our son from his sickness. That was the first time

I laid hands on anyone and prayed for their healing. God was doing something with me, but I was not there yet. I began to think to myself, why didn't I pray for him when they said he had a hernia, maybe he would not have had to go through that operation. I still think about that today. I was learning about the power of God, and the gift of the Holy Spirit He had blessed me with.

The boys began to grow they were beautiful babies. Everyone wanted to hold them. They are my heart. When they were christen our Pastor reach for them to hold them in front of the congregation. I handed him one and he motioned to me to give him the other one also. He looked as proud as I was standing there holding them. After all the fuss I made when Gere told me that she was pregnant, now I wanted to be with the boys all the time. The lord God had really done something to me, I was a changed man. I was a new creation. I had a new heart, and a new direction, a new walk.

Gere did not return to work at the church, and she also stopped attending church services. She said that she wanted to find another church. I continued to go. When I would miss a Sunday my Pastor would call and check up on me. I thought that was very thoughtful of him taking time out of his busy schedule to call me. He also was interested in how the tournament was coming. I had appointed one of the members to run the tournament in my absence. The tournament was not as successful the second year. There was not a good turn out.

During this time we began to have problems with the investor who helped us get the house. He doubled our house note. I told Gere that we were not going to let him rip us off. We agreed and decided to find another house to move in. We moved into a larger house with a lake in the back yard. It was a nice quiet area. We liked the house and the surroundings. I had attended a seminar at one of the theological seminaries where Sister Pat was working. I wanted to go to school to learn more about God and His word. I had not made up my mind about the direction I wanted to take in the church. I was searching for guidance, I needed direction. The seminar was good, but it was focused on those who were ministers, or those who were going into the ministry. I was not interested in becoming a minister. One of the older gentlemen was setting next to me made a comment about me to the group. He asked me what I was waiting for, Why haven't you answered you call? I did not know what he was talking about. What call? Who called? I did not here someone calling me to the telephone. I looked at him in amazement. He said you are getting older and there won't be a lot of time left for the Lord to use you. What he said resonated in my spirit for a long time; I could not get it off of my mind. One day while I was in my little room where I would go to pray, I told the Lord if he would allow me to get in school and if I do well I will give my life to you to do your will. I will join the ministry. When I had finished praying and came out, Gere said that she heard clapping coming from the room where I was praying. She said it sound like a lot of people were in there. I told her that I did not hear anything, and that I was not clapping. I told her what I was praying about. She looked at me and smiled.

I was on a journey now to see what the Lord's will was for me. I went to my old Pastor the one I use to sneak out of service on and go to the football games. He was a professor at Morehouse College. I did not want to attend Morehouse, but I wanted his advice. I respected him very much and I knew he would give me good advice. I met with him and told him that I wanted to attend Bible College to learn about God and His word.

I did not tell him that I was considering entering the ministry, because I did not know for sure at that time. He recommended me to Beulah Heights Bible College, and he said that he would give me a letter of recommendation. I am off on this journey now. I made an appointment with the Dean of Admissions at the College. We met, he was very nice. I will never forget his name Dr. Kealer. I told him that I was interested in attending the school, but I was concerned about my age.

Also I was not a good student in high school. To be honest I barely graduated. I had a c- average in High School. He told me not to worry about that. He said "that he had found that people do better in school when they get older than when they are young because they study harder, and that they are more committed to their studies." He said "don't be concerned about your age, that they have people of all ages enrolled in the school." He said "that they even have some Pastors attending." He said that I would have to get a copy of my transcript from the high school I attended and then they would admit me. I was forty five years old now; they probable have thrown away my transcript. He told me where I could go and get a copy.

Off I go. I procured the transcript and carried it back to the school and then I enrolled.

I had one more task to perform, I had to go and talk to my Pastor. I was going to leave the church and start attending the church where Gere was attending. I made an appointment to see my Pastor. When we met I told him that I was going to leave the church. I told him that I was going to go to school and that I thought it would be better for me to attend another church because of the associations I had made in this church. I needed to go where no one new me. I felt that if people new me that would hinder me from achieving the goals I was after. He tried to talk me out of leaving, but my mind was made up. As I sat there talking with him I had tears in my eyes. I new I could not be focused with Gere in one place and my being in another place. I did not need anything else to crowd my already minute mind. I thought where Gere was attending I could get better trained. So off I go again.

Gere was already attending the church. I asked her what she thought about the church. She told me that she really liked the services, and that she thought that we could learn a lot there. I thought it would be a good thing to set up a meeting with the Pastor to let him know our intentions, and see if they would be willing to help us on this journey. Gere was already an evangelist, but she wanted to go through their program. We sat up a meeting; they told us when we should come in. I thought that we were going to meet with the Pastor, but we meet with one of the assistant Pastors. When we met with her she asked us about our selves. We told her about the church we attended, and some of the things we were involved in. I told her that I had enrolled in Bible College, and I told her that a good friend of mine who is the Pastor of the church where I attended before I met Gere advised me to go to the College I would be attending. We told her that we would like to enter their ministers in training program. We talked for a while, and then left. I did not feel right in my spirit about the meeting. There were things said which I did not like, but I thought it was just me.

I went with my family to my first service there. I really enjoyed the quire and the atmosphere. It was a large church, but it was comfortable. I was ready to join that Sunday, but when the Pastor got up to preach I had to rethink my decision. He said that he hated for people to come into his office telling him who they know and where they come from. I knew he was talking about me. I said to Gere I have not been in that man's office and I surely have not met him or spoken to him.

She said that the associate minister must have told him those things. She said that I should not get angry and let's give this a chance. I said ok but I still had reservations. You think it got better, read on.

We did join the next Sunday. We had to go through their new members classes. I was quiet in their classes. I listened to others speak. The only time I would say anything was when they would ask us to introduce our selves. Sometimes Gere would introduce us, and I would not say a word. I wanted to see, hear and not be heard. That only lasted a while. When the Lord is inside of you, you can not hold your peace, or you will burst open.

We had joined the church, started ministry training, I had started school and I was working building houses. Sounds good doesn't it? When you give your life to Christ to do his will you would think that everything is going to get better in you life. Well for some people it probably does. My life was already having its ups and downs, and my friend it got worse. I was in for a war. A war which would be worse than any man could go through. And my family would have to go through these struggles with me. The word of God says that God will not put on you more than you can bear. 1 Corinthians 10:13. I was beginning to question that scripture. I could not have made it if it were not for Christ Jesus presence in my life.

I was really enjoying school. I was very interested in learning all I could about the early days of the Bible. I had some very good instructors. The one which stood out the most in my life was Brother Moore. He was hard, but he was very fair. He instructed us in the history of the Bible, the formation of the Bible and the Old and New Testament. I always had questions. I would talk to him a lot after class. He was very helpful. Dr. Kealer was one of my favorites also. He instructed us on the synaptic gospels (Matthew, Mark, Luke and John), He was a humorous instructor. I studied hard, and I always went to the library doing research. I was very surprised at the difference in opinions of Theologicians on topics of the Bible. If the men and women who were supposed to be the experts on the Bible could not agree on certain topics, where does that leave the novice? I believe that is why Christ said; "Nor are you to be called teacher, for you have one Teacher, the Christ." Matthew 23:10. And He also said: "All this I have spoken while still with you. But the counselor, the Holy Spirit, whom the Father will send in my name, will teach you all things, and will remind you of everything I have said to you. John 14:-26... I have heard so many times people say, "This one says that and that one says something different. Every church **teaches** something different. Who do you believe?"

The Apostle Paul said in 2 Corinthians 2:15, **study** to show thy self a proved.

Studying means more than reading. Some people open their Bibles with a dictionary beside them, and then say that they have studied. No you read, you did not study. Studying requires more than reading a topic, or looking up words in a dictionary. Studying requires research on that topic. When you study a topic you are looking for the five W's who, what, when, where and why. This requires reference materials, a trip to the library, meditation and prayer.

In order to get something out of a bowl, you first have to put something in the bowl. There are so many people today that will lead you astray if you don't know God's word for yourself. And they are good at what they do. I once went to a bible study in one of the neighborhoods we lived in. These people had formed an organization where the ministers ministered by video and telephone. I attended the study; they were so good at what they say that I started having doubts about the things I know. I caught myself and said this is wrong, I know my bible. I have not only read my bible but I have studied the word of God. What I am hearing here is wrong. Suppose I had not studied? Then I would be open to receive their false doctrine because It sounded convincing. Isaiah 29:13, the Lord says: "these people come near to me with their mouth am honor me with their lips, but their hearts are far from me. Their worship of me is made up only of rules taught by men." If you know the word of God for yourself, you can go any where and not get caught up in their false doctrine. You can do like I do when I hear something false. I say to my self; lie, lie, lie, boy that was a lie.

Has God ever told you to carry a message to someone, and you were like Jonah you did not want to go? Well that happened to me. The Lord gave me a message to carry to one of out associate ministers. I said Lord this lady has been in the ministry longer than I have. She has gone through school, and she has a higher position in the church. She stands before the church on Sunday s and ministers to the multitudes. How can I go to her and tell her the things you are showing me. Then the Lord allowed me to watch her showing me what he said was true. I watch her when she was ministering, and when she was just setting in the pulpit. I saw that everything the Lord told and showed me was true. But I still did not want to go to her. I liked her and I did not want to carry the message. I fought with this thing for a while. The Lord would not leave me alone. My obedience was being tested. I was not like some people who could at the drop of a hat run and tell someone, thus says the Lord. I was learning. I was a rookie. And I was afraid of what might be the repercussions if I had heard wrong. Boy there was a battle going on in side of me. I talked to Gere about the task I had been given. I even told her what to look for when we would see the minister on Sundays to confirm if I was seeing right. She confirmed the fact that I was seeing correctly and said that I should go and tell the minister.

She said that what the Lord had given me to say could possibly help her. And that you don't want the Lord mad with you. I did not say angry, I said mad. I could deal with angry; angry may not be too bad. But you don't want the Lord to get mad with you then you are in for it for real. Just ask the children of Israel. I prayed asking the Lord to give me the strength to carry the message, and that I would go.

He is so merciful that He even showed me where the place would be that I would talk to her. We were at church for a meeting in the chapel. Everything was as the Lord had shown me. Right down to the pew we would be sitting in. I approached her and said that I have something that I would like to talk to you about. I began to talk to her giving her the message. Then I asked her if the things I was saying were true? She acknowledged that what I was saying was true. But then dumb me softened the message. I did not give the message as I was told to.

I added to the message taking some of the power out of the message. Because I liked her, I with hold the most important part of the message. Well I guess you know what happened to me? What would you do if your child disobeyed you? I got punished, boy did I get punished. I learned that when the Lord gives you a task do it just as He says. Do not add to the message, or take any thing away from the message. Just do as you are told, and let the Lord do the rest. I messed up. But like I said I was learning, I was a rookie. I guess you know after the Lord finished dealing with me, I never did that again. What ever he told me to say to you, you got it brother and sister. Just as the Lord told me to bring it, Better you that me.

I would imagine she told her husband and the pastor, no I know she told the pastor and her husband, because the next Sunday the pastor in his message said that he was against parking lot profits carrying messages that the Lord did not give them, hurting people. I knew he was talking about me, and boy did I feel small. My feelings were hurt. I could not even enjoy the rest of my Sunday, I was down. Why did he call me a parking lot prophet? Gere once again had to come to my rescue. She told me that what he did was not right, but don't let that deter me, and don't let it get me down.

You know my God is awesome. They had been announcing about a well renowned profit coming to the church. A person they held in high esteem. They were remarking about the books he had written, and his remarkable prophecies. We had a special Wednesday night service when the prophet was to speak. We were there and during the end of his sermon he began to prophecy. He brought the minister forward and began to prophecy to her everything the Lord had told me to say to her. He also told her that someone here as already told her these things. The minister, her husband and the pastor looked directly at me. I just smiled. The parking lot prophet just smiled. I was praising God. You know the prophet even told her the part I messed up. I was very happy. I got punished for messing up the message, but God had someone to come along to confirm the message, and to even clean it up. The Lord's word will be confirmed by two or three witnesses. By now you would think that things got better for me wouldn't you? Nah! I am still in the tunnel.

I had this friend who worked for the company where we bought building materials for my company. My friend was a Christian, and he was having problems in his marriage. He wanted some information on Demonic forces. I knew of some books, but I had never read them myself. I told him that I would look into the matter and get back to him. I knew Gere had some books on the subject. I conferred with her and she told me what to get for him.

I went to the book store and asked the sales person where I could find the book. He took me to where the book was. I purchased the book, carried it to my friend and said that I hope that this will help him. I told him that if he needed me to just call. And I also told him that we would be praying for him and his wife. I was happy that the Lord had put me in place to help someone find what they were looking for.

I thanked the Lord and felt really good about the situation. The next Sunday at church the pastor during his sermon said that instead of people getting books on demonic forces they need to be getting books about God, learning more about Him. He made a whole sermon on the topic. I sat there burning up. I did not even remember seeing him in the book store. If he was there why didn't he speak to me? Why didn't he come to me and talk to me in the book store, then I would have told him that the book was not for me, but for a friend. Why did he wait until Sunday and preach about me and the book over the pulpit. Why not face me man to man. I was hot. Gere look at me. She knew I was mad, not angry, but mad. I could not be still in my seat. I said that he was not going to get away with this. I was going up to him after church was over and talk to him. Service was not over fast enough for me. He would always stand at the front of the pulpit speaking to people after service. I went up to him and told him that I was not buying that book for myself, but a friend. I also said that if he would have said something to me at that time I would have told him. He just looked at me and smiled not saying a word. I turned and walked off still mad. Here comes Gere once again cooling me off.

When I was in the army part of our training was to study our advisory. We were taught to try and learn everything we could about our enemy. This would give us an advantage over the enemy. If we knew the enemy, then we would be able to know where and when they were going to attack. This would give us an advantage. We could prepare being ready to repeal the invasion and to counter attack. Foot ball, basketball or any competitive sports team studies videos and any diagrams about their opposition before the game looking for their opponents' weaknesses. Knowing their weaknesses helps them to format a plan to win their game. A politician studies his opponents' weaknesses looking for any thing to gain an advantage over him or her to win the votes of the people. Only your enemy does not want you to have knowledge of him and his tactics. What a better way to foil his plans if you know about him. Getting all the information you can about him can be beneficial to you, and can keep you alert to his tricks and tactics. Only the devil does not want you to know about the devil. My people are destroyed from lack of knowledge. Hosea 4:6... When a strong man, fully armed, guards his own house, his possessions are safe. But when someone stronger attacks and overpowers him, he takes away the armor in which the man trusted and divides up the spoils. Luke 11:21-22. Do not be naive my brothers and sisters. The devil and all his forces know all about you and your life. He knew you before you were born. He was in Heaven when God and Jesus Christ wrote the book on you life. He knows your weaknesses and you strengths, and he will use them against you. If he knows my weaknesses and my strengths, wouldn't it be to my advantage to know his.

"Be always on the watch, and pray that you may be able to escape all that is about to happen, and that you may be able to stand before the son of man." Luke 21:36. "Watch and pray so that you will not fall into temptation. The spirit is willing but the body is week." Matthew 26:41. There is no better way to spoil the plans of your enemy than to know him and his weaknesses, and even you knowing, your weakness can be an advantage to you in this war over good and evil.

When you combine the knowledge of God, and the Lord Jesus Christ along with the knowledge of yourself and your enemy, you can and will be prepared to meet any challenge which comes along in life. Above all seek knowledge, wisdom, and understanding; these are part of the keys to life. God through the Lord Jesus and His Holy Spirit are the main keys. We God's children need the whole set in order to make it through life's journey. Let no one deceive you my children learn all you can, so you will be equipped to meet the Lord Jesus Christ when He comes.

I was in a war, a real spiritual war. At night when I laid on my bed and in the day when I was awake. I was having these dreams or visions, which ever makes you feel better, but they were real to me. I was having these confrontations with the devil himself. The first time when I said that I would give my life in service to the Lord Jesus for Him to use me as he pleased, that night I had this fight with the devil. He came to me and talked to me. He told me that he was not going to let me go, that I was his. I began to cry out to the Lord Jesus for help. The devil started to turn me a loose, but it was like his hand was holding on to my leg stretching to hold on. The next time as I lay asleep, I was in this room with all these people walking around me. They were like zombies walking back and forth. They started crowding me on all sides. I could actually feel them pressuring me. I felt the pressure all around me. I began to cry out again, and this angel in the form of a man came to me and told me to start rebuking them using the name of Jesus. I started rebuking them in the name of Jesus and they started going away. I was happy and boy it was on then. I would say, I rebuke you in the name of Jesus get out of here. I rebuke you in the name of Jesus. They were leaving, but all at once they started coming back. The room was becoming filled again. I began to cry out for the angel. Before the room was over crowded he came and took me out of the room. I asked him what had happened. Why did they come back? He said it was because of my lack of faith. When I awaked I wondered about that, my lack of faith. The next time I was once again in a room filled with people and we were sitting on a bench. This time the people were not crowding me. They were just setting there. All at once this black cloud covered the whole floor, and I felt these things biting me on both my ankles. I actually felt the pain. I knew they were evil spirits. I would rebuke them; they would go away and return again. They did that all night long until daylight. When the daylight came they left me alone and went away. When I awaked I knew that the Lord was showing me that the enemy would always be there no matter how many times I rebuked Him in the name of Jesus Christ he would leave for a little while only to return again. The devil told me one time that he was leaving me now, but that he would return and I did not know in which way he would return. There were other times he visited me in my dreams, he was trying his best to hold on to me. He knew that I would do my best to allow the Lord Jesus to use

me to wage war against him, stopping anyone I could from entering his kingdom. The war was on now, No longer was I in man's Army. I was in God's Army now; I was an am a soldier for the Lord Jesus Christ.

I liked the people at church. We became friends with some nice people. One of my coworkers from a long time back had joined. They had assigned me to work with the youth. I really enjoyed that. I dismissed all the things that happened. I said that I was not going to let the devil run me off. I was there to learn, and I would accomplish my goal. My wife was happy there, and that made me fill good. One man does not stop a show. I attended school with one of the Associate Ministers. We would set together during class. We became good friends. I would go to the church sometimes and we would study together. I was trying hard to fit in. I wanted them to like me. Gere would always warn me to be careful, that I could get hurt. What does she know? These people are my friends. Yea right!

They would move the ministers in training around from one ministry to the other. They wanted to expose us to different ministries in the church. They assigned Gere and me to the prison ministry. What prison ministry? They were disorganized. There leader was not a leader and incapable of holding that office. The only thing she knew was to go into different prisons sometimes and preach. There was someone whom I thought was more capable to chair that ministry than she was. I do not know why they appointed this person over him. When we started the program I asked to see their by laws. I was told that they did not have any. I asked to see their purpose in writing. They did not have any. I asked what do you have in writing to show new prospective members. I was told nothing. I went to the Associate Minister who assigned us to our prospective ministries and told her the problem I saw. She told me that the ministry needed organizing, and asked me to be responsible for organizing the ministry. I said that I would. We started having meetings at our home until we had put together a program in writing. After we had completed the process of organizing the prison ministry the Associate Minister asked me to come to a meeting with her. When I arrived she thanked me for the work we did in organizing the ministry. She said that it would not be right for me to chair the ministry. I asked her about the Minister I thought would be a good candidate to chair the ministry. She did not agree. She told me that they had already chosen someone to chair the ministry, and asked me to work with him turning everything over to him. She said that they had chosen a captain of the police force. I said ok. What else could I say? I did not agree with her about there choice. I saw it as being political. Why would you have a police officer heading a prison ministry? You are asking the person who locks people up to go and preach to them. Yea right. That would be like a shark coming back to you and saying I'm sorry I ate you, you were just there at the wrong time, and I was hungry. Maybe I am wrong, but I thought that a ministry that goes around preaching to prisoners should be headed by a minister who at lease knows the word of God, or is in training to

become a minister. I could be wrong though. I am not saying that a police officer can not be a minister. I do think it is a conflict of interest though. I will lock you up and preach to you. Or after shooting someone the officer goes over to the person kneels down and begins to pray over them.

Who am I, and what do I know. I am just learning. After I turned everything over to the new chair of the ministry they sent me to the men ministry. I did not like that. But I was obedient.

Things started happening very rapidly after that. I had completed my first semester at Bible College. I received my grades and was completely surprised. I had made all A's and two B's. One or the students came and told me that my name was on the board in the office. I went and looked. I saw my name on the honors board. I was tenth in my class out of the whole school. I was totally taken off my feet. Me who was a C- student in high school made the honor role in Bible College, and not only did I make the honor role but I was tenth in my class. I was so happy that I did not know what to do. I told Gere when I got home she was happy for me. I could not take any credit though. I began to praise and thank God for the miracle He had done through and in me. You see every day when I got in my car before I left the driveway on my way to school I asked the Lord to bless me with the Holy Spirit, and I asked that His Spirit would be with me as I attended school teaching me His word and opening my mind to learn. I prayed this prayer every day I attended school. How could I take credit for something I did not do? It was the Spirit of truth and the living God that opened my mind and gave me knowledge and understanding. I will never take His glory away from Him. I knew that I was not that smart. Can you believe a dummy like me making the honor role? Well I did. My high school teachers would scream.

I started my second semester and then the bottom began to fall out. We were about three months into the second semester when everything started going bad. We were on our way to Wednesday night service when a deer ran out of the woods. When the deer saw the car he tried to jump over the hood of the car, but he did not make it. He landed on the top of the hood of the car. The hood and the whole front of the car was damaged. We did not get hurt, and by the grace of God the car was able to take us back home. We had only gone about a block away from home. I would see those same deer in my back yard when I would go up on a hill to pray and practice preaching. We had moved into a really nice house that Gere had found. Behind the house were two small lakes and a pasture where the owner kept some cows. There was a wooded area adjacent to the lake where I would go up to the highest point to pray and practice preaching. I would often see this small group of deer in the pasture.

They knew I was there, but they would never run away. They grazed for a while and then they would walk away. That same area where I would go to pray is where New Birth Missionary Baptist Church is today.

All the time we would go to Wednesday night service, we never saw those deer. Everything happened so fast that I did not have time to react. I was thankful that he did not try to jump over the body of the car and land on the top. He would have crushed the top in. The Lord was truly with us. One of my professors had a Cadillac Servile, and he let me have it in exchange for me doing some work for him. The car was real nice in side and out. The only problem was the car did not have a reverse gear.

When ever we needed to back up Gere and I would have to put our feet out the door and push. We would try to park the car in spots where we did not have to use the reverse gear.

After we came out of that ordeal we were told that we were going to have a preaching class on a Saturday. We were to give a fifteen minute sermon, and then the class would critic us along with our instructor. We had a lot of fun during the class. It was enjoyable listening to all of us novice trying to preach, some trying to out preach others, and some trying to show off. I had a good time though until. That next Sunday at church our pastor took the opportunity to embarrassed our class in front of the church. He said that he could not preach a fifteen minute sermon. He rubbed it in. He also said that he was tired of training people and then they would leave the church. He went on and on about our class. I just sat there and listened. I had never seen him training us not one time while I was there. And Gere and I fatefully attended every training session. I was use to him by now and I wasn't surprised about any thing he said or did by now. I considered the source. But my respect for him was dissipating. Aren't you supposed to build up your people instead of tearing them down? Again what do I know, I am just learning.

My company suffered some misfortunes while we were building houses for this organization. We lost a lot of money. My partner bankrupt the company, so that left me without a job. Gere had stopped working to take care of the boys, but we were not worried. I had contracted with a family to build a house for them on my own without a partner, but I had tied up their down payment in the last house I built with my partner. Before my partner bankrupt the company I had filed a lean on the house to get the moneys owed us. But my partner got a lawyer, and the lawyer told me that I had to take the lean off of the property. I called my partner and asked him why he allowed the lawyer to do that. He told me that everything was in the lawyer's hands now and that I should talk to him. I said forget it. Our pastor told me that they were going to do some remodeling to the church and that he wanted to hire me to over see the operation. I consented to help them out. He also told me that if I needed anything to come and see him. One Sunday our pastor was bragging about how he had given this young man a thousand dollars to by a house. I said that he wants me to do something for them. I need them to do something for me. Sound good to me. I saw his assistant and asked him to make an appointment for me to see the pastor. All I needed was two thousand dollars to start the house, and I could pay the money back after the first draw. This would be a way for me to continue building and support my family.

I felt real good about my proposal. The church was always asking me to do something for them, and now I needed help. I waited for a week and I went back to his assistant and asked him when I could see the pastor. He said that the pastor had not given him a time yet, but he will ask him again. When ever he wanted to see me I would always make myself available. Now I wanted to see him and he was putting me off. My time was running out along with my money.

I had those people's money and now I can't produce the product. Not only that we wee getting down to our last. I waited another week and then I said forget it. I was mad now. I said that I don't want to be involved in a one sided church, wanting you to do something for them but can't do anything for you. I was fed up. I told Gere that I was not going back to that church anymore. I did everything they asked of me, but when I needed them they turned their back on me. I quit. I had to face those people and tell them that I had lost their money. I explained everything to them. They were angry and I don't blame them, but the husband told me that he would not hold that against me. He said that he knew that one day I would pay him back. I thanked him for being so understanding. He told me that he was just getting into the church and that his life was changing. I did not know what to say, I was hurting inside. I told him that I would give him his money back. The young man that introduced me to him said that If it were him, he would sue me. This same young man was supposed to be a real Christian, sang in the quire, and was supposed to be a real good friend. I built his house and added a lot of things with no cost to them. I helped his wife get financing for the loan to build the house when she had some financial problems. I helped them out and now this so called Christian friend said that if it were him he would sue me. People for get what you did for them so quickly. Some friends, some Christian.

Gere and I said that things were not working out for us in Georgia. We decided to put our things in storage and leave the state. I had a basement to finish, and we said that when I finish the basement that we would move to Charleston South Carolina. Why we picked South Carolina I don't know. When I finished the job we had three hundred dollars left. I had been taking draws from the job to support my family, so when the job was completed three hundred dollars was all that was left. We said that we could make it on that. Our objective was to go there get a place to stay and immediately get a job. We had planed the whole journey out. We knew we could make it happen. We packed up the car and headed for Charleston South Carolina.

The trip was going fine. We were in South Carolina headed to Charleston. We were about fifteen miles out side of Charleston when I got tired and told Gere that she would have to drive. I pulled off the road and stopped the car. We exchanged seats, and Gere got ready to move the car and it cut off. She tried to start the car and it would not start. I told her not to try again because she could run the battery down. I got out to see if I could repair the problem. It was about two or three o clock in the morning and there was hardly anyone going our way.

I checked the car and found out that there was a blockage from the fuel tank. The tank was full of gas so there was nothing I could do to repair the car on the expressway. While I was explaining our situation to Gere a State Trooper came up. I told him about the car, he said that he would call a wrecker and have the car towed to a repair shop. He also said the he would carry us to the nearest motel. We thanked him for his assistance.

We arrived at the motel, got a room sat down and counted our funds. We had a little over two hundred dollars left. I was hoping that they wouldn't charge us too much to repair the car. I looked at the telephone number the wrecker driver gave me to the repair shop. The number had three sixes together. I immediately started praying and rebuking the devil. The next day I called about the car and they told me that it would be ready soon and that they would send some one to bring me to the shop. When I arrived at the repair shop they said that there was a blockage in the fuel line, and they had to drain all the fuel out to repair the problem. They also said that my battery was bad. I said that there was no way that the battery could be bad. That was a new battery. I told them that when the car stopped we only tried to start the car a few times and that could not kill the battery. I said in any case if the battery had run down it was new and it could take a charge. I told them that I used to be a mechanic and that I know about cars. They gave me the keys to the car and charged me Two hundred dollars for the repair work and the tow. I said you charged me two hundred dollars to drain and open a fuel line? That was a rip off. I immediately thought about the three sixes in their telephone number. I took our car and left. When I picked up Gere and the boys we had just enough money to get some gas and that was all. We decided that we would still drive around and find a place to live and go back and get our furniture and come back. We did find a place to stay, but we did not have any money to give the lady for rent. We told her that we had to go back to Atlanta, and that we would come back and rent the apartment.

Our money was gone. I felt real down. I had my family up here and we were out of money and food. We decided to sell some blood to get some money. I needed to feed these babies. I was desperate. We found out where the blood bank was. When we got there the blood bank was closed. I did not know what to do. It was getting late and we did not have a place to stay or any food to eat. We found a little store and bought two peaches with the change we had. We gave the boys the meat of the peaches and we ate the hulls. We went to a restaurant and Gere asked the manager to let us have some food for the boys and he said that he could not. We prayed and said that God would take care of us. We went into a motel parking lot where we said that we would sleep for the night. We got as comfortable as we could and began to fall of to sleep. I heard someone knocking on the window of the car. I looked up and it was the night watchman. I thought he was going to tell us to leave. I told him what had happened to us, and asked him if it would be Ok if we slept in the car in the parking lot.

He told me that there was a room that had been flooded
and that we could sleep in it, but we would have to be out
of the room before the day people came on. He said that
he would come by when it was time for us to leave. He
took us to the room and opened the door. The floor was
full of water. I had to carry the boys first into the room
and putt them on the bed, and then I had to carry Gere
In and put her on the bed. The room smelled so bad that
I could not sleep at all. I lay there the rest of the night
awake. When morning came I was happy to get out of
that room. We went back to the car. I closed my eyes for
a little while to get some rest. We rode to the water front
and walked around the park. We let the boys play for a
while. They were so peaceful during the whole ordeal.

I was so proud of them. They did not make a fuss at
all. I was proud of my family, but inside I was crying. I
prayed Lord why did you bring us to this place? We have
had nothing but misery since we have been here. Please
help us, show me what to do. My family needs food and
a place to stay. Our money is gone. We need you Lord,
right now.

We stayed in the park the whole day until it started getting
late. The battery in the car was getting weak. I don't know
what those people at the garage did to the car, but we
were having battery problems now. We could drive the
car as long as we did not turn on anything. I checked the
car out and found out that the alternator was bad. The
car also had a leaking radiator. I would put stop leak in
the radiator to stop the water from running out. I had to
put stop leak in regularly, the leak was getting worse. We
could drive about ten miles and then we had to stop and

get some water. One time when we stopped to put water in the car it was so hot that when I slowly took the cap off the pressure inside the radiator pushed the cap off and the steam from the radiator burned my back. I really wanted to cry now. My back was burning and I was hurting on the inside and now on the outside. We drove to a strip mall near a parts store and I went in to check on the cost of a battery and an alternator. We had decided to call a friend and ask him to help us. I did not want to call my friends, but we were desperate now. I felt awful inside when I made the call. I told my friend our situation and he said that he would help. He told me to go the parts store and have them call him and he would charge the parts. I felt better. At lease we could keep the car running. But we still had the problem of the radiator.

I repaired the alternator and replaced the battery. It was late now, so we got comfortable as well as we could and spent the night in the parking lot. That morning a lady came to the car and told us that she owned the restaurant in the plaza where we were parked. She told us to come in and have some breakfast. We went in and she said that she had noticed us there that night when she left. She said that she saw the boys playing in the car while I was working on the car.

She said that when she saw us still there that morning she knew that we had slept in the car that night. Gere told her what we were going through, and they talked for a while. We thanked her for the food and went back to the car. I called another friend. The minister that I thought should head the prison ministry. I told him where we were and asked if he could help us? He said that he did not have any money right now, but he said that he has a daughter living in the area. He said that he would call her and ask her if we could stay there for the night. He called back and said that she said it would be ok for us to come to her house. He gave me the number and told me to call her and get directions. I called her and she told me how to get to her house.

When we arrived at her house she welcomed us in. We talked for a while, and she said that her husband did not really want us there. They were having a hard time financially, and they could not offer us anything. We told her that we just wanted a place to stay for the night and that we would leave in the morning. She said that was fine that he was on duty that night and he would not be there. I asked her if I could use her telephone to call a friend. I called another friend and asked him to loan me some money to get a radiator. I told him that we were stranded In South Carolina. He said that he would wire the money and that I should have it the next day. The young lady prepared us a place to sleep on the floor of her living room. We were so grateful that we did not have to sleep in that car another night.

The next day she carried us to pickup the money and the radiator. I repaired the radiator, and we gave her some money for allowing us to stay there. My friend had sent us more than I asked for, so we had enough money to get the radiator, give her some money, and buy a box of chicken for our trip back home. During that night we decided to go back to Atlanta. We had enough of South Carolina. When we decided to come to South Carolina we both prayed and asked God for direction. We both were in agreement about going to South Carolina, but now we were wondering was that God telling us to go, or who was that? It did not matter now we were headed back.

We left with half of a tank of gas, and a box of chicken. I knew that a half tank of gas would not get us back to Atlanta. I told Gere that we would go as far as we could. I had a new portable radio; I said that we would stop in a truck stop and sell the radio for gas so we could make the trip back to Atlanta. We started back I was driving. I got tired and asked Gere to drive while I get some sleep. After a while she woke me up and said that the gas was almost gone. She asked me what I wanted to do? I saw a sign for a truck stop and told her to pull into the parking lot. I went to some of the truckers trying to sell the radio. No one wanted to buy it from me. I told Gere that I was not worried someone was going to buy the radio. We left the truck stop and went to the next exit.

We pulled into a service station where a lot of cars were getting gas. They also sold food. Gere and I left the boys in the car and went in different directions looking for someone to sell the radio to. I did not get out of sight of the car. I was close by the boys, they were asleep. I saw this church van with a lot of people in it. I went to the driver's side and told the driver that I wanted to sell the radio to get some gas for the car. I told him that my wife and babies were with me and we were trying to get back to Atlanta. He looked at me and said" We don't do that." Then he let up his window. I told him the radio is not stolen and I am not trying to get some drugs. I said that he could come and see my wife and children. He looked the other way and would not let the window down to talk to me. I heard Gere calling me, and I left to go and see what she wanted. She was smiling from ear to ear. When I arrived she was standing next to a man. He said that Gere had told him our situation, and he wanted to help us. He said that he was not a Christian, but he was trying to clean up his life.

He asked us to pray for him that he would do better. He really touched my heart. He reached in his pocket and gave Gere some money. He said that we could keep the radio. I told him that would not be right and asked him to take the radio. He took it and said that he was glad he could help us. He not only gave us enough money for gas to get us back, but he also gave us extra so we could get some food. We were very happy and began to praise God, and pray for the man. God had sent someone to bless us, and he was not a Christian.

We had encountered many so called Christians on our journey that would not help us. We were at a rest stop trying to make a call back home. We needed twenty five cents to make the call. Gere approached a man who said he was a Christian, but he told her that he would not give her the money. He told her that she should go to the Salvation Army for help. A man who was not a Christian gave us not only twenty five cents; he gave us enough to make two more calls. I began to ask God why did we make this journey? We only had hardships and misery during this whole trip. I began to meditate on the events that happened. I remembered all of the people that helped us. Every person that helped us in South Carolina was not a Christian. Every person we asked for help who professed Christianity would not help us. These things weighed heavily on my heart. The only people who were Christians that helped us were my friends in Atlanta. I even thought about the church we were attending. If they had helped us we would not have taken the trip in the first place. I began to cry out to the Lord, something is wrong with this picture. I began to remember the story the Lord Jesus said about the Good Samaritan Luke 10:25-37, on one occasion an expert in the law stood up to test Jesus. "Teacher he asked, "what must I do to inherit eternal life?" "What is written in the law?" He replied. "How do you read it?" He answered: Love the Lord your God with all your heart and with all your soul and with all your strength and with all your mind and love your neighbor as yourself." "You have answered correctly," Jesus replied. "Do this and you will live." But he wanted to justify himself, so he asked Jesus, "And who is my neighbor?" In reply Jesus said: A man was going down from Jerusalem to Jericho, when he fell into the hands of robbers.

They stripped him of his clothes, beat him and went away, leaving him half dead. A priest happened to be going down the same road, and when he saw the man, he passed by on the other side. So to a Levite, when he came to the place and saw him, passed by on the other side. But a Samaritan, as he traveled, came where the man was: and when he saw him, he took pity on him. He went to him and bandaged his wounds, poured on oil and wine. Then put the man on his own donkey, took him to an inn and took care of him. The next day he took out two silver coins and gave them to the innkeeper. Look after him he said, and when I return, I will reimburse you for any expense you may have. "Which of these do you think was a neighbor to the man who fell into the hands of robbers?"

The expert in the law replied, "The one who had mercy on him." Jesus told him, "Go and do likewise."

Here is one even I am guilty of not fulfilling. Give to the one who asks you, and do not turn away from the one who wants to borrow from you. Matthew 5:42. We often prejudge people when we are asked to give. We look at them and try to size them up. We have an attendicy to foretell their need, whether it is for alcohol, drugs, or some other mischievous deed. We judge them on the bases of what we see, and think we know. True if a person smells like alcohol, we should not help him continue to destroy himself by supporting his need. But what if he smells like alcohol and he asks you for money for some food what should we do? I found the best thing to do would be to tell him or her that I will buy some food and give it to them. If their request is honest they will say ok, but if not they will walk off. I remember going to the grocery store and a Latin American woman had a piece of paper in her hands asking me to read it, she was begging. I looked at her and continued to walk away from her. She took a few steps with me and continued to say please. I walked on not saying anything. I only had three dollars and I wanted to buy some ice cream. I was convicted as I walked and I knew I should have given her at least a dollar.

I still would have enough to by me a small quart of ice cream. I put the dollar in one pocket to give to the lady when I leave the store. I purchased the ice cream and looked for the lady, but I could not see her anywhere. That really tore me up. I had missed my opportunity to help someone. I felt really bad inside, and I began to repent, asking God to for give me. I have never seen a

Latin American begging before. If she was begging she was desperate and really needed help. I still remember her face today. I had an opportunity to be a small blessing to someone and I blew it.

The scripture quoted: to give requires wisdom and prayer. God will give you wisdom about who you should give to if you ask Him. Only He knows the heart of the recipient weather it is pure or devious.

I find that talking to a person can help you make the right decision when approached. As I listen I am praying for guidance. This has never failed me. A liar, deceiver and thief will reveal him or her self. The Lord God will make what is hidden come to the light. I don't want God angry with me for disobeying His command to give. The money belongs to Him anyway. I had seen what it was like to be hungry. I had seen what it was like to be homeless with your family with you. I had seen what it was like to be rejected by the church and those who called themselves Christians. I began to cry out: Lord where are you real children? Where are the real Christians? I had heard people say that they had gone to the church they supported and asked for help and the church told them that they did not have funds for that. Why not? If I support the ministry, shouldn't the ministry support me when I have a ligament need? One lady told me that she went to the ministry where she attends and asked for some money to get her baby some pampers and they turned her down. How could they do that? And this was a large church with twelve thousand members. They could not find five dollars to give to this lady to buy her child some pampers? Is the church in the business of receiving and not giving?

I always hear ministries on Sundays asking you to give, and now they are on television asking, but I hear so many who have gone looking for help being rejected. I'm not saying that all churches are like that. There are some who really help. But there are too many who are turning people away. It is no wonder so many people are refusing to be supportive of the church and stay out side of the church. If the church sets a bad example, what do you expect the people to do?

I had no doubt that the Lord had sent us on this journey. After we had returned back to Atlanta I was praying about the whole trip. I knew He was testing our obedience to Him. Would we go where He sent us no matter how hard the journey may get? He also allowed me to see the church, his true followers. I had learned a lot. I was learning what ministering was all about first hand. I found out that some lessons are more difficult than others. This not only applies in the natural world, but in spiritual world also. When God wants to use you for some great task, you may have to go through a great learning process which could be very painful. But never forget that God said that He would not give you mare than you can bear. 1 Corinthians 10:13

After we had returned to Atlanta one of my friends that had sent us some money had a vacant house and he allowed us to live in it. We stayed there until Gere and I got a job. After finding work we moved to the north side of town. We moved into a townhouse. After all we had been through I was ready to settle down and just be happy with my family. I did not want to return to a large church, not at the present. We talked with Sister Pat and told her that we were back in town. She told us that she was going to start a church. She asked us to help her. We said that we would. She was a good friend, and a very spiritual person.

How could I turn my back on someone who was there for me when I was trying to find out my purpose for being. We began to have bible study in their home. Sister Pat would always challenge me during bible study. One day she said that she did not know why she was so hard on me. I did not mind her challenges, she was only making me study more, and to dig deeper into God's word. If I was going to Minister God's word I needed to know His word, and be able to stand up against all those who would challenge me about the word of God. I loved to be challenged; you can challenge me, but not God's word. Even after I had stopped going to school I never stopped studying and researching the word of God. I would read the books I had when I was in school from the beginning to the end. Something I did not do when I was in school. I had a thirst to know more. We would go with Sister Pat when she would speak. Sometimes Gere could not go, so I would go alone. I did not like the style of the denominational worship she was in. It was to dry for me. I had joined a dry church at one time and I said that was it for me no more dry churches. I still went along with her anyway. We told her that we did not like their style of worship, and she said that when she got started that she was going to be more crismatic. We had been with her for a while, and I kept questioning her about when was she going to get started?

She kept saying that she was waiting for them to give her a building. I said that we needed to get started because there were people out there who needed our help. This went on for a while. I was getting impatient. I wanted to work for God. Let's get started even if it is in a house like the early Christians met. Why wait for a building? She would say just be patient that they were going to give her a building soon.

We continued to have bible study, and then the meetings began to lessen. One night I had this dream about building God's house. I was even given the name of the church, Tabernacle Of Faith Ministries. God's House Of Faith. I prayed and meditated about the idea of starting a church before I mentioned it to Gere. When I was sure that this was the leading of the Lord I told Gere. We agreed to start having our own bible study and then continue on from there. We started putting out flyers in the neighborhood, and we invited everyone we would meet. We decided that we would rent a suite at a hotel to have our bible study. But before we would start bible study we decided to have our first church service in an adjacent hotel. We made arrangements for the service. We were going to have a Good Friday Service. I took all of the money from a job I was working and put it toward the service.

We needed a good car, but I put the service first. We made up some more flyers, told all of our friends; I even got my pianist from the church where I first joined the choir to play for us. Another of our good friends was going to help us with the service.

People were saying that they were going to come. Everything was going well. We were about to have our first church service, I was very excited.

The day came and we were on our way to the hotel, we were ready. When we arrived at the hotel the parking lot was almost full. They did not tell us that they were having another function in the foyer of the hotel. We were in one of the ball rooms across from the other party. We had to go through their function to get to the ballroom. I was angry, why didn't they tell us that this was going to happen? We were in the ballroom trying to worship God, and out side of the room they were partying. I did not like that at all. And to make things worse, the parking lot was almost full. It was hard even for us to find a spot to park. I began to think about the people we invited, would they look for a place to park and come in or would they go back home because the lot was almost full. I was having a hard time.

The time came for the service to start. There were only ten people there. I was very upset. Where were all our friends and the people that said that they were going to come? I had spent all this money on this event and only ten people came, and five of the ten were children. I was having a hard time, and I could not hide it. My friends tried to comfort me, but I was still down, more hurt than anything. Here I go again was I really hearing God when I decided to take this step, or was I out on a limb alone?

All kind of things was going through my head. We made it through the night, and with the help of Gere and my other good friends the event wasn't a total flop. Later we found out that people did come but could not find a place to park so they left. One couple even went to the wrong hotel which was across the street. After hearing that I felt a little better, but I did have Gere to write the hotel and voice our complaint. They should have told us about the party and we would have gone somewhere else.

I decided to start the church by having bible study first, and see what would happen from there. We started having bible study and our good friends came with their family. The next bible study some more people came, and then after that I told Gere that we may as well start having our Sunday services. The Sunday services were great. We were very small but we enjoyed the services. As we continued to meet our numbers begin to grow, but we did not grow over fifteen people.

Everything was going fine, I was working, and Gere was working. We weren't making a whole lot of money, but we were happy and we had a roof over our head and food to eat. If you have been following my life closely you know that every time things are going well something is about to happen. Well you are right.

The ministry was small, but we knew that we would eventually grow. We had a beautiful program and visions for growth. We knew that it would take time, prayer and commitment in order to grow. We worked together as a team. I was very proud of my family. One day Gere told me that she had met this young lady at work, and her husband was a Bishop. She said that they had moved here to help one of their satellite churches. The Bishop was sent here from the mother church to assist the satellite church. She said that the Bishop could help us grow. I met him and his wife one day after Gere got off work. He seemed to be a nice person. We would talk in the evenings when we arrived at Gere's job. I enjoyed talking to him. He told me about this ministry he was working with in the City of Atlanta. He invited me to come to some of their meetings. They would go out into the neighborhoods on Saturdays delivering food and praying for people. They were located in one of the project areas of Atlanta. He told me that I could build the ministry with people from the projects. He told me that the people in the projects who would start coming would be very committed. Some of the things he said I did not like because I saw that some of his statements could be construed as exploitation. I did not like the idea of exploiting anyone. I wanted to help people, and not to use them just to grow a church. I did not like people using me, and I surely was not going to use anyone. If I found out that a person was using me, our relationship or association was over. I felt strongly about this issue because on many occasions people would try to use me. I have a kind heart and people would try to take advantage of me because of my kindness. I knew first hand how exploitation hurts.

Gere and I started attending some of their Saturday services. They were different but nice. I was learning street ministry. We would go from house to house giving out food and praying for the people in the community. We had a good time. I found out that this was what ministering was all about. I would minister to the homeless and the sick, those on drugs, and alcoholics. It was a real challenge, but I liked that kind of ministering. Sometimes when Gere did not go with me on Saturdays I would go back visit and pray with some of the people. I saw people get healed, and come off drugs. I saw people get jobs and move out of the projects. Working there was the best thing that could happened to me. Coming out of a large church, we never went out into the field like this. I talked to one lady and she told me that some churches come out on Saturdays, and talk to the people and fill their heads about helping them, but they never come back. I heard so many sad stories that sometimes I wanted to cry for the people. I was so involved that I would go visit people after I would get off work. The people always welcome me into their homes, and into their lives.

The Bishop wife had told Gere that they had to find another place to stay. We talked about allowing them to come and stay with us. We moved the boys into the bedroom with us and gave them the boy's bedroom.

After not having a place to stay ourselves, we wanted to help. We thought that we would not be much of a Christian if we would not open our doors to someone in need. After all when we came back to Atlanta, and we needed a place to stay and a friend of ours allowed us to stay in his house, so how could we turn them down? We talked about our stipulations for them moving in and we all entered into an agreement.

Once they moved in the Bishop started talking to me about the ministry. He said that he would help me grow the ministry. Ok. Then he started telling me that I would have to make a decision on becoming a full time pastor going out every day seeking new members for the ministry. Gere and I discussed the idea and she said that she would work while I worked on growth the ministry. The Bishop and his wife were supposed to help us with the rent, so we believed with their help we could make it. What a big mistake.

I quit my job and started going to the ministry where the Bishop was working with homeless men. They had me doing some bible study classes, and I was also assigned to do bible study classes in the projects on Wednesday nights. They would have meetings and classes with the homeless guys during the week. I worked with them, but I did not feel right in my spirit. Something was wrong, I did not know what, but I knew that something was wrong. I began to pray and ask God to show me why I was feeling this way. Things began to unfold very fast. The Bishop and his wife had lived with us about three months now, and they were not living up to their part of the bargain.

They never paid us the portion of the rent that we agreed upon. Gere would talk to his wife and she would say that the Bishop would pay us. We never saw a penny. I wondered how he was going to pay us when he was not getting paid from the ministry where he was working. I was getting very concerned. One night while I was lying on my bed I felt like a suction pump was placed over my mouth and I was sucked right out of my body. I was taken to the building where we were ministering down town. I was taken down the hallway between the room where they gathered for church service and the living area. The hallway was dark a real black dark. I felt this evil in the hallway. Then I was taken back to the main room where they held service, once we arrived in the room I was taken straight up out of the building. I was going straight up and I looked down and saw this white cloud with a red ball like fire in the center. I was terrified and began to cry out: Jesus, Jesus, Jesus. I heard the Holy Spirit say; "don't be afraid." We reached a level and we stopped quickly. There were these twin doors like in a hospital going to the operating room. The doors swung open and I saw these gurneys lined up on both sides of the room with white sheets over them. I looked to the right and these doors swung open and there was a black man operating on a person with a sheet over the person he was operating on. I looked again and the sheet fell of the man, and I saw that the man who was during the operation was fitting the man with mechanical legs and arms. I looked in the outer room and all the men were fitted with these same mechanical arms and legs.

I began to cry and then the Spirit carried me back down to my room. When we entered my room I looked down and saw my body laying there. The Spirit put me back into my body and I laid there meditating on what had just happened. I began to pray and seek God about the incident. He told me that they were making robots out of the men in the shelter.

The next day I told Gere what had happened to me. I described the whole trip I had gone through. I was very concerned, but I did not know what to do. I knew that I would have to stop going down to that ministry because I did not want any part of what was going on. The next Saturday I was with the Bishop and his wife on our way to the meeting and I told him part of my dream. I already new the answer, but I just wanted to hear his version. He could not give me a clear interpretation of the dream, and when I told him that the Lord had already revealed the dream to me, he got very angry. He quoted a scripture to me; "touch not my anointed, and do my profit no harm." He said that if I already new the interpretation of the dream I should not have asked him. I said that I wanted to hear his interpretation. He was angry and did not say anything else. That evening I went to visit some of the people in the projects and caught the buss home.

From that point on they would come home and go straight to their room and would not say a word to Gere or myself. This went on for about three days and I called him and told him that they had to move because our agreement was not working.

He said that they were not going to move. I told him to come and get his things or I was going to put them out side. He said that he was on the way and that I had better not put his things out. When he arrived he had three guys from the shelter with him. They began to carry their things to the truck they were in. He stood by the steps and looked at me, and then he started coming toward me wanting to fight. The guys with him broke us up and we went out side. They got between us again and then they left. He called me back and apologized saying that he was under a lot of stress. I accepted his apology but I said I was finished with him.

We had opened our house to them hoping that we could work together and make the house a comfortable place for all of us. We had even taken our boys out of their room and made an area for them in our room. Once again I began to see false Christians. Here was a person who claimed to be a Bishop using people and provoking fights. I felt sorry for him. I stopped going to the ministry where he worked after that. I never saw or talked to him since that day.

There were some nice people we meet in the projects, one of them became a good and dedicated member. When I met Sister Catherine she was suffering in her body. We prayed for her and the Lord heard our prayers and healed her of her affliction.

She was full of fire for the Lord. Her affliction had hindered her from getting out, but after she was healed she was on the go. I never will forget the second time I went to her house to pray for her, Sister Catherine's husband told me that I should leave the area before night, because the gangs were rough, and I could get hurt. I told him that I was not concerned about the gangs. I said that my Father in Heaven watches over me, and I am not afraid. The next Saturday I went to visit them her husband was all bandaged up and I asked them what happened to him. They told me that he got beaten up by some of the gang members in the neighborhood. I thought to my self, he warning me to be careful he lives here and he got beat up, I don't live here and they have never bothered me. I would sometimes see the young men on the corners. I would always speak to them, and they would always speak back. They were always respectful. I knew that they were selling drugs on the corners I just watched them and went on my way. They spoke, I spoke and that was that. The Lord gives you wisdom when you are on another person's turf. There was a police prescient right around the corner from where they were selling drugs, I never saw a policeman walking through the projects in order to hinder them from their activity. The police left them alone and so did I. I do not go where the Lord does not send me. When I go, I want Him with me, and then I know He has my back.

There was another family that I would go and visit. The first time I went to their house I saw this little boy I thought he was about four years old. He was attached to a stand with an I V in his arm. He would walk around the room pulling the stand. He could not talk, he just made mumbling sounds. They told me that he was seven years old.

I could not believe he was that old. I began to pray for him and the Lord told me that his mother was using drugs when he was conceived. His grandmother and aunt were in the room. I asked them who was using the drugs. The aunt said that it was her sister-in-law. The grand mother looked at me and said that was true. They said that she was no good and that she was a crack head. I asked about the husband who was the brother and son. The mother immediately went to the defense of her son. She said it was the mother; her son would not do drugs. I told her that both the mother and the dad were doing drugs. She said no way; my son does not do drugs. I looked at the sister; she dropped her head and said that the son does drugs to. The grandmother said well the daughter-in-law probably started him. I said that it was the other way around, that the son started using drugs first. She did not say a word after that. I told them that I wanted to meet the mother and dad. They said that they would let them know. The following week I had the opportunity to meet them. We talked about the child and his condition; they told me that they were both using drugs and that the husband introduced them to the wife. She had stopped using after the child was born. She was very sorrowful about what she had done to her child. They were a young couple in their early twenty's high school drop outs living the best they new how. They had three more children, and they could not care for the boy, so they left him with his grandmother and aunt. I would visit them and pray with them, I even helped her with her reading.

We would read portions of the bible. They started coming to church. I felt sorry for them. They were children raising children. Who was going to train their children? What would become of them? Who would inspire them to make something out of their lives? They had an uphill fight. Would they make it? I pray they will. I continued to go and pray for the little child. They said that he was making improvements. They told me that his teacher was surprised at the improvements he was making. He had started saying words legibly. Every time I would go to see them he would come to me, and he would not leave me until it was time for me to go. I shed many tears for that child.

The ministry was going fine. We would rent a van to bring people from the projects to church. All of the people we would pick up eventually moved out of the projects. Sister Catherine got a job, bought a van and started doing fine. I was very happy for her. She was at every bible study, and she did not miss a Sunday coming to church. She also made sure her children came to church. I will never forget her smile. She was an inspiration to me. God had healed her body and she was full of smiles and happiness. I truly miss her. Not only was she a good member, she was a good friend. Good friends don't come along often.

Sister Catherine moved away to take care of her dad. Some of the others I would pick up from the projects stopped coming. Our membership started declining. Gere would bring ladies home from her job for me to minister to.

One lady she brought home had been in an accident, and as a result of the accident she had back problems. She had to ware a brace for her back, and she had pain in her neck. We prayed for her and her pain left her. I was hoping she would come to the church, but she stayed in the church where she was attending. This happened quite often. People would come to be prayed for, or wanted to hear a word from the Lord, get healed, get their mail and then leave. I felt badly. I did not want to be used like a psychic. I was not a psychic where you go get a message or get healed and then off you go. I felt like I was being used. Although the power was not mine, it was the Lord using me, but I still felt like I was being used. I thought how Christ must have felt. People would come to him by the thousands. He would heal them, teach them, feed them and they would crucify him. If they used my Savior what would they do to me? I never said no to anyone who came, even though most of them never came to church. I realized we were small, we did not have a nice building, we did not have a large crowd attending services, and we did not have a quire, but we did have the Spirit of God. It is bad that people are drawn to the building, the quire, and the stuff. I understood that if you do not have these things it is hard to grow a church. I was going to try anyway. I did not call myself. I never wanted to be a minister let alone a pastor. But I was given a job to do, and I was going to do that job. People would always tell me, "God will supply if you are doing His will." People will make you question your relationship with God. I began to as God, Lord is this your will? Are we doing what you would have us to do?

Every time I began to doubt someone would come to the church needing help or just to visit. I would not quit. It was hard though there were so many times I wanted to through in the towel, but God knows that I am not a quitter. I would stay with the ship bailing water if necessary. We had gotten down to Gere, the boys and I. We would sing, pray and preach all by ourselves. We were determined to carry on. The Lord Jesus said, "For where two or three are gathered in my name, there I am with them." Matthew 18:20.

Even in our small gathering we knew that the Lord Jesus was with us. We had attended small churches that had more power and anointing than large churches. It is not the size of the church that manifests the power of God. It is the anointing which comes from the obedience to God that brings s about changes in the lives of people. A small gathering can have more of the power of the Holy Spirit than a large church if the small church is fulfilling God's will for His Church. If either is not obeying God, and the power of the Holy Spirit is not being manifested in the building, then the gathering is just a social event. It is the anointing that breaks the yokes. If the power of God through Christ Jesus and the Holy Spirit is not present then there will be no healing, deliverance or salvation. People will come in the door and leave just as empty as they entered. Some people come to church looking for a life changing experience, and when they don't get the manifestation of the Spirit they are looking for they turn to other sources for the things they need.

I say some people, because not all people who go to church are searching for Christ. Some have their own hidden agendas. I feel sorry for those who have never experienced the presence for the Lord Jesus.

We were doing fine as a family so I thought. Gere worked and I stayed home careering for the boys. I began to feel badly about her going to work and I was not working. We did not have a car and she would walk to the bus stop in the rain and snow to support our family. When she got off the bus she had to walk about half a mile to get to her job. We would walk to the grocery store and carry the groceries in the boy's stroller while they walked with us. I felt very guilty inside. I was not sick and there was not any thing wrong with me that would stop me from working. I had listen to man tell me that I should stop working and build the ministry, and the one who told me that turned out to be my enemy. I really felt badly when my boy's had to ware torn underwear. I said that is enough, I need to get a job and support my family. The church was not growing and my family was suffering. I wanted this to stop. Before I could get a job Gere decided that she had enough. She told me that she was leaving me. I could not blame her for wanting to leave. I did not put up a fight, but said ok. I was really hurt though. I loved my family and I did not want to be separated from them. To take my boys from me was like cutting out my heart. But I knew I was wrong and that I would have to take my medicine. I had made my bed and I would have to sleep in it.

Gere and her manager at work had become good friends. Her manager came to the church one Sunday and danced for us. She have us the money to incorporate the ministry. We even went with her to minister to some wayward youth. I thought she was a nice person. Gere told me that they would pray together at work. I liked her manager.

Little did I know that she was stabbing me in the back. She was telling Gere to leave me. She had left her husband. They had started a church and it did not survive. She told Gere how hard it was trying to be a pastor's wife and the dirty chores she had to do. She convinced Gere to leave, although Gere denied it I knew what happened. Gere left me and about a year later Gere and her manager were having problems. Gere told me that her manager was trying to get her fired. She had done some things to Gere that were against company policy and Gere could have sued the company. The company in turn fired Gere's manager. She tried to get Gere fired and they fired her. God does not like ugly.

Before Gere had left me she brought this lady home for me to minister to. She was having problems at home with her husband. She told me about the things she said her husband was doing to her. They had three children. I told her that she should leave her husband if he was doing the things she said he was doing. She would come every week for counseling. I was young in my position and I should not have told her to leave her husband. I was wrong. They had three children; they should try to work out their differences for the sake of the children.

Because I ministered incorrectly without following the Lords word, the Lord separated my family. I really believe that. After the lady left her husband she started talking about marrying a minister at one of the large churches. She would not come to our church, but she came to me every week to be counseled. She started talking about buying a large house and she wanted me to confirm the fact that God would let her have it. God had started showing her to me. She did not want her husband because he was not making the money she wanted, and she wanted to be in the lime light. I would not confirm her mess and she stopped calling and coming by to get counseling. Gere told me that she had to go back to stay with her husband and that she said while she was there he forced himself on her and she was pregnant. Now she was going to have four children. I was glad she was out of my life. I felt badly about telling her to leave her husband. I only heard her side of the picture. I never asked her to bring her husband over so I could hear his side. No matter I should not have told her to leave. God had to punish me for my ignorance. He separated me from my family. Boy did I learn a lesson, one I will never forget as long as I live.

When Gere left me I was without a job. I told my land lord that I needed time to get to work and then I could pay him his rent. I told him that my family had left me, but I was not depressed or feeling sorry for myself. My focus was on taking care of my responsibilities. He told me that he understood and that he would give me some time to pay him.

I thanked God for touching his heart and allowing me to stay where I was. That week I got a job. I had to ride a bicycle to work since I did not have a car. The job was not to far away. I started making five hundred dollars a week. That job lasted for a month. I had made enough money to buy a little used car for three hundred dollars. It was not in good shape, but it got me where I needed to go. From that job I started working for a contractor making more money. Then I was able to purchase a better car. When that job was completed the Lord blessed me to get a job making a thousand dollars a week. I went from no money to five hundred dollars to one thousand dollars in five months. I went from no car to three cars in five months. I sold one of the cars the first one, the transmission went out on the second one, and I drive the third one back and forth to work. God was surely looking out for me. That Christmas I carried my boys to the toy store and told them to pick out anything they wanted and they could have it. I spent over two thousand dollars on them for Christmas. One lady told me that I was crazy for spending that much on my boys. She did not know what we had been through. There were times that I did not have any money to spend on them and I felt really bad. I was just giving them some of the things they had missed during our struggles. I was not spoiling them; I was just expressing my love and sorrow. I even bought Gere a ring for Christmas. I let her pick out the ring she wanted and I purchased it for her. I was not looking for anything in return, I just felt good to be able to give my family a good Christmas.

Although I was making good money now, the money did not bring me happiness. I would cry every night when I got home. My day consisted of prayer, work, praising God and crying. I really missed my family. I would have the boys every other weekend, and when I took them back to Gere I would cry on my way back home. One day I began to pray to God and I said Lord I know you have blessed me to make good money, but you can take all this money back just restore me to my family. I said that the money is not bringing me happiness; I would rather be with my family. All the money in the world could not replace the love and misery I am felling right now. I would pray this prayer every day. It was going on two years now since we were separated. I never stopped praying and believing that the Lord God would restore my family to me. At work I would sing and pray all day long. I was spraying insulation in house attics. The boards I had to walk on were 1and ¾" wide. I had to drag this long hose from the opening of the attic across the top spraying insulation as I went along. I would be praising God singing and dancing on those narrow boards holding this large hose in one hand and a flashlight in the other. That is how I would spend my day. At night before I went to bed I would cry and pray. One day while I was on my knees praying crying out to the Lord asking Him to bring Gere and I back to gather, I heard Him say that we will be back together soon. I prayed Lord when I see her and she says that we will never be back together again let me be attentive to your voice and not hers. Let me believe what you say and not what comes out of her mouth, because my faith is in you and not in the things of mankind.

Gere had told me that we would not ever be back together again. She had gotten a lawyer and filed for a divorce. Her attorney called me and asked me what I wanted in the divorce. I told him that he would have to talk to my attorney. I did not have an attorney at the time but I procured one. I was given the name of an attorney from a friend. I was given an appointment to meet with the attorney to discuss the divorce. When we met I told her that I wanted to oppose the divorce. I said that I wanted my family back. She began to ask me the usual questions about my finances, my stability and about infidelity.

I told her that my finances were good, my stability was better and I was a faithful husband, I never had an out side affair. Never had one, and never wanted one. I said that I was faithful to my God and my wife. She told me that she would handle my case and that I would have to give her five hundred dollars up front. I wrote her a check for the five hundred dollars and gave the check to her. Then she started talking about her life. She told me that she was single, and she commented about all the men who wanted to marry her. She began to tell me personal things about herself. I began to wander what was going on. I thought for a minute that she was making a pass at me from the way she was talking. Gere always said that I was naive to the ways of women. I was always open and friendly. I would take you for who you say you are until the Lord showed me different. If that meant I was naïve, I guess she was right. The attorney and I talked for a long time. I listened and kept my distance. I did not know if she was just bragging, boasting trying to be impressive, or if she thought she was God's gift to man. I was puzzled and I was not going to try and connect the pieces. When I left it was late we were the only persons left in the office. I thought about our meeting all the way home.

In Georgia when you filed for a divorce at that time you had to go through mandatory counseling by the state. I received a notice for the date we were supposed to go through counseling. I called my attorney and asked her what was this all about. She told me and she said that she was going to contact Gere's attorney. A couple of days later Gere's attorney called me and wanted to talk with me about the session. I asked him if my attorney had been in communication with him. He said no. I gave him the name and number of my attorney and told him that he would have to talk to her. It was about two weeks before we were supposed to go to the counseling sessions that Gere called me and told me that she was having car trouble. I repaired her car and that Friday she invited me over to watch television. It was raining very hard that night, and she told me to stay over. The next night I was invited back over this time I was asked to stay. The Lord had put my family back together just as he said he would. I was very happy to be back with my family. I called my attorney and told her my good news, she said that she would have to refund me some of my money, and that she would mail it out to me. To this day I have not received that check, it must have gotten lost in the mail. I called on occasion, but she was never in nor did she ever return a call. I just gave it into the hands of the Lord and left it alone. Gere had told me that she was having a hard time with her attorney also. He did not want to refund some of the monies she had paid him. The lost of the money was not important to me. Being back with my family meant more to me than the lost of the money.

We had been back together for two weeks when I started having problems with the man I was subcontracting from. We would get into arguments about him keeping up the equipment. My helper and I would get to the job site and have everything prepared to insulate a house and the machine would break down. This became very frustrating. We would have to be at the shop by six o'clock in the morning load the truck get our assigned houses and then travel to the areas we were to work in. Sometimes we would not get to our first house until ten o'clock that morning. We were paid by the number of bags we blew in a day, so when the machine was not functioning correctly we were not making any money. The next day when we arrived at the shop I told the man who owned the truck and machine that I was not going out until he repaired the problem. We got into an argument and I quit. Before I quit the owner of the company told me that if I quit working for the man he would give me a job with him. I took him at his word. He lied. The next day I remembered the prayer that I had asked God; that He could take the money away just restore me to my family. I told Gere what I had prayed, and all I could say was that God had answered my prayer. I learned from that to be careful what you cry out to God about. The money was gone, but I was back with my family.

We had two cars now, and the boys were in school. I started contracting again, although I wasn't making as much money as I was, but I was happy. We started the church again with people from the apartment complex where we were staying. They were really nice people. I met Sonya from doing some work on a house she bought. She became a very faithful Christian. We were having service in our apartment. We grew to about twenty five faithful people. We started making plans to start a nursery and pre school. We set up a board of directors and had monthly meetings.

We were on our way to really establishing the Lord's house. The people who came to church were more than members, they were friends. I saw God do many miracles in their lives through the Lord Jesus and the Holy Spirit. I was so proud of them. One of my deacons, Sonny was a hard worker talking to people trying to get them to come to church. He really wanted to see the church grow. He was my hardest worker and my biggest headache. I would always have to explain things about the message that he did not understand after service. I got use to the work I had to do with him and I did not mind setting down with him trying to get him to understand. He was just getting into going to church and I did not want to do anything to deter him even if it meant setting down with him every Sunday and going over the message again. We became good friends. He was always there when I needed him. I remember once when I was invited to go attend a service with a group that called themselves prophets and prophetesses. After the speaker finished speaking he called people up to pray for them. I had already told my deacon what was going to happen, and I told him to just watch and listen. He went up for prayer anyway. They would lay hands on people and some they were trying to force to be slain in the spirit by pressing their heads back or pressing hard on their stomachs. He went up and when they laid hands on him he fell back and they laid him on the floor. When he got up and came back to where I was setting I asked him to go outside with me.

When we got out side I asked him about the experience. He told me that he fell backwards because he felt that was what they wanted him to do. I laughed and we went back into the room until the service was over.

There was a new thing going on in the church. Everyone wanted to show that they had the power of God and His Spirit by the laying on of hands and slaying people in the spirit. There is a famous Pastor on television that has captivated people by the laying on of hands. Now everyone wants to show that they have the gift also. I have watched some Minister's literately force people's heads back trying to make them fall down. I was in one service and the minister called for the young men of the church to come up for prayer. He approached one young man and laid his hands on his head and was forcing his head backward and the young man would not fall. The minister kept forcing the young mans head back father and father the more he forced the more the young man was resisting. Finally the minister gave up. I was setting there laughing to my self at the event. I was at another event and the speaker called for people to come up and receive prayer and these young men would go and when the speaker laid hands on them they would hit the floor. I sat there and watched and the same young men would go up there over and over again as if it were some game. I have seen some ministers lay hands on people and pray for them over and over again just standing there with their hands on them waiting patiently for them to fall. I guess the person finally gave up and fell backwards. On another occasion this lady pastor would holler at the people telling them to get in the spirit. I did not know that you could get into a spirit. I always thought and read that the spirit has to enter you. Maybe I am wrong, but I don't think so. No, I know that I am right. No don't get me wrong, I do believe that people can be slain in the spirit.

I remember the first time I went down. I was at the ministry I told you about earlier. I was attending one of the Saturday services. We had just returned from ministering in the projects. A group of men that had gone out with us asked me to allow them to pray for me. They gathered around me forming a circle around me. I was in the center of the circle and Tom the man I went out with laid hands on me and began to pray for me. Some of the other men behind me laid hands on my shoulder. As Tom began to pray I closed my eyes, as I closed them I saw this huge hand coming toward me and hit me right in the chest. I could not help myself and fell backwards. They laid me on the floor, I opened my eyes and I saw this man walking in and out of the circle looking down at me. I knew it was the devil. He would appear in and out between the men and just looked down and stared at me while Tom was praying. I waited until Tom finished praying then I got up off the floor, when I got up I looked for the man but I could not find him in the whole room. I told Tom and the Bishop about the man, I described him to them and they said that they don't remember seeing anyone that resembled the person I saw. That was my first time and last time seeing a hand pushing me down. The next time I was prayed for in the same building the head of the ministry prayed for me because he said that there was something going on with me and I needed prayer. He was right there was something going on with me, but he did not ask me to talk about the problem. He began to pray for me and I just fell backwards.

I was not slain in the spirit; nor did I see the hand I had seen the first time. I was angry and I just wanted them to pray so I could get over my anger. It was their custom that when they prayed for you they wanted you to fall, so I fell. When I got up I was still angry. The prayer did not help me at all. When I got away from them I prayed for myself and then I got better. Remember I said that I do believe that God can slay you in the spirit. God can do anything, He chooses to do. There is nothing impossible for God. I remember one Saturday when I was at the same ministry. We had returned from going out into the neighborhood. It was a rainy day; water was coming into the auditorium where we would gather after returning from ministering. There was water on the floor in places. They called people up for prayer, and asked me and some of the other ministers there to pray for the people who came up. There was a puddle of water behind the people that I began to pray for. I just touched this young man in the chest, and before I could say a word he began to fall backwards. I reached out my hands to catch him. I caught him before he fell into the water. He said that had never happened to him before. He did not know that was knew to me also. I had never laid my hands on anyone and they began to fall. It frightened me as much as it did him. I was concerned because I did not want him to fall into all the water that was there. I began to pray after that telling God that I did not want that gift. The next person I prayed for that day, I laid hands on him, and I began to feel him being lifted up off of his feet. I felt him going up and my hands and arms going up with him. That made me feel real good. I felt as though God was raising him up to Him instead of laying him down on the ground. I felt more joy and satisfaction out of him being raised up, rather than falling down.

I have read the bible from Genesis 1:1 to Revelations 22:21 and I can not find a place where Christ or anyone else prayed for a person and they were slain in the spirit. Everyone that Christ laid hands on and prayed for was healed, and the bible does not say that they were slain in the spirit. Even the Apostils after Christ the bible does not say that they prayed for people and they were slain in the spirit. As we do today, laying hands on them and they fall backwards. What good does it do to wave your hands over a congregation and they all fall out? To me it is like false baptism going down wet and coming up wet with no change in the person's life. To me if God wants to slay a person in the spirit He has a reason for the person to lie out, not just to show off His power. Mind you I did say that I do believe a person can be laid out. I do not deny the gift, but too many people are playing with the gifts of the Holy Spirit for their benefits of showing off. When ever I am ministering I always have someone stand behind the person I am praying for and I tell them to not let the person fall. I want them to be raised up and not fall. I have had people get weak in the knees sometimes when I pray for them, then I ask someone to hold them up. That's just what I want when I pray for someone. I want them to be raised up instead of falling. I will always remember what happened to me when I went down. I can still see the man moving in and out of the circle even today. Once I wanted the gift, I thought it was something when you lay hands on a person and they go down, just to touch them and poof they are out. Now no, that's not for me.

I would rather pray and poof they are healed, or poof they are delivered (saved), or poof they are blessed receiving God's blessing for something they are asking the Lord

Jesus for. That is my poof. I can't see myself laying hands on a person praying for them, praying and praying, and praying waiting for them to fall. Ok Lord lay them out now, or ok, welling get into the spirit and fall. Even pushing their head back almost breaking their necks. I get more satisfaction when a person says the pain has gone, I am healed, or thank you Lord Jesus for the blessing. I am not looking to rob God of His glory. Slain, Webster defines it as to slay, to kill or murder. I don't want to kill or murder anyone. Help me I could not find the word slain in the bible dictionary. That is my two cents worth. It may not mean much to you but that is what I see.

We were having a great time in church. Mr. Sonny, Ms. Lorrie, Ms. Brenda, Robert, Sonya, Gere, David, Daniel and myself. We met together every Sunday. Occasionally we had visitors. Mr. Sonny was always looking for someone to bring to church. We were a happy family. We worked on growing and having a school for the children. I was very proud of my family. When they started coming to church I saw the Lord God bless them all with good jobs and raises. Within one year all of them had received jobs and raises except me. I was very happy for them. It was a sign to me that the Lord Jesus was really in charge. Our services were very Spirit filled. The power of the Lord God was there to heal and bless. What more could you ask for?

Mr. Sonny's sister had heard about the things the Lord was doing in the ministry, and about accomplishments Mr. Sonny was making. She called and said that she and her husband were coming to Atlanta to see for her self. She called me and we had a beautiful conversation. I looked forward to seeing her in person. She wanted me to meet this prophet she knew in Atlanta. I said that I would call him. I did and later we met in person.

When the prophet and I met he prophesied to me about some things that I knew God was telling me, and about the growth of the ministry. I accepted the messages because most of them were true. I highly believe in the gift of prophecy. I believe that God can use anyone to speak for him. That is why I listen to anyone who talks to me. I weigh the message throwing away the things that are false, and receiving the things that are true. I believe that sometime we go a little too far in delivering prophetic messages. Adding to the message or as I did one time subtracting from the message. To add to the message or to subtract from the message can alter the message robbing the message of the power God had intended the message to carry. This can and will bring the wrath of God upon the messenger. Deuteronomy 18:20, "But a prophet who presumes to speak in my name anything I have not commanded him to say, or a prophet who speaks in the name of other gods, must be put to death."

Jeremiah 23: 30-32, "therefore," declares the Lord, "I am against the prophets who steal from one another words supposedly from me. Yes, "declares the Lord, "the Lord declares indeed, I am against those who prophesy false dreams, "declares the Lord. They tell them and lead my people astray with their reckless lies, yet I did not send or appoint them. They do not benefit these people in the least," declares the Lord. I am very careful when I open my mouth telling anyone thus says the Lord. Most of the time I will say, "I see this or that." I do my best to speak the truth. When I am witnessing to something the Lord has told me about the person's life I will always ask them if the message is true. It is very hard for me to carry a message because I do not want the wrath of God on me.

I have had enough troubles in my life and I don't want to do anything to cause anymore. I am not saying that I want speak when I am sent by God, no I am not saying that. But I will pray very hard before I open my mouth. If other people would fear the Lord God in this way there would be no false messages or prophets.

The prophet started inviting me to come to some of the meetings he was having. He was forming an organization of prophets. He would have meetings at his home and in other places at times. I did not agree about some of the ways they ministered. I would set and watch a lot of time until he would ask me to pray for someone. I never got up on my own. They had a lot of people who would jump up at the mention of laying hands on and praying for people. I watched a lot of people in their group literally beat up on people. Pushing, hitting people on the head, and almost wrestling with people. I did not find that kind of ministering Godly.

Sometimes he would bring people to me to pray for them, and sometimes he would call me up to pray for people. I would never go on my own. There was enough showmanship going on, they did not need me. As I said before I fear God, and I will not do anything to discredit Him or His name.

The prophet was a very funny man, but I liked him. When we would go out to a restaurant to eat, he would holler loudly, "The Lord is coming soon, get ready." The first time I heard him do this I wanted to hide under the table. After a while I just looked and smiled. People would look at him, some would make comments and others would just look in bewilderment. I found out that he was not doing it for a show, he was very sincere. It can make you uncomfortable about going out to dinner with him, because you don't know when he was going to stand up and holler out the Lord is coming soon. Can you imagine being in a nice restaurant and someone gets up in the middle of diner and hollers across the room, "Repent for the Lord is coming soon?" If the management doesn't throw you out everyone will think you are just as crazy as they are. Association brings on assimilation. I believe everything must be done decent and in order to draw people to Christ, and not to scare them away. There is a time and a place for everything. If the Lord has me to do that I hope before I close my mouth He will show up. Don't leave me hanging Lord please.

I started inviting the prophet to speak at the church. He was a good speaker. He knew how to hold the attention of the people. The only problem I had was that he would go to far ministering during alter call. Two of my best members had some problems and he began to minister about them openly. This began to cause problems. They felt uncomfortable about coming to church when he came to minister. I would always have to talk to them after he left. I was able to calm them down the first time it happened, but I guess it was to much the second time it happened and they left the church. I had lost four of the best members we had. We were very small and to loose four people was a tragedy. From that time on things started going down hill. We had a lot of things that took place during that time which I could have stopped, but I did not. I regret that even today. We were left with just one faithful member and that was Sonya. She remained faithful. I wanted to move from having our services in our apartment after that. I told Gere that I wanted to move back into a Hotel conference room. We started having meetings in one of the hotels, but things weren't the same anymore. We would have people come by sometimes. They were visiting in Atlanta and just stopped in for Sunday service. Our numbers were not being added to, but we kept on meeting.

Things were getting hard at home. Gere was working, but I was not working regularly. We had gotten a nice van, but we did not keep it a year before we lost the van. I had an older van that I worked out of so now we were back down to one vehicle again. Every now and then I would get a good job, but by the time I collected on the job we were so far in the hole that the money I made did not catch us up. We had to move again. After we moved I got an offer to build a large house.

It took me a while to work up the plan. During the time I was working up the plan we had to move again. We had to move three times in one year. I was very sad, but we stayed together as a family. When we moved this time I told my family that we would not have to be forced to move anymore. I said that the next time we move we will be moving into our own house. I had this good offer to build a large house and I saw our future getting better. So I thought.

I would pray constantly asking God, why can't I give my family the things I had when I came up? I even asked why I couldn't give them the things I had as an adult. I had houses and cars. I even had boats, even a brand new boat. Why can't I give my family who I love these things? One thing He always brings to my attention was that when I had these things I did not know Him or serve Him. I worked hard for the stuff. I did not have Him in my life nor did I want Him in my life. I wanted the stuff, and that is what I worked for. He allowed me to get the stuff, and then He allowed me to loose the stuff. I was on a train going no where. I worked hard and harder trying to get the things of the world only to eventually loose everything. What good did my hard work accomplish me? I was chasseing after the wind. I look at all the things I bought in life where is the stuff today? "But seek first His kingdom and His righteousness, and all these things will be given to you as well." Matthew 6:33.

I did not know the steps to keep the things we acquire in life. I thought the stuff come first. I had to be taught a lesson because God loves me. God's lessons are hard, but if you study, remain faithful and obedient you will see the rewards of your suffering.

I thought our financial suffering was over. We had moved into a nice town house and I was getting ready to build the largest house I had built in my life. Not only that but I had a dream about my dad. Remember when I told you earlier that every time my dad came to me in a dream something bad happened; well this was the first time I thought was different. I had this dream and my dad said that I would be making a thousand dollars a week. I knew that I would not be getting that much off of the house I was getting ready to build because I told the owners that I wanted to receive five hundred dollars a week until the house was finished. If the dream was true something else would have to come my way, and it did. I started work on the first house and while I was working on the first house I was asked to build a house across the street. The people across the street were working with someone that did not know how to build a house and he was taking their money. He had started grading their land before I had gotten started on the house I was building. I was ready to start pouring my foundation and he had not done anything. The work he had done was wrong also. When the owner's wife came over one day and asked me if I would build their house to. We negotiated and I began to build their house. I asked for a five hundred weekly draw until the house was finished, this wood give me a thousand dollars a week just as the dream had said.

We were very happy; I finally could support my family. Gere had stopped work to stay at home, to home school the boys. I was working and bringing home the bacon.

Well you would think after all we had been through that our ship had finally come in. Well guess again. We were doing well as I said. But I was having a hard time with the people I was building for. The people I was building for on the left side of the street were crooks. And I found out that the ones on the right were crooks also. Remember what I said that every time I would dream about my dad was a warning that something bad was about to happen. Well though I did start making a thousand dollars a week on paper, it was like pulling teeth to collect. I was in a world of mess.

I wanted to quit building the house for the people on the right almost every week. They were very difficult. They wanted something for nothing. I was giving them a really good price to build their house. I was building their house way below the cost that builders charged for building a house this large. And still they wanted more. The husband and I were always in an argument up to the time I completed the house. The wife played the good cop, but she was sneaky. I lost a lot of money and I had the hardest time I had ever had building a house. The ones on the left were just as bad. It was surprising to me how they talked about each other and the one was no better than the other. Without going into any detail I lost a lot of money dealing with them also. In all I lost over ten thousand dollars between the both of them. I got a lawyer to sue them and guess what? The lawyer took my money and did nothing. Here we go again.

We lived well for about a year, bought a new car which I should never have bought. That's another story. Stay away from those side car lots. They are out to take your money. If you need a car save your money and buy one with cash. Keep doing that until you graduate up to a new car. A word to the wise will suffice.

Well here we go again. We had to move again. This time we moved into an old house which needed a lot of work. I told the lady that I would do the work on the house for us staying there. I found out that she wanted me to work on the house buy the materials and then give her six hundred dollars a month also. That was not our deal.

By this time Gere was fed up. She had all she could stand with me. She started getting real nasty toward me, and decided she was going to leave me and take the boys. I did not want my family to be broken up again, but what could I do? You can't force anyone to stay with you. She started saying things to me that really hurt. I wandered how could a person professing to be a Christian could be so evil and cold. I know that she had been through a lot being married to me. But what could I do? It wasn't like I had planned to go through these things. I did not want things to happen the way they did. I cried out to God everyday asking Him to bless me, to provide for me and my family, and to keep us together as a family. Every time I thought I was going to have a break through, someone allowed the devil to use them and they cheated me out of the funds I was supposed to receive. Although broken hearted I never gave up. I was compelled to keep on going. I know, and I did not say believed, I said that I know that my God is going to bless me after I go through the storm.

Marriage is one of the hardest things God has given to man. It was this union between a man and a woman that sin became dominant in the world. And this started all the way back with Adam and Eve. God made man and woman to love each other work together and reproduce and fill the earth. It is this love that has prompted the devil to destroy mankind. The devil does not care about you or me. He hates love, and consequently those who perpetuates love in their lives. God is love, His essence is love, His creation is based on love, and it is this love that the enemy hates. If you get down to it, it is not the premises of love that he hates, but the author of love. We are just there in his way as he tries to destroy God. He will try to use anything and anybody to help him fulfill his purpose. When we wake up and see him for who he is and recognize his tricks and traps, his deceptions, we can avoid the pitfalls he has set up. If you are like me you hate for anyone to try and trick you, using you for their pleasure. When I find out that a person is trying to use me for their sick purposes without any regard for my feelings, I am finished with them. I would rather you spit on me than to use me. I can wipe off the spit, take a bath and wash off the spit. But to act like you are my friend just to use me, you have gone too far. I will pray for you, because that is what you need, but I am finished with you. Father forgive them for they know not what they do, or whom they are doing it to. Although I will never pray for the devil, I will pray for those he uses, and allow themselves to be used by him.

God instituted marriage, and marriage between **a man and a woman whom God has joined together can be a beautiful thing.**

Let us look at this for a minute:

1. Between a man and a woman:

In Genesis 1:27-28, "So God created man in His own image, in the image of God he created him; **male and female He created them.**" **God blessed them and said to them**, **"Be fruitful and increase in number; fill the earth and subdue it**. Rule over the fish of the sea and the birds of the air and every living creature that moves along the ground."

As you can see God never gave the command to increase in number to a man and a man, or to a woman and a woman. We have been equipped with reproductive organs which are to be used to reproduce a species of our origin. This union originally was to copulate and bring about increased numbers on the earth. God new that the animals would increase in number, and in order for them not to over populate the earth and put man in submission to them man had to reproduce and increase also. If man did not increase the shear numbers of the animals would be too much for Adam and Eve to handle, to maintain. Man was never intended to lay with man. Nor was woman ever intended to lay with woman. This is an abomination in the Eyes of the Lord God. Sodom and Gomorrah were destroyed because of homosexual acts. Genesis 18: 1-33, 19:1-26. God also destroyed the house of Benjamin for attempting to have sex with a Levite. Judges 19:1-30. Leviticus 19:23 do no lie with a man as one lies with a woman; that is detestable. Leviticus 20:13, If a man lies with a man as one lies with a woman, both of them have done what is detestable. They muse be put to death; their blood will be on their own heads. I know we do not kill people anymore for these acts. But God was and is serious about men lying with men and women lying with women.

Today aids is a by product of homosexuality. People are dieing every day from this dreaded disease. I have personally visited with and seen people die from aids. God is very serious about this sin as with all sins. People will say that was in the Old Testament when God made these laws. But they do not know the bible or the Power of God. Nor do they know God's wrath. "Though you already know all this, I want to remind you that the Lord delivered His people out of Egypt, but later destroyed those who did not believe. And the angels who did not keep their positions of authority but abandoned their own home, these He has kept in darkness, bound with everlasting chains for judgment on the great day. In a similar way, Sodom and Gomorrah and the surrounding towns gave themselves up to sexual immorality and perversion. They serve as an example of those who suffer the punishment of eternal fire." Jude 1:8-7 New Testament. The bible is filled with scripture warning us to keep from unnatural sexual acts. I remember when a person would hide the fact that they were a homosexual or lesbian. We called them closet queens. But to day society embraces them giving into their perverted acts. I was invited to attend a church service by a person practicing lesbianism. I thought they attended a regular church where there were heterosexuals, homosexuals and lesbians attending, since so many churches are filled with these mixes. When I arrived and went into the sanctuary I noticed that the men were setting with their heads laying on other men and women were setting close to other women with their arms around them and their heads together also.

They were pared off men with men and women with women. I had never been to a church service where the whole body was filled with homosexuals and lesbians. I was shocked. When the service started two men came down the aisle and lit three candles in front, followed by the pastor and his assistant. When the pastor got up to preach, his message was about his soul mate packing his bags to go on a trip. He was trying to speak as a woman would. I said to myself that is a shame that even the pastor and his assistant are homosexuals. How can the people know they are in sin when the head of the church is just as much a sinner as they are? There was nothing mentioned about the bible. I did not think there would be. At the end of his sermon they had communion. I was asked by the people who invited me to participate, they told me that I did not have to if I did not want to, and I declined. They went down front men and men holding hands and women and women doing the same. The pastor gave them communion as they drank out of the same chalice. I felt sorry for them. At the end of the service the person who invited me said to me, "that did not hurt you did it?" I did not know what to say. I wanted to say something but I kept quiet. In my whole life I have never seen that before. I did not know that homosexuals and lesbians have a church where only they attended. They think they are going to heaven, but they don't know that they are on their way to hell.

It surprises me the way homosexuality is embraced in a country which was first populated by Christians from England. The Puritans came from England along with their cousins the Pilgrims. Pilgrims and Puritans were cousins who came to America to populate the new land. You know the story it is taught in schools everywhere.

But did you know that the Puritans were Christians. They were a group of people who broke off from the Catholic Church in England under the leadership and writings of John Calvin. They came to America to establish a new church and to worship God under strict laws for worship.* Their numbers grew from 17,800 in 1640 to 106,000 in 1700. Religious exclusiveness was the foremost principal of their society. The spiritual benefits that they held were strong. This strength held over to include community laws and customs. (Taken from Kay Kizer). Puritans were very strict in their worship of God. We today have evolved from a society which was very stern in their worship to a society where anything goes. Maybe the Puritans were wrong in some of the ways they enforced their worship. But they did lead this country into a healthy state of morality and Christian ethics putting God first in their lives. Look at this Nation Under God today. What God empowers this Nation today? I am not finished with this; I have more to say on this topic later.

A man and a Woman Whom God has joined together:

This is the Lord Jesus talking: He told her, "Go call your husband and come back." "I have no husband" she replied. Jesus said to her. "You are right when you say you have no husband. The fact is, you have had five husbands, and the man you now have is not your husband. What you just said is quite true. John 4:16-18.

It is my belief that God has chosen one person to be our wife or husband just as he made Eve for Adam. He did not make two or three wives for Adam, nor did he make two or three husbands for Eve. We enter into marriages without the will or consent of the Lord God, and these marriages turn out to be disastrous. Marriage is hard enough and when it is not the consent of God it will fail. Then when the one fails we continue doing the wrong thing because of our need for companion ship, or loneliness. Sex also has a part in our desire for marriage. When I came up if you were lying with a woman you needed to get married to her, this was the respectful thing to do. It did not matter what God's will was, because no one ask God anyway. In order to respect the young lady you need to marry her. The Apostle Paul says, "But if they can not control themselves, they should marry, for it is better to marry than to burn with passion." 1 Corinthians 7:9. Paul is not saying that you should go and find a person to marry just because you can't control your sexual desires. No; as we know, to have sex without marriage is a sin. Galatians 5:19-21 If you did not know it I am telling you know. So now if you have sex without obeying God's laws on marriage and without getting a certificate of marriage (obeying the laws of the land) you are in sin and in danger of hell's fire. There are too many people sharing the same bed and they have even gone as far as living together having children without a certificate of marriage or God's blessings. This is sinning in the Eyes of God. You will not prosper when you are being disobedient. What good is it to gain the world and then loose your soul? If you can't control you bodies, but your bodies are in control of you then you should ask God to give you a wife, and then you should go to the church and receive counseling to make sure that the person is the one whom the Lord is blessing you with.

If your church does not have a person gifted in counseling, and I mean spiritually gifted, then seek the Lord for direction to lead you to where you should go to receive real counseling. This is very important, and can save you a lot of heart aches in the future. People today do not know or obey God's laws on marriage. Here are a few and they are found in the New Testament with the exception of one.

1. Matthew 19:8-9, Jesus replied, "Moses permitted you to divorce your wives because your hearts were hard. But it was not this way in the beginning. I tell you the truth that anyone who divorces his wife, except for marital unfaithfulness, and marries another woman commits adultery.

2. 1 Corinthians 7: 10-11, to the married I give this command (not I, but the Lord): **a wife must not separate from her husband**. But if she does, she must remain unmarried or else be reconciled to her husband. And a husband must not divorce his wife.

3. A woman is bound to her husband as long as he lives. But if he dies she is free to marry anyone she wishes, but he must belong to the Lord.

4. Malachi 2:13, Another thing you do: You flood the Lord's alter with tears. You weep and wail because He no longer pays attention to your offerings or accepts them with pleasure from your hands. You ask, "Why?" It is because the Lord is acting as the witness between you and the wife of your youth, because you have broken faith with her, though she is your partner. The wife of your marriage covenant. Has not the Lord made them one? In flesh and spirit they are His.

5. And why one? Because He was seeking godly offspring's. So guard yourself in your spirit, and do not break faith with the wife of your youth**. I hate divorce**, "says the Lord God of Israel, and I hate a man's covering himself with violence as well as with his garment. "Say's the

Lord Almighty. So guard yourself, and do not break faith.

6. Matthew 19:4-6, "Haven't you read," he replied, that at the beginning the Creator made them male and female," and said" For this reason a man will leave his father and mother and be united to his wife, and the two will become one flesh. So they are no longer two, but one. Therefore what God has joined together, let man not separate."

A wife must not separate from her husband; in today's society when a man leaves his family he is considered the lowest thing on the face of the earth. A man is considered a deserter, a low life, irresponsible, and just plain worthless. The court system is very hard on a man who deserts his family. But if a woman leaves her husband she gets around the criticism by taking the children with her. This still throws the blame on the husband because everyone will say that the man did something to her to make her leave and take the children. Then the man still becomes the victim. There are rare cases when the man is allowed to keep the children in a divorce or separation. The man has to prove that the woman is irresponsible or using some sort of habituates be it alcohol or drugs. In the eyes of God both are wrong and are in sin. A man should not leave his wife, and a wife should not leave her husband.

There are too many couples that say that they need a break from being together. They should have thought about that before they said I do. Separation can bring about sin, marital unfaithfulness. 1 Corinthians 7:1-7. This is a way the enemy uses to bring about adultery breaking

God's laws on marriage. Marriage is sacred in the eyes of the Lord God.

Most marriages are broken because of finances. The lack of finances can lead to arguments, hatred, and separation in the bedroom which leads to adultery. People forget about the vows they took when they first got married: to love, to honor, to respect, to care for, for better or for worse, through sickness, for richer and for poorer. Most people remember for richer, but don't remember the poorer part. It is like they put up a mental block when the minister said poorer. And I am not just talking about the woman; there are men that feel the same way. There are even churches that minister: "check his finances before you get married." Because a person has money now does not mean that they will always have money. If you remember in the bible there were times of plenty and times of famine. If you are only in a marriage for good times the marriage is doomed to break up. And just because a person is poor now does not mean that they will be poor for ever. People put their security in finances, houses, cars, land, things, and people rather than in the Lord Jesus. Being financially stable can not and will not save you or get you into Heaven. If you remember the children of Israel, they choose the prosperity of the nations around them rather than God. Prosperity is in God alone. We should not look to man for stability or finances.

The only way for a marriage to survive is love, unconditional love. Love can conquer all things. If you marry a person because they look good now, or they are as we say fine now. What is going to happen when the wrinkles come, and the drips start showing up in places? Will you through the person away? Did you marry them for their looks, their finances, or did you marry them because you love them from your heart? If you love the person from your heart then no matter how old they get, no matter what their bodies look like later you will continue to love them. But remember no one wants to marry a person who looks like a movie star and then later look like a bag of potatoes bulging everywhere. So do your best to exercise and stay healthy, then your husband or wife's eyes want wander for from home. 1 Corinthians 7:28, but those who marry will face many troubles in this life. This is a true saying. As I stated earlier the enemy hates love and happiness. Marriage is based on love and happiness and the devil will do all he can to bring about division between the two of you. He wants to destroy love in the relationship. Love means happiness and joy. Love means sacrifice and servitude. When you love someone you will put their needs and desires before yours. Take your children for instance. You will do all you can to see that your children are provided for. You want the best for them in life. You put their needs before your own. When they hurt you hurt also, and you want to get to the bottom of the problem to find out what is the cause of their pain, and you will do all you can to relieve or alleviate the pain. You don't like to see them crying, because when they cry you cry inside also. If this is how you treat your children, why don't you treat your husband and wife the same way?

You say that they came from you bodies. God says each of you came from the same body, and you are one. Not two people but one person. Christ said that He came to serve and not to be served. Mark 10:45. He came to be a sacrificial lamb for our lives. Psalm 40:6-8, Mark 10:45,

John 10:14, John 10:17-18, Romans 3:25-26, Ephesians 5:2, Hebrews 9:26, Hebrews 10:5, Hebrews 10:10, 1 John 2:2, 1 John 4:10. Christ came as a suffering servant. He loved us so much that He was willing to suffer that we may be reunited to God our father. He set us an example which we should follow not only at church but at home also. If we would be committed to serve each other in our house holds then no one can call himself the leader. We would look to God for guidance and directions for the family. We would know that it is Christ who is the head of the house; we would recognize Christ Jesus as the leader praying to Him for direction and guidance. Just as Christ loves us without stipulations, we would also love each other in the same way. Then the house will be whole. Then we will be able to withstand the attacks of the devil. When trouble comes, or when our marriage is being tested. We will be able to pray together, stay together, and when it is all over we will stand.

Another thing look at your children what are you doing to them. I have heard to many times people saying that it was better for the children that we broke up. They say that they argue a lot with their spouse that it has to be affecting the children so it was better for us to separate. You would break God's law for the sake of your child instead of trying to find the root cause of your differences.

You would disobey God rather than seeking counseling. You would rather sin and put your life in jeopardy of hells fire than to pray for the Lord Jesus to save your marriage. Then you say well God will forgive me. Yea Right. You don't know what your punishment will be. You don't know if God will require your life the minute you walked out of that door. And think what you are doing to that child. Or do you care? Are you more concern about your self than you are about your children? Are you more concerned about you peace than you are your children? What if Christ felt that way we would still be outcast separated from Our Father God. Are you willing to suffer to go to Heaven? Exodus 3:7-9, the Lord said, I have indeed seen the misery of my people in Egypt. I have heard them crying out because of their slave drivers, and I am concerned about their suffering. So I have come down to rescue them from the hand of the Egyptians and bring them out of that land into a good and spacious land, a land flowing with milk and honey, the home of the Canaanites, Hittites, Amorites, Perizzites, Hivites and Jebusites. And now the cry of the Israelites has reached me, and I have seen the way the Egyptians are oppressing them. Luke 18:5-8, then Jesus told His disciples a parable to show them that they should always pray and not give up. He said: "In a certain town there was a judge who neither feared God nor cared about men. And there was a widow in that town who kept coming to him with the plea, Grant me justice against my advisory." "For sometime he refused. But finally he said to her, 'Even though I don't fear God or care about men, yet because this widow keeps bothering me, I will see that she gets justice, so that she wont eventually wear me out with her coming!'" And the Lord said, "Listen to what the unjust judge says.

And will not God bring about justice for His chosen ones, who cry out to Him day and night? Will He keep putting them off? I tell you, He will see that they get justice, and quickly. However, when the Son of Man comes will

He find faith on the earth?" If we continue to cry out to God about the situations in our house holds in stead of taking the matter into our own hands God will work things out for us. He can change hearts and minds and restore the peace love and joy in a house hold that was there when you first said I do. The first thing we need to do though is take inventory of our selves. Is our mate the problem or are we the problem. Some people want to change their mate when they need some reconstruction themselves. That is why there is a need for a spirit field counselor. A person who will pray and allow God to reveal the problem, and then offer suggestions for healing and restoration. Remember the Lord God is serious about Marriage and divorce.

You may ask who am I to give advice? I have been a law breaker. I know what it means to have the wrath of God on you. I know first hand His love, mercy and His wrath. Would you go to a person who never stole if you want to know how to steal, or would you go to a real thief a convicted felon a law breaker? I am not proud of what I did. I want to spare you the pain of my Ignorance of God's laws. A word to the wise is sufficient.

Right now I am alone, but not really alone for I know that the Lord is with me so I am at peace. As I write these last pages I am in a one room extended stay motel holding onto each and every day. I believe in the blessings of the Lord God. I believe in prayer, receiving what you pray for through obedience to God. I have come too far to turn back now. I love my family, but I love the Lord God more. Family may desert you, but He promised that He would never leave me, that he would never leave me alone. And I hold on to His promises. One day my family will be back together again because that is my prayer. The Lord Jesus said in the gospel of John "I tell you the truth, anyone who has faith in me will do what I have been doing. He will do even greater things than these, because I am going to the Father, **and I will do what ever you ask in my name**, so that the Son may bring glory to the Father. **You may ask me for anything in my name, and I will do it.** John14:12-14. Also: You did not choose me, but I chose you and appointed you to go and bear fruit, fruit that will last. Then the Father will give you whatever you ask in my name. This is my command: Love each other. John 15: 16-17. Also: **If you remain in me and my words remain in you, ask whatever you wish, and it will be given you.** This is to my father's glory, that you bear much fruit, showing yourselves to be my Father's disciples. John 15:7-8. I live by these words. I believe in them with all my heart. Even though you may not see the things you ask God for right away, that does not mean that you should give up on your prayers. God is working things out for you so you can receive the blessings.

I always say do the math take inventory:

1. Look at what you are asking God for. How will your blessing benefit not only you, but others? Is your prayer self centered.

2. Obedience is greater than sacrifice. Are you obeying God in all areas of your life? Not just at church, but at home, at school, at work and on the streets and highways are you being courteous?

3. Are you covetous, or exhibiting jalousies toward you friends and neighbors?

4. When you sin do you repent immediately asking God to forgive you and do your best not to make the same mistake again?

5. Are you kind and respectful to all God's creation no matter who are what they are? Devil excluded.

If you can answer yes to all these questions then why would God withhold your prayers? Just have faith and hold on to the promises of the Lord Jesus. He said that He would give you what ever you ask in His name. Do you believe Him, or is it just good reading?

This is not the first time the Lord God has separated me from family and friends. It hurts but I have come to except His will for my life. He has blessed me with special gifts. He has allowed me to see things no ordinary man has seen. He has allowed me to do things no ordinary man can do. He has allowed me to suffer and in my suffering He has brought me closer to Him. My suffering has taught me humility love and an understanding of mankind. Do you remember when the Apostle Paul cried out to God to take away his suffering? God told him that His grace was sufficient for him.

2 Corinthians 12:7-9. Many times I have cried out to God to reunite me with my family and friends, but I know that I have to be alone to receive from Him training and direction that I may do His will. It is for you that I suffer so I may be a witness, and that I may have a testimony about the Love and mercy of the Lord God, Christ Jesus,

and His Holy Spirit. He has taught me humility. I know without a shadow of a doubt that I am just a vessel for Him to use. All power belongs to Him; I can do nothing on my own. I can pray for you all day, but is the Lord who has to answer my prayer and bless you. I know that without Him, or apart from Him I am nothing, I can do nothing on my own. When the Lord Jesus was on the cross the chief priest and the teachers of the law mocked him among themselves. "He saved others, "but he can't save Himself! Mark 15:13. I remember the first sermon I did. I cried out to God that I have seen others being blessed through my praying for them. I said that I don't want to be out side looking in, I want to be blessed also. I was hurting inside when I ministered and I poured out my heart. I want to love and be loved. I want to have God's blessings to be able to take care of my family to give them a good life. I would love to be financially prosperous so I may share in the gifts the Lord has blessed me with. I am no different from you, I don't like suffering. But when I cry out I hear the words He said to the Apostle Paul, "My grace is sufficient for you. I have come to live with my suffering for what else can I do?

Someone has to suffer so others can be saved.

I believe there is a light at the end of my tunnel. King David saw it, and I see it to. One day I will be delivered from my suffering, in this life or in the life to come. It does not matter which one. My joy is knowing that He will not allow me to suffer always. I know He hears my cry and He will deliver me from my suffering when I have fulfilled His will for the life He has given me. Then my joy will be complete, but until then I must remain hopeful, faithful and obedient. My suffering has brought me closer to Him. My obedience has brought Him closer to me. I will not do anything to separate myself from the love of my God and my Savior the Lord Jesus Christ, and the communion of the Sweet Holy Spirit.

Now faith is being sure of what we hope for and certain of what we do not see. Hebrews 11:1, NIV. My life is and has been a life of faith and faithfulness. He has instilled faith in me. He has taught me faithfulness. The name of the ministry I was Pasturing is Tabernacle Of Faith Ministries. God's House Of Faith. In order to minister faith you must have faith. I did not choose this walk. My life was laid out for me before I was born, before I was conceived in my mother's womb. He knew my failures and my successes before I was born. He knew the road I would travel before my name was called. Oh Lord here I am I have come to do your will. Let not my will be done, but let your will be done with me. Mold me and make me into the person you would have me to be. This is my prayer. Amen.

Finally I would like to address some issues that He has allowed me to see that are dividing the body of Christ, His Church.

There are many things today which are being propagated into our society that are bringing about division into the body of Christ. These issues are growing day by day. Division is nothing new. Man has always sought to be diversified in his thinking and actions. This need to seek answerers to questions about the unknown has driven man on a quest for knowledge. To seek knowledge is a good thing, but the usage of the things found can become a bad thing if not used correctly. With knowledge there must also be a quest for wisdom. Wisdom will correctly propel you in the usage of the knowledge found. Without wisdom knowledge is futile. When I was in service they taught me about a rifle. The many parts of the weapon, how to dissemble the weapon and put it back together, how to load and unload the weapon, which ammunition the weapon uses, the proper way to hold the weapon and the end the projectile(bullet) comes out of. They taught me knowledge of the weapon I was to use. Along with this knowledge I had to seek and gain wisdom about when and where to use this weapon. To use the weapon unwisely could endanger the lives of my fellow soldiers causing irreversible harm even death. Knowledge and wisdom must go hand and hand.

Diversity is a by product of knowledge. One man believes this and another man believes that. I am always surprised how man can read the same thing and come up with different answers or interpretations of what's read. It is as if they were reading different topics. And from their different interpretations they formulate different theologies.

It is these diversities or theologies when vocalized into society are the catalyst causing divisions among people. All topics searched require a preponderance of information (knowledge) to effectively evaluate and then transmit the information found correctly. The information we transmit can and will affect the lives of others. Someone will believe the information we transmit whether true or false. Some people are to busy, so they say, to research information for them selves, so they rely on others to do the work for them. If the information found sounds good and reasonable they believe what was said and then they even transmit the information to others. This is a gathering of knowledge from someone else without using wisdom to make sure the knowledge found is correct. We hear, we choose sides, and then we react. It is the reaction by some that causes divisions weather in the church or out side of the church. This is man's drive, to know, to understand, to be an authority, to manipulate, to have his voice heard, to gain power over his listeners.

I had heard that the bible was first translated into the English language by King James. This is not true. The bible was first translated into the English language by John Wycliffe in 1384. I was also told the different stories about King James and his dictatorship and persecutions. In my research I found out that there were many King James's. It was King James1 who had the bible translated in 1604. It was King James VIII who was the first to legally translate the bible into the English language.

It was this King James who broke off from the Catholic Church because the Pope would not allow him to marry his mistress. He denounced the Pope and made himself Pope and had the bible translated for spite. There were many people who translated the bible before King James VIII who were martyred for their works and their beliefs. These men sought the truths in the word of God not for their own self gratification, but to give the people the true word of God. It is recorded that the bible was hid in bottles and in caves to prevent its destruction. This preservation of the bible and its translation brought about the first separation into denominations in England. But was this the first sign of denomination? No by no means, by the definition of denomination we will see that denomination existed way before the church was divided in England.

Denomination – A religious denomination, (also simply denomination) is a large, long established subgroup within a religion that has existed for many years. The Jews were divided into religious groups during and before Christ came to earth. These groups were called Pharisees and Sadducees. The Pharisees and Sadducees are a division of the Jews that were formed during what we call the four hundred years of silence that is the period between Malachi and Matthew. These Pharisees and Sadducees were different from the Pharisees and Sadducees during the time of Christ Jesus. They were the ones who secretly held the Jews together during the time of persecution of the Jews during the four hundred years of silence. They secretly met together holding onto the laws of Moses and teaching the Jews secretly the Torah under duress and threats of death for their religious beliefs. They also hid the scrolls in jars and in caves to preserve them. But as the times changed and their numbers were added to and the persecutions stopped they became the persecutors of their own people and those around them.

They began to change God's laws through their own interpretation to fit their own selfish ambitions. Thus they became denominationalized. **<u>Hosea 4:7, the more the priest increased the more they sinned against me.</u>**

Denomination has had it's affect on the church for decades. Man has sought change and a better way of worship. It is sad to say that Religious beliefs have caused many to die because of differences or beliefs. Many have become out cast for their difference of opinion. Many have been burned on the stake, hanged expelled from the church and had their heads cut off by the church because of their pursuit of different perspectives on religious beliefs, (matters of the laws of God). Man has used denominations to establish his own religious society or social order. It is these differences which have brought about persecutions and segregation. If you don't believe as I do then you are against me, and I don't want to have anything to do with you or your beliefs. I will gather my followers and speak openly against you in public gatherings.

They tried to denominationalized Christ Jesus, to put Him in their social order, but when they could not they wanted to get rid of Him. He came teaching the way of truth. Truth takes no sides, it stands alone. Truth does not need a witness, for truth is a witness unto it self.

People do not understand truth, and they try to make truth a matter of society's regulation. They comprehend truth as the combined beliefs of man, what man coming together through his combined intellect has formulated as truth. Christ came showing that man's limited intellect was driving him far away from truth. Man was using his interpretation of truth to bring his fellow man under bondage and servitude to himself.

Man was manipulating truth for his own personal gain, distorting the real truth. It was this social club that Christ Jesus came to destroy, and because He would not join and become a member they wanted to discredit Him even kill Him.

There are many different denominations in the world today. I found out through research that there are denominations even among what we call pagan beliefs. Not only are those who consider themselves Christians denominationalized but it seems that Christians and non Christians alike share differences in their religious beliefs. If we trace these beliefs back to their source we will find out that they come from one mans search for knowledge and then voicing his findings to others and getting them to belief in the information found, thus causing division in his social group. Then as time passes and this group grows in numbers a denomination is formed.

I do not believe in denominations. I do believe in a search for the truth. I believe that God wants us to be a progressive people, and not to be stagnant. We should always search for God wanting to find the truth. It is this search which brings us closer to Him and His purpose for our lives.

But we must be careful in our pursuit for truth and God that we do not misinterpret the information found which could lead to bondage in stead of freedom. We should not be mislead by our own intellect, but always pray for guidance, direction and wisdom in our pursuit. It is only through prayer that we will have a clear understanding of the information (knowledge) found and how this information (knowledge) should be applied to our lives today, or if the information (knowledge) found is for the past or for a later date. Remember what God told Daniel; He replied, "Go your way, Daniel because the words are closed up and sealed until the time of the end. Many will be purified, made spotless and refined, but the wicked will continue to be wicked. None of the wicked will understand, but those who are wise will understand." Daniel 12:9-10. Christ came to free us from bondage, and some with there pursuit of knowledge are trying to put us in bondage all over again. Knowledge should not be used to cause separation. Knowledge found should be evaluated and then consult God for questions about what He wants us to do with this new found knowledge. Everyone may not be ready to accept the information God has revealed to us. We make cause irreversible damage to others by transmitting the information found to fast. I believe that God reveals Himself in levels; stages as we mature in Him, just as a baby who learns to crawl, and then later begins to walk. We also start of as infants in our search for God. We must learn to crawl before we began to walk. There is a stage where we are feed milk. And there is a stage for solid food.

Everyone is not ready for solid food. Everyone is not ready for some things God has revealed to us, they are still on milk. If He feeds them solid food to fast they will reject the food as nonsense and then rebel turning back into the world from which they came. It is our responsibility to bring people closer to Christ, not causing confusion, or putting heavy loads on them which we are not willing to carry ourselves. **Hosea 4:7, The more the priest increased the more they sinned against me**.

2. Speaking In tongues:

Mark 16:15-18, He said to them, "Go into the world and preach the good news to all creation. Whoever believes and is baptized will be saved, but whoever does not believe will be condemned. And these signs will accompany those who believe: In my name they will drive out demons; **they will speak in new tongues**; they will pick up snakes with their hands' and when they drink deadly poison, it will not hurt them at all; they will place their hands on sick people, and they will get well.

Acts 2:1-4, when the day of Pentecost came, they were all together in one place. Suddenly a sound like the blowing of a violent wind came from Heaven and filled the

whole house where they were sitting. They saw what seemed to be tongues of fire that separated and came to rest on each of them. **All of them were filled with the Holy Spirit and began to speak in other tongues as the Holy Spirit enabled them.**

These are verses that many organizations have used to bring gilt on those choosing to come to Christ. They say that if you don't speak in tongues you are not saved. They say that speaking in tongues is a way of professing you salvation. How can you be saved if you don't speak in tongues?

There are churches (denominations) that have incorporated this into their church doctrine. There are even churches that will teach you how to speak in tongues, what to do to get the gift of tongues. They make those of us who do not speak in tongues feel guilty, left out and questioning our salvation. I had a friend who started attending a church where they use tongues frequently. She could not speak in tongues. She wanted that gift so badly that she told me that one morning she was lying in bed and

she started spitting on the floor beside the bed. She said that the saliva kept coming up out of her mouth and then she would have to spit it out right there on the side of the bed.

She said after a while she began to start speaking in tongues. As she was telling the story to me I could envision her spitting beside the bed, and I thought to myself how nasty to spit on the side of the bed. If you have to spit why not go to the bathroom. Is the spirit limited only to the bedroom? Will he go away if you said excuse me I need to go to the bathroom so I won't be so nasty spitting on the floor?

I could see this pool of spit lying on the floor. Her husband was not saved at the time, what if he suddenly came home and saw her in bed spitting on the flood? Would he think she was sick, and if not sick would he think she was crazy? Then an argument may pursue. Would God put you through this to give you a gift? Is your mouth so filthy that He has to purge you this way to bless you with a gift? Are has your desire become so grate that you would try anything to achieve your goal, weather God wants you to have the gift or not.

I was talking to a so called pastor one day and he was telling me about his church. He was very critical of me. I told him about our ministry and the fact that we were not meeting right now. He said the same things I have heard from so many. "I don't know why people want to start churches when God is not in it." He said, "When God starts a church the church will grow and prosper, and God will have people to just come along and give you money." He said that because I told him that we did not have the funds to continue, and some other things stopped us from coming together. I wasn't going to tell him everything because that was not his business. He told me that their ministry was a deliverance ministry. He said a few words in a tongue and said that is how he delivers people who are demon possessed; because that is the language the devil understands. He also told me that he was hearing God tell him to tell me to go on a fast for seven days then eat for seven days then go on a fast for seven more days then I would have the give of speaking in tongues. He said that he is hearing that I have never fasted in this way before. When he spoke in a tongue I asked him to translate what he was saying. He said that he did not need to translate it because the church was not meeting. I thought to myself that Christ said that where two are three are gathered in my name there I am with them. I was there, a police officer was there, he was there, and we were talking about Christ and the church. Why wasn't the church meeting? Did we need a building?

He and I went back and forth in our debate. He said that I was argumentative. I did not consider myself as being argumentative because I did not agree with what he was telling me. If God wanted me to go on a fast, God knows all He has to do is tell me. God knows I hear His voice. He talks to me, and I get my orders from Him.

Lord Jesus said, "My sheep listen to my voice; I know them, and they follow me." John 10:27, also, "I am the good shepherd; I know my sheep and my sheep know me." John 10:14. I do consider myself as being one of the Lord's sheep. I do not need another man to speak for the Lord to me. All another man can do is confirm the message the Lord has given me. I am not stubborn, nor am I deft, but when someone speaks I am praying for the Lord Jesus to show me his word (the Lord Jesus word) and allow me to hear His voice (the Lord Jesus voice). Then and only then will I say Amen. People are being lead astray because of the teachings of mankind. You need to know the Lord and His word for yourself. Isaiah 29:13, The Lord says: "these people come near to me with their mouth and honor me with their lips, but their hearts are far from me. Their worship of me is made up only of rules taught by men." I do believe in the gift of tongues. It is in the bible, God's word. I have heard my spirit speaking in tongues as I was praying. I once really desired to speak in tongues. But now I am happy with the gifts the Lord has blessed me with. If the Lord chose to give us all the gifts of the Holy Spirit how awful we would be. Remember Satin how he was the most beautiful angel in Heaven. How God had adorned him with all kinds of gifts and beauty. Look what he did.

He was so gifted that he tried to take over God's kingdom. Do you think God is going to allow that to happen again? I don't think so.

When I was in school I was very interested in the gift of tongues. I attended a church where the people spoke in tongues. The gift fascinated me. I wanted to learn all I could about the gift. When you are trying your best to please God, you want to make sure you are on the right track. I knew what I was hearing from man, but I wanted to hear from the Lord. So I sat out on a journey to be educated.

The first thing I learned was that tongues are a gift from God. 1 Corinthian 12: 4-11, there are different kinds of gifts, but the same Spirit. There are different kinds of service, but the same Lord. There are different kinds of working, but the same God works all of them in all men. Now to each the manifestation of the Spirit is given for the common good. To one there is given through the Spirit the message of wisdom, to another the message of knowledge by means of the same Spirit, to another faith by the same Spirit, to another the gift of hearing by that one Spirit, to another miraculous powers, to another prophecy, to another distinguishing between spirits**, to another speaking in different kinds of tongues**, and to still another the interpretation of tongues. **All these are the work of one and the same Spirit, and he gives them to each one as he determines.** I learned that speaking in tongues are a gift from God through Christ Jesus and are given to us by the Holy Spirit as He determines. Man can not give you the gift of speaking in tongues. Man can not teach you how to speak in tongues. Man can not give you what he does not possess. Man did not go to the store and purchase the gift, so he can not give the gift away. Man can not teach you what God does not want you to have, or to learn. You will be just saying words which have no meaning, like hitting a bell and making no sound, or making a sound with no anointing, no purpose, and no power.

The second thing is that tongues are a sign for unbelievers and not for believers. Read 1 Corinthians 14: 22, "Tongues, then are a sign, not for believers but for unbelievers: prophecy however, is for believers, not for unbelievers. There must be an interpreter when tongues are spoken in public so the unbeliever will become convicted and change their ways. If there is no interpreter people will think you are crazy, out of your mind." I have the gift of interpretation. God has blessed me to know when he is speaking through someone or they are just showing off trying to look holy. I may not be able to speak, but I definitely can hear God's voice speaking by His Spirit.

The third thing I learned was we all do not possess all of the gifts of the Spirit. 1Corinthians 27-31. "Now you are the body of Christ, and each one of you is part of it. And in the church God has appointed first of all Apostles, second prophets, third teachers, then workers of miracles, also those having gifts of healing, those able to help others, those with gifts of administration, and those speaking in different kinds of tongues. Are all Apostles? Are all prophets? Are all teachers? Do all work miracles?

Do all have gifts of healing? **Do all speak in tongues? Do all interpret**? But eagerly desire the greater gifts." Where would the church be if one person possessed all the gifts? There would not be a need for the body. If the eyes possessed hearing there would not be a need for the ears. If the ears could smell there would not be a need for the nose. We are the body of Christ and each one of us has a part in the body. It is true that some have more than one gift. But that does not make them more important than you are. Some have suffered tremendously to receive those gifts, and God has allowed them to have multiple gifts because He knows they will not prostitute the gifts, and they will give Him all the glory and Praise He deserves. Just as we have five fingers and five toes, God may allow you to possess multiple gifts. But be careful what God gives, He can take away just ask King Saul.

The third thing I learned is that people do not read the entire chapter before forming an opinion. Everyone wants to quote Acts Chapter 2:1-4 when talking about the gift of tongues. They forget about verse 5-11 where it names the different nationalities that heard the disciples speaking in their own languages. What's with that? They heard them declaring the wonders of God in their own language. Men of different languages. All of them who heard them thought they were drunk and crazy. The Apostle Paul talks about unbelievers hearing you speak in tongues. You need to take some time and read 1Corthians chapter 12 and 14. Apostle Paul gives a good synopsis on tongues.

Read and study these chapters and allow the Holy Spirit to teach you. Stop believing you are not saved because of the things of some men. Man will lead you to hell, but want lift a finger to stop you from going in. Pray to the Lord Jesus your savior for a better understanding on the topic of tongues if you still are confused. God is a God of order, and not disorder. Those who are playing with the gift should be careful one day they will have to give an account of their actions. God is the only one who can save. With man this is impossible. Man can not save himself, then how can he save me. Man does not know who God will save or who will go into the firry furnace.

Man has been given the job to pray for his fellow man, to do his best to dissuade him from going to hell, to cry out to Christ to save their souls. But today so many have become a hindrance, on their way to hell and trying to carry you and me with them. When a thorough bread horse is in the starting gate, and the gate opens who can stop the horse from completing the race? Who can hinder him on his journey? There is a destructive spirit loosed in this world today, who can hinder it from completing its course, who can stop it from running its race?

Just think about this for a minute. When I was lost in the world I had a tongue filled with lies, cursing, slander, cheating, dishonesty, pride, adultery and stealing. Now I have been given a new tongue through Christ Jesus saving me. I no longer talk the way I used to talk. Christ has filled my heart with love, compassion, forgiveness and honesty. And out of the abundance of these things He has placed in my heart, they flow out from my tongue. I am a new creation thanks to the Lord God who saw my wretchedness, who saw me in my dirtiest form, who saw me on my way to hell, who had mercy on me and sent His one and only Son the Lord Jesus Christ to save me, and no one can take that away from me. No one. Amen

Women in Ministry:

Women have come a long way in history. Today they are making great advancements in all areas of life. They have evolved from mere house wives, baby breeders and babysitters to become leaders in business and government. There leadership abilities are even being applied in the church.

Woman have made great strives to show the world that she has a brain and can use it. Her warmth, compassion and spirituality have made her a great catalyst of the church today. You will find more women in church then men. It does not matter where you attend church, or what denomination you are affiliated with, one Sunday just look around you and count the ratio of women to men. You will find out that the women out number the men two to one, and in some churches the number is even higher. It is because of this ration that some are using women for their personal gain. They are using her for the very same thing Satin used Eve for, to gain power, domination, personal wealth and the destruction of man. They are praying on her emotions, kind heart ness, compassion and love to trick her as Satin did Eve. Nothing is new under the sun the same trick the enemy used on woman during the time of Adam and Eve are being applied even today.

Woman has made herself known. She has stopped being the oppressed, and now she has become the oppressor. Man has become an object of her disapprovals of life. She has deserted the call God had given her and now she has set her own priorities, her own goals and direction.

I will have to admit woman has had a hard time through out history. Even the animals were considered more important then she. You could take his wife, but you had better not take his cow or he would kill you. And even his neighbors would help him destroy you over his animals. But if you took his wife they would just say that she ran off with another man and let that be it. Her importance was to bare children to help with the work of the land. She was a mere thing for sexual pleasure, and to feed man when he was hungry. She was not permitted to speak out at home or in public. Her opinions did not matter. Man was the master of his castle. She was traded like animals, sold, raped, abused and then when she got old she was let out to pasture while man sought a younger acquaintance. Truly she has gone through. Truly she has been persecuted, and not for righteousness sake. But once again I say that the persecuted has become the persecutor.

She has fought for her freedom and now she has become the task master. Even during the time of the Apostle Paul she was strongly scold. She was told not to ware jewelry, not to cut her hair and to keep quiet in the church. You will find these discords in 1 Corinthians. She was not even to be with the men in the Temple. Women had to watch from the balcony. What the man learned at the synagogues he would have to instruct his wife when he got home. Even in the church she was not recognized as a solvent being a person of notoriety. She was not even chosen as one of the twelve with Christ, but she was there taking care of the needs of the men. But once again I say that she who was persecuted has become the persecutor.

Thought out history her importance has been noted. Sarah Abrahams wife though she made a mistake by trying to rush the blessing of God by giving her maidservant to Abram. God still bless her with a child Isaac the child of the promise. Leah and Rachel through whom the twelve tribes of Israel were born, the catalyst of the promise of God to make Abraham in to a nation.

Potiphar's wife though her intent was evil God used her to elevate Joseph. Pharaoh's daughter who raised Moses as her own child, who would eventually become the shepherd of the children of Israel. And then there was Miriam Moses sister who was a prophetess. Rahab who hid the spies when Israel was getting ready to cross the Jordan to come into the Promised Land. Deborah the Prophetess who judged Israel when there was no King in Israel. Naomi and Ruth all the way down to Elizabeth who was the mother of John the Baptist and Mary the mother of Christ Jesus. There are many more women of importance in the Bible. There were prophetesses during and after the time of Christ on the earth. There were evangelist and deaconess during the time of the Apostle Paul. These are just a few to let you see women though they went through they were still important in God's plan for salvation. Again I say that she who was persecuted has become the persecutor.

Women have played an important roll in the rise and fall of nations. Her beauty and her special gift which God equipped her with have conquered man from Adam until today. And she has used her beauty and her special gift to rule and dominate man. Man in his naivety has always though that he was in control. But his lust after woman has made him subjected to her. Even though she was not allowed to speak out in public, or vote don't think that she was not in behind a lot of decisions that were made. There were probably more important decisions made in the bed room than were made in public chambers. Because man could not control his sexual lust for woman she used this to her advantage. Though she was not in front of the public gathering her voice was being personified. If man did not agree with the way she wanted things to go all she had to do was withhold her special gift from him and eventually he would give in. Women are smart and they know how to get their way. Some are even considered to be devious.

I think God that there are Godly women, women who hold to the principles and teachings of God. I have met a few in my life. There are women that know why God brought them on this earth, and they are willing to be submissive unto Him and His will. It does not mean that you are weak because you are submissive. I believe as the Apostle Paul says "who is weak, and I do not feel weak. You don't have to be ashamed of your weakness. You don't have to put on a posada of strength when you are weak. If I acknowledge that I am weak I know that I need a power greater than I am to watch over me, to protect me, to guide me and I know that I must be submissive to that power because I know that He is my strength. My strength is shown in my weakness. I must come down below you to raise you up. If I am above you I can only step on your head driving you father down. That is not why I was born. It is my job to lift you up to Christ, and not to drive you into hell. What is wrong with being a servant? A servant is greater than the one being served. A servant knows what to put in front of you at the table, and when to put it there. The recipient can only eat what the servant has prepared and placed before them. The servant knows how to prepare the meal so it will be enjoyable for the guest and good for their health. A servant is always about his masters business making sure everything is ready for his return. "I did not come to be served, but to serve." Matthew 20:28

If you have been oppressed and abused through out history it is a natural instinct to fight back once you have received your independence. If you cage a dog for a long time, once you let him out of the cage he will began to run all over the place with no concern for where he is going or the dangers ahead of him. His only focus is on the fact that he is free. His new found freedom can become detrimental to him if he runs out into the street in front of an on coming car. What he considered was his freedom in turn, turned out to be his death. No one likes to be oppressed or abused. Oppressions and abuse can and will bring about anger and vindictiveness'. We want to turn against those who are the perpetrators of our abuse. We want them to feel the same oppression we went through, the hurt and the pain. We forget about the scriptures that say that we should forgive them, Matthew 6:12, Matthew 6:14-15, Matthew 18:21, Matthew 18:35, Colossians 3:13.

I have heard people say that they can forgive but they can not forget. If I can not forget then I am hovering resentment storing it up in my heart to be used at a later time or date. What if God stored up our sins after we repented to be used against us if we slip again? How many times shall I forgive my brother? Matthew 18:21.

Man through out history has been the catalyst of the emotional state of women. Man has not treated women with the respect she deserves. It is funny to me how they will come to the defense of their mother but not their wife. Both are women, both are a part of their life. It is no wonder woman has taken the attitude she has toward man today.

I have heard women in their meetings; groups and gatherings talk down about men. It always bothered me to listen to them. Some talk about the abuse they have gone through from their husbands or boy friends, even their dads. I could feel their pain, but does that give them a right to become abusive themselves? Does that give them a right to group all men into the same category? She who has been persecuted has become the persecutor.

Woman has fought for her place in our society. Today they have excelled to some of the most prominent positions in the world today. They have become judges, lawyers, doctors, senators, governors, and heads of state and even in some countries rulers. They have even taken high positions in the church. Some have propelled themselves to be pastors. I can not speak for the world, but I can not find a single place in the Bible where God called a woman to be the head of His church. If the Bible is our book of guidance and we are to search the Bible for direction in our lives, then how can a woman become the head of the church. I have attended churches where women are the pastors. Most of them I have observed minister harshly and without compassion. I have heard them hollering at their congregations embarrassing people from the pulpit. I have noticed where women are pastors their entourage are women. In most cases where women are pastors, mostly women run the church. I have noticed where women are pastors there are mostly women in attendance. I heard one woman say "though she is the pastor of the church, she is submissive to her husband when she gets home; he is the head of their house." I guess when they go home they leave God in the church building. I was talking to a woman who was a pastor about this because I wanted to know. I asked her did she hear God tell her to become a pastor of His church. She paused for a while and then she told me, no. I know some women who are pastors of their church and their husbands are the deacons. I knew two woman pastors and their husbands are the associate pastors. I was praying for the church one morning and the Lord Jesus spoke to me and said that His church was not made up of brick, wood and motor. God's house His church is made up of people. If I leave God in the building who goes home with me? If God is not the head of my house, then who is? If a woman is the head of the church, then it does not matter if it is the building where we meet collectively as a group, or where her family resides, she has to be the head of her house also. Christ said "Where two or three come together in my name, there am I with them." Matthew 18:20.

Christ does not need brick, wood or stone for His church to meet. The problem is that we limit the church to a building. This is what the Lord say's: "Heaven is my throne, and the earth is my foot stool. Where is the house you will build for me? Where will my resting place be? Has not my hand made all these things, and so they came into being?" Declares the Lord. Isaiah 66:1-2. When Christ was on earth He moved all around the country side teaching and healing. He did not limit Himself to the Temple or the Synagogues. People want to put Christ in a box limiting Him to a place and a time which we have set up. If a person needs healing, prayer, deliverance, counseling and salvation should they wait until Saturday or Sunday morning service, or when the building opens for business? I pray not. Christ has set an order for his church, and people today are no different than the Pharisees and Sadducees were during His time on earth.

Everyone wants to be the head, and no one wants to be the tail. People believe because they can sing good, play instruments, and speak well they should be pastors of Gods house. Your talents do not make you a pastor. Pasturing brings great loneliness and suffering. I never wanted to be a pastor. I continue to pray to the Lord God and ask Him why I should be a pastor when there are so many churches in the Atlanta vicinity. It seems as though there is a church on every corner. Why should I be a pastor? I would rather work with someone helping them minister and leave all the headaches of pasturing to them. But at the same time I will not be disobedient, I am not here for myself, I am here for his purpose. 1 Timothy 3:1-7, Here is a trustworthy saying: If anyone sets his heart on being an overseer, **he** desires a noble task. Now the overseer must be above reproach, the **husband of but one wife**, temperate, self-controlled, respectful, hospitable, able to teach, not given to drunkenness, not violent but gentle, not quarrelsome, not a lover of money. **He** must manage his own family well and see that **his** children obey **him** with proper respect. (if anyone does not know how to manage **his** own family, how can **he** take care of God's church?) **He** must not be a recent convert, or **he** may become conceited and fall under the same judgment as the devil**. He** must also have a good reputation with outsiders, so that **he** will not fall into disgrace and into the devil's trap.

This may seem contradictory but listen and pray about this. I do believe a woman can be an associate pastor as long as there is a man over her. I base my conclusion on Adam and Eve. Eve was made to be a helper to Adam. It was Eve's job to care for the things of the house. She was placed over the children in the house hold, male and female. The children of a house came under the mother of the house. In the Bible when there was no husband and there were children it was the responsibility of the church to take care of the family. They did not mean for the pastor of the church to commit adultery, but the church would see that they were fed, clothed, and they had a roof over their head. I guess that was just good reading in the bible.

When a snow ball is rolled from the top of a tall mountain, what will stop that snowball from becoming an avalanche? What will hinder that avalanche from its destructive course?

There are many things today that are causing division in the church. I know you can think of many more. How can we put an end to these things? We can not, what is set in motion must be. These things are the beginning of the end. The things we see today must be in order for prophecy to be fulfilled. These things will bring about the return of Christ and the destruction of this earth as we see it. If we could bring about a positive change then the bible would be a lie. It is the wickedness of man which will bring about his destruction and the eventual destruction foretold. Everything prophesied must be fulfilled. Just as it was in the time of Noah, Isaiah, Jeremiah and all the prophets who prophesied destruction these things must come to pass. But we who are the children of God will see these destructive things from a distance, as though looking through a window. God has promised to protect us from all harm, and gather us to Him. Christ words were, "My prayer is not that you take them out of the world but that you protect them from the evil one." John 17:15, "Holy Father, protect them by the power of your name – the name you gave me - so that they may be one as we are one. John 17:11. It is not for us to fear the end, because we will have to leave here collectively or singularly. We should rejoice that God loves us so much that He will not allow us to continue to suffer in this world. In this world there will always be suffering and persecutions for the children of God. As long as there is good and evil these things must be. But we whose names are written in the lamb's book of life can rejoice because Christ Jesus has already prepared a better place for us, a place of love, joy, peace and harmony. We don't have to fear what is going to happen tomorrow because no matter what happens Christ said that He would be with us, and he would not leave us alone. It is our faith in Him, that He will keep His word to us just as His Father kept His word to Him when he said "Therefore my heart is glad, and my tongue rejoices; my body also will rest secure, because you will not abandon me to the grave, nor will you let your Holy one see decay." Psalm 16:9-10. I am not saying that some of our bodies will not see decay. There is a possibility that some will and some won't. That does not matter; the important thing is that Christ will not abandon us in this life or in the life to come. I wish there was no evil and that all men could live in harmony with each other. I wish that man could turn their heart to God and worship Him obeying Him and doing His will. I wish that every child will not know pain, suffering or loneliness. I wish that every household would be filled with laughter and joy. What a beautiful world this would be.

January 12, 2009. I thought I had completed this manuscript. I thought that by now it would be published, marketed in book stores on book shelves. It has been six years now and I am still writing. And guess what? I am still going through my tunnel. BUT,,, I am stubborn I am not a quitter I can not give up. As long as the Lord has the breath of life in me I will not give up.

I want to take you back to February 1, 2008. I would like to take at look at Salvation. I title this, Salvation In Its Spiritual And Physical (Natural) Form:

When will it end? How long must I cry out? When will the pain stop? When will the suffering go away? How long must I carry my cross? These are the questions many gave asked, many have prayed. How ling oh Lord will you watch the misery of your people? When will you bring deliverance? Just as Jeremiah, Hosea, Job and many other prophets cried out, we are still crying out today.

Many have cried out for themselves, and many have cried out for others, the pain can seem almost unbearable when we cry out for a loved one, especially for our children.

I have been through so much with my boys (David and Daniel). Doctors saying that David would not be born, both boys were being born premature, David being born with a hernia and thyroid sickness, David breaking his arm and wrist, then being separated from them three times. What else Lord? How much more must I go through? I really love my boys and the pain seems so unfair and hard to bare. It is hard to watch them grow older and I can only watch from a distance. I hope one day as they grow older and get their drivers license they will be around me more. This is my prayer. I do not want to take them from their mother, but I would like them to be able to spend some of their time with both of us. I do not want them to be forced to be with me or their mother. I want them to know that we both love them and want them to feel free about being with me and her. Most parents when divorced or separated want to choose which parent the child is to be with. The child grows up without the love and affection of one of their parents. Did the Lord God intend it that way? If so why did he take two to make one? We as humans decide which parent the child is to be with. We set up days and hours of visitation. We set up our rules with out any input from the child. The child grows up being twisted back and forth between both parents. When they become teenagers they have their own social lives, places where they want to go to be with their friends. It is not fair to them when they are forced to spend all of their time with mom or dad depriving them of their outlets (time away from their parents). Their lives are so regimented IE, school, homework, chores; church, time to go to bed and time to rise (get up). We plan their lives with out their input. It is no wonder that so many children rebel against their parents. We direct and guide according to our desires, wants and wishes, not taking time to discuss their activities with them. We never think about the affects this will bring on the child as they grow older. Are we concerned about the welfare of the child or for ourselves? What I am saying may sound contradictory to scripture, Proverbs 19:18 – Discipline your son, for in that there is hope; do not be a willing party to his death. Proverbs 23:13 – Do not withhold discipline from a child; If you punish him with the rod, he will not die. Proverbs 29:17 – discipline your son, and he will give you peace; He will bring delight to your soul. Proverbs 22: 6 – Train a child in the way he should go, and when he is old he will not turn from it. These scriptures talk about discipline, not about depriving a child of be with both parents. When a child is born the Lord God gave the responsibility of both parents to raise and train the child, to teach the child love, respect, and responsibility. A child does not know right from wrong when it enters the world. It is our society which destroys the child. We have been given the responsibility of the child to train the child in the way they should go in this life. God gave that responsibility to both parents not one, and He holds both parents responsible. It is hard enough to raise a child when God is in the house.

It is impossible to raise a child correctly when God is not in the house. We must lie at the feet of Christ day and night, praying for our children and our spouse asking the Lord God to place a hedge of protection of His Angels around our family day and night, asking Him to protect them from all sin and harm, and asking Him to bless them as they go out and come in. We must know when to be stern with our children, and when to show compassion. Jeremiah 31:3 - The Lord appeared to us in the past saying; "I have loved you with an everlasting love; I have drawn you with loving – kindness". Loving your child and showing kindness should not be misinterpreted by neglecting to discipline your child. But I believe if we began to train our children when they are young. Then our discipline will not be as stern when they grow older. What you instill in your child when they first start to understand right from wrong can and will be an influencing factor on their lives for the rest of their lives. When they are away from you, you can have peace in your spirit that they are conducting themselves in a respectful way. And you did not have to beat respect into them. You have grafted respect into them through your instructions and your Godly actions. Godly instructions grows Godly children I am not saying that they will do what is right more than what is wrong. By no means am I saying that. There is a nature which is dwelling in all of us trying to get us to rebel against God and His laws. Thanks to the Lord Jesus and His Holy Spirit who are there inside of us working on our behalf helping us to reject the wrong and cherish the right. This child does not know nor understands this. God gave it to us his parents to help the child along. If we are not obeying the Lord Jesus, how do we, or how can we expect the child to obey the Lord God. A child learns by listening and seeing. You the parents set the example for the child to grow by. If there are Godly parents at home then the child will have a chance out in society. If there are not Godly parents at home then the child is domed to fall. Share with them the things about life, listen to them, pray for them, then after we have done all we can do God will watch over them, and take good care of them. Then and only then can we be at peace whoever they are, and whoever they go. When ever David and Daniel are with me sometimes I just set and watch them from a distance, listing to their conversations with out interjecting. I look for their reactions to the things they are doing and saying when they are watching television. You can learn a lot about your child just by watching them, and listening to them. I do not enter into their space unless what they are doing or saying could get them into trouble, or harm them or someone else. You can not be around your child all the time (24/7), although we know God can. But we can pay attention to them when they are around us listening to them, watching them and interacting with them when needed. This will help us to learn more about them. Then we can see signs of trouble before it happens and be able to redirect their energies into another area that is not destructive and harmful. If I am constantly talking, directing, scolding, and not listening, how will I know if they are receiving or ejecting? How will I know what I am doing is benefiting their lives.

Let us look at a car. When a car is not running correctly we take it to a mechanic. Before he takes action the first thing he will do is listen to the car to determine where the problem is. Then after patiently listening and observing (observation), he maps out a plan for correction. After the corrections have been made he listens again to see if the corrections were successful.

This same principle applies with our children, listening, observing, determining a cause of action, implementation (correction), and observing and listening again, praying to God to guide you through every step. Then we can have peace where ever our children may go. Discipline is needed, but when it is given it must not be given in anger but in loving kindness. Think about the way you would want God to discipline you. Do you want Him to be harsh, cruel, not giving you time to respond, asking for repentance and most of all not telling you why he is punishing you? Don't you want to be justly punished? Then you should treat your child justly also. You have feelings and they have feelings also. Do you remember the parable about the unforgiving debtor Matthew 18:21-35? Read it sometimes. There is a time to be stern, there is a time to punish, and there is never a time to be harsh. In all you do, remember how you would want to be treated. Then do the same for your child. Whatever you do, do it with love. What you do today you will see the results tomorrow. Think about this. Let it resonate in your computers hard drive. How can you raise you child and set Godly examples when you are doing wrong yourselves. Did not the Lord God say "I hate divorce, I hate separation"? Check this out in the Bible; do not take my word for this scripture.

With all my heart I never wanted to be separated from my children, from my boys. I have prayed many times for my family to be put back together again. For years I have cried out for restoration. Now I cry out that the Lords will be done. Do not misunderstand what I am saying. I know that it is not the Lords will that families should be broken up. But I do know that sometimes the Lord will use separation to punish us, and to fulfill His purpose for our lives and others. Look at Abraham for a minute. God told Abram to leave his father's house hold, family and friends and to take Sarai his wife and go to a land where He was leading Him. Do you think that did not hurt Abram to leave his father, family and friends the people he grew up with and take a journey to an unknown land? To leave his place of safety to go a place he knew nothing about? Was God punishing him? Or was God using him for a greater purpose. We do not always understand the things God allows us to go through in life, but one thing we can be sure of, that everything works out for his good purpose and will. And you can count on this, that in the long run we will see the blessings of the Lord after the suffering of our souls. Suffering is for a little while, but joy is eternal.

I have found out something in this life which took me a while to comprehend. No matter how much you may love someone, you can not force them to be with you. I do not want anyone to be in my life that does not want to be there. People should not try to hold onto people when they want to go. You can not force someone to love you. If is not in their hearts to love, then there is nothing you can do or say that will change things. You will only make their lives miserable and yours also. No matter how much it hurts, you must let them go. Would you want to live out your life wishing you were somewhere else? Hateing the sound and even the smell of the person you are with? Does God make you love him? Does He make you serve Him? Will He not let you go if that is your desire? Are you greater than He is. You know really, He could if He wanted to. There is nothing impossible with God. But remember he is God, and not man. Everything works out for His will and purpose. He is the one who made your heart, and He can harden or soften your heart according to His will and purpose. If you do not believe that ask Pharaoh (Exodus 4:21). But once again I ask you, are you the Lord God. What is your purpose for wanting to make someone love you? I want someone to love me from their heart. Not for whom I am, or what I have, or who or what I may have someday. I told a friend one day, that I want to be loved as though I am naked. Not having a thing in the world, just me. Can you love someone that way, if they have nothing, if they are blind, cripple, death mute, not as smart as you are, do not have as much as you have, not as pretty as you are, old, young, poor, black, white, red, can you love them from your heart? Guess what? God does. Jesus gave His life for all of us. He did not make any specifications about who could come to Him (blind, lame, cripple, death mute, rich or poor, black, white, red or any other color or disability, pretty or ugly). He sacrificed His life for us all. Yet we have our specifications. We pick and choose who we are going to love and be around. Are we greater than the Lord our God? Some times I wonder.

I know that my boys love me as much as I love them. We share a love that can not be broken even though we are not together. When I am around them I do not want to leave them. It hurts very deeply. I watch them as I go until I can not see them anymore. Hoping to get that last glance, that picture that will resonate in my mind until the next time I see them. The pain sometime fills my eyes with tears. But through it all I am not angry with their mother or God. I do not blame anyone but me. What I must go through, the path I must walk, the valley, the journey, the suffering

I must endure, I must carry on. I must be strong. I thank God for the time I can spend with my boys. It means a lot to me. I thank God that their mother and I are not confrontational. We do not get into any disputes when I am around. I know how to stay away from arguments. I told you once before that I can see and cense spirits. I know when it is time for me to leave and not over stay my welcome. I know what to say and not to say. In other words I know how to shut up and mind my own business. I will not give the devil a foot hold, a place to sneak in. If I can not be with them all the time, then part time will have to do. A little bit is better than nothing.

In about October of 2007, the boy's mother carried David my youngest to the doctor. He was getting tired quickly when he and Daniel would walk from school. He would have to stop for a while, and then continue on. They did not have that far to walk. They wanted to walk rather than ride the bus. David could not play like other children, he would get exhausted fast. In school he could not play basket ball when they took physical education, he would just be too exhausted. He could not run for fear of passing out. He began to see blood in his urn. His mother carried him to the doctor to have him examined. After they ran test on him the found out that he had PNH a rare blood disorder. The disease is so rare that only a few doctors are able to diagnose and treat the disease. The doctors here knew that the disease affects the white blood cells, red and the platelets. They told us that the disease destroys the bone marrow which produces blood for the body and eventually would take his life if not treated. I cried out "Lord how much must I go through? How much must

I bare? When will it stop?" How much must this child suffer? What has he done to go through this suffering?

I began to think back to one of their birthdays. I had bought Daniel and David new bikes. We had a party for them, and I took the boys and their guest to a trail where we could ride. We would have to stop along the way to wait for David. When he caught up he would have to stop and rest. This was when he was about twelve years old. I was very concerned for him then, but we did not consult a doctor at that time because we thought the problem was possibly coming from him being premature. They had told us when they were born that the bays would not be able to perform as well as other boys their age. They said that their development would be slower. So we believed that this was just a part of his development. We did not worry about it. When David was fourteen, he began to see blood in his uren. He had to have physical exams for school and they said he was healthy. We did not know what was really going on inside of his body. After his sixteenth birthday his mother decided to carry him to find out why he was getting so tired, and why he would sometime pass blood? When she told me what was going on I began to cry out" Why Lord? What has he done to be going through this? Hasn't he suffered enough?"

If you knew David you would say that he is the most loving and mannarable child on earth. He would give you the shirt off of his back. He thinks about others before himself. I had to talk to him about his giving. He would give students in his school his lunch money so they could eat, and he would go hungry. I told him to be careful and prayful, because there are those who would abuse your good nature. Some people would see your good heart and try to take advantage of you. The Lord wants us to give, but we must be wise in our giving. You would not give an alcoholic money to buy alcohol, or a drug addict money to buy drugs. It is good to have a giving heart, but don't let you giving cause someone else to sin. Do not aid them in their sinning. I will not change what God has placed in his heart. I will not rob him of his blessing. But in all things I want him to be wise.

I began to cry out to the Lord, why? Is it something I have done, or not doing to cause my child to suffer this way? I would rather suffer myself than to have my child go through this. I cried that the Lord would take the disease away from him and give it to me. I deserve to be punished. He has not been here long enough to have sinned to cause these things to be happening to him. I began to cry out Lord please tell me why, I am hurting inside? This was my daily prayer.

We had to carry David to the doctor twice a week for them to examine him. On one occasion he would have to get blood transfusions to bring his blood count up. He was under the care of specialist. They were conferring about his case around the United States. I felt confident they were doing all they could to help my child. But this did not ease my pain. I wanted to know why? I would not stop asking God until He spoke to me and tell me why?

We had to carry him to Scottish Rite and Egleston children's hospital that only specialized in the care and treatment of children.

Some of the doctors were very good, but there was one or two that I wanted to throw into the garbage disposal. I do understand that doctors have a hard job to do. I know that they are held responsible for what they say and they do not say. Doctors like ministers walk a thin chalk line. People are listening to your words and advice. Saying the wrong thing could get you in a lot of trouble, doctors with man, and ministers with God and man. Doctors have to pay out a lot of money for their insurance because of their hypocritical oaths. Ministers have to pay with their souls. Doctors can be sued and loose their license. Ministers can loose their souls and find themselves in hell. I do understand, and I am sympathetic, but there are some in both fields who seem that their hearts are made of stone (solid rock). David had one, and I did not like her, and I knew that she did not like me. I did not care though; this was my child and not hers.

I can not mention her name, but I wish I could. She had to me, the worst bed side manner of all the doctors I have come across in all my life. I have heard people talk about doctors with bad bed side manners, but she was the first one I had personally experienced. She was hard and cold. I felt the coldness in her spirit. When we would be in consultation with her, she would look at David's mother rather than me. Not directing her conversation to both of us. She focused more on David's mother. This did not bother me because I knew her spirit. If you are ever in a conversation with a person that has an unfamiliar spirit watch them, they will rarely look you in the face. They will look at anything or anyone else but you. She would talk about David dieing looking right at him. She would say if we would not allow him to get a bone marrow transplant he would die. She also said that even with a bone marrow transplant he may not make it. I was getting angry, well lets say mad setting there listing to her talking to my son about dieing. Who made you God? Who gave you the authority to say who is going to live or die? I sat quietly that time and let her talk, after she left I talked to David and told him not to believe what she was saying. I told him that she was only speaking from her prospective. Only God can give life and take it away. I told him not to be frightened just to have faith and believe in the Lord God. He looked at me humbly and said "OK dad". I told his mother that I would not allow him to be in the room with her again if she begins to talk that way. The doctor and I began to get into clashes. As I said I could not stand her bedside manners at all. I told her that I would not allow David to be in the room if she would continue to talk about him dieing. She told me that he had a right to now what was going on. I told her it was not her place to talk to him about dieing. That was solely up to me. Any information she had about his condition should be discussed with myself and his mother first, then we would make a decision what would be passed on to him. I wanted that made clear. It is not right to put the idea of dieing in the head of a youth. That you as an authority tell them inters their mind and becomes imbedded into their thoughts. This can be a disaster. If you tell me I am going to die, what hope do I have that maybe I will live? How many people have died that could been cured because they gave up on life. I hear doctors tell patients not to give up on being cured, to hold onto life.

I also heard Doctors say, there was nothing they could do for a certain patient because they wanted to die. You hear of people being so heart broken that they give up on life. I was not going to let this happen to my son. I wanted him to have a positive attitude about his illness. Do you remember, or have you read about the Thessalonians during the time of the Apostle Paul? They had given up on life waiting for the return of Christ Jesus, waiting to die and be resurrected. Paul had to chastise them for giving up and tell them that they need to get back to work, do something with their lives. No man knows the day, the time, or the hour when Christ will return again. We do not know when our time is up, only God knows. God is still a miracle worker. He is performing miracles every day. If He has not told me that I am going to die, then your words mean nothing to me. God will always tell His children when He is going to bring them home, read your Bible. I could give you passages, but I am not. There are something's you need to look up in scripture for yourself. You need to read your Bible instead of skipping through it. You miss a lot, and you are not well informed by just skipping through the Bible. I hear people say all the time "Oh I did not know that was in there". I guess you did not if you are just skipping through the Bible instead of reading it. Try reading the whole Bible instead of looking up scriptures. There is a time to look up scriptures to reformulate yourself, after you have read the whole Bible. "My people are destroyed from lack of knowledge". Hosea 4:6.

Later I found out that the information the Doctor was giving us came from another Doctor in Tennessee. I found out that she was not an authority on the disease. She was only transmitting information. When I found that out I wanted to take David to the doctor who specialized in the field of PNH. I wanted to contact him. We discussed the matter with one of the other doctors who would see David and they told us that the Doctor who specialized in the disease would only see extreme cases. I said to Gere', "my child's life is a risk, how much more extreme can this be. Then they told us that we would have to make an appointment, and after acceptance we still may not see the doctor only one of his assistance. I began to thank about praying. Do I have to make an appointment to see Christ Jesus? Can I go to Him or do I have to see someone else, Maybe Gabriel? I am glad that God is not like man. We would be in big trouble.

We had to carry David back and forth to the Doctor once or twice a week to have his blood count checked. He had to stop going out in public. He could not go to school, Church or any where else where he could come in contact with other people. He would have to ware a mask and gloves at all times. When people would see him they would stare at him. I did not blame them though. Whenever I would see a person wearing a mask I would stare at them also. Now when I see someone wearing a mask I began to pray for them. It does not matter why they are wearing the mask that is not my business. I know that there is some sort of sickness that has caused them to have to protect themselves, and I immediately feel sorry for them, so I began to pray for them.

We as human beings do not understand the power in our words. If I constantly tell you, you are going to die. Then the power in my words can feed into your spirit, and then you will give up on life based on my words.

When I say my word, I am talking at the moment about doctors words. There are also others in other professions who do the same thing. Take a minister for instance. If a minister continually tells you, "you are going to hell". If that is where I am going, why should I try to get to Heaven? I am lost, and will forever be lost. There are those who will seek a second opinion as they should. But what about those who do not seek a second opinion like Children? You have planted a seed into their minds which can destroy their bodies. You continually tell a child they are dumb. What happens? If I am dumb why should I study? Why should I try to do better? You are lazy and no good. Then I should act that way. That's what you expect of me anyway. How would you want some one to address you? Think before you open your mouth. What harm am I going to do by the words that come out of my mouth? Shouldn't I try to build you up, instead of tarring you down? How would you want to be treated? Look in the mirror at your self, and then you will know how to treat someone else.

I am an adult I know how to pray and seek the Lord God for myself. God is my first and second opinion. Others who do not have that personal relationship seek other authorities. I am not saying that is a bad thing. What I am saying is always see the Lord God even after you have received an opinion from man. We need Doctors they have their place in our lives. Some are good and some are bad, as with all things in the world we live in. Always remember though that they are men and women, they are not God. Listen to Doctors, they have spent many years researching and studying the human body, its functions, its many parts, and how it works. It takes a lot of years of schooling before they become certified and licensed. But when my life is a risk after I have consulted man, who do you think I am going to? Who made this body, who can heal and restore this body, who can raise the dead back to life?

They told us that David has to have a bone marrow transplant. They consulted with us and asked us what do we want to do? I thought that was dumb. You tell me that my child could die if he does not get a bone marrow transplant, and then you ask me what do I want to do. That is like asking me if I want my child to live or to die. What a dumb question. We said that we wanted him to have the transplant. We as humans can be so smart and at the same time we can be so dumb.

We returned home, they told us that they would let us know what actions were to follow after David's lab test comes back. During the time while we were waiting I would anoint David from his head to his feet, praying over him as I anointed him, praying for the Lord my God to heal him. I have seen the power of God heal people through my anointing, laying hands on them, and praying for them. I anointed him, and I prayed for him twice before his lab test came back. I was praying that his lab test would com back negative. I did not want him to go through the procedure. I wanted God to heal him right now. I would cry out Lord heal my child, take this disease away from him.

One of the tests they had to do was, to put him to sleep and take a long needle and insert it into his hip bone and draw marrow from it to see if the disease was present in his body. They said that they would put him to sleep and that he would not feel a thing. Although I knew that this had to be done. I did not like the idea of them sticking a needle into his body to the bone. I did not object openly though, while hoping that the test would come back negative. I was praying and crying out to God that the results from the test would show that their diagnosis was wrong. When the test came back positive I began to ask God why? I know that my prayer was in faith. I know that I did not waver in my faith. I knew that I have faith as great as a mustard seed. I knew that I had been used By God to pray for others and see them healed. But my son David's test came back positive. Why Lord Jesus? I began to look at myself. What have I done, or what have I not done that you oh God have not granted my request? All sort of questions began to go through my mind. The scripture kept coming to me, "He saved others," they said, "but he can't save himself". Matthew 27:42. I used to lay hands on others and pray that they would be healed, but my child, my flesh and blood was still carrying this disease. I did not question my faith. I did not question the reality of the Lord God. I wanted to know what I was doing or not doing? In times like these we look for answers. Job looked for answers also and he questioned God about him not having done any thing to suffer as he was. I did not do that, I looked at me. My focus was on me and not on anyone else. I cried out, Lord what have I done, or what am I not doing that you did not fulfill my request? I know that you are there; I know you hear my prayers. Why Lord? Why? Please tell me why must my son go through this? I had made up my mind that I would not stop crying out until the Lord answered me. This would be my daily prayer. For two and a half months

I cried out day and night, and I did not get an answer. I was determined to find out why. I was not going to give up until the Lord answered me. At Church I would listen closely to the sermons seeking an answer. I would pay close attention to godly people talking to me, praying all the time that God would speak through them to me. I would pay special attention to my dreams, hoping that the Lord would answer me in my dreams. I would fast and pray, five days without food and water, sometimes seven days without food and water. I was on a mission and I was not going to give up, I was not going to back down.

Almost three months had gone by and there was still no answer. During this time they were checking Daniel, David's twin brother to see if he would be a good match (donor) for the transplant. I had told them to check me out also. I did not want Daniel to go through any pain or suffering from the procedure. I wanted to spare him from this. They said that since they were twins that Daniel would be the best candidate for the transplant. They said that they would have to run some test on him to see if the disease was not present in him also. Daniel's test came back as a good match, and they did not find any traces of the disease in him. I was very happy, but very sad at the same time. I wanted to do this for my child. I would lay down my life for my children. They told us that because Daniel was David's twin, Daniel would be the best candidate. They said that David was lucky because he had a twin brother who is a perfect match and that his body possibly would not reject the new bone marrow. That is one of the concerns they have about transplants. Taking parts from one body and transferring those parts to another body. We were told if the body does not recognize the added part it could reject the transplant, then they would have to look for another donor. That could be timely, costly and disastrous. They talked about luck. I do not believe in luck. **Luck - defined by Webster – A force that brings good fortune or adversity. The events or circumstances that operate for or against an individual.** Luck takes away the control of God. Luck states that things happen by circumstance or by chance. The Lord God is in control of all things past and present. Nothing happens in this universe by luck. God knows what has been, what is, and what will be. God directs and controls the present and future. Not some mysticism or mystic.

We talked to Daniel to see if he would be willing to do this for his brother? The doctors explained the procedure to him. He would have to have surgery, they would put him to sleep and take two long needles inserting them into both his hip bones and draw marrow from them. The surgery would take four hours. They told him about the pain he would suffer after surgery, but they said they would give him something for the pain and it would go away. The pain would not last long. They were very through explaining everything to Daniel. Taking him through all of the procedures, and his mother and I also. Daniel consented and said that he would do that for his brother. I was very proud of him. I wanted to cry. Daniel said that he wanted to see his brother well. **John 15:13 "Greater love has no one than this that he lay down his life for his friends"**. Daniel is more than a brother to David, he is his best friend.

We had to go from Scottishrite Children's Hospital to Egelson Hospital at Emory, where the procedure would be preformed. For a while were going back and forth from one hospital to another. They would see David once and sometimes twice a month. As the time for his surgery came closer the visits were frequent and long. Everything at this time was transferred to Egelson Hospital at Emory. The Doctors and Nurses at Egelson were very nice and informative. They held counseling sessions explaining everything that David and Daniel would go through. They made me feel very secure. I was glad that we were there and not at Scottishrite. I did not feel good at all at Scottishrite. Do not misunderstand me. There were some nice Nurses and Doctors at Scottishrite also. There was one Nurse that would always smile and talk to us. It was a joy to see her. It was just the one Doctor that pushed my button. Her assistant was very nice though. I liked him very much. He had good bedside manners, a very concerned and knowledgably young man. It is a shame that in this life the good has to work with the bad. And that is bad.

The doctors, Nurses and staff at Egelson would always greet us with a smile. They wanted to make sure that we knew everything that would happen. Before David was admitted we would spend all day long for a week going to different counseling sessions, going to different examinations. They were very informative and I really appreciated that. They made us feel very comfortable. Egelson is a large hospital with different wings. After a while I knew my way around the whole hospital.

The Doctor who specializes in the Disease was not going to do the procedure, but one of his colleagues who new as much about the disease and worked closely with him would do the transplant. We met her, she was very nice also. She told us step by step what to expect. She was good. She addressed a lot of my concerns, and eased my mind, and I had a lot of questions and concerns. If a question came to mind, I asked. I wanted to know everything. What was going to happen now, and what to expect later. Tell me everything. I do not want any surprises.

The big day came January 2, 2008. David was going to be admitted. We were ready to get this over. We had been going back and forth since September of 2007, Talking, listening, examinations, getting angry, praying and crying. I was tired of my child going through this now. Let's bring this to an end. Isn't it amazing, when we are in the mist of our suffering we want to rush to see the end. Not only to see the end, but to end it. The faster, the better. How many times do we stop and think about the lessons we are learning while we are going through. What is the Lord God teaching us? He does not allow us to go through things in life just to be going through. God is not that kind of a God. God has a purpose for everything that happens in our lives. He is not a God that will play with our lives just for sport. Everything that happens to us is to, correct us, to punish us, to challenge us to be and to do better, to strengthen us for the challenges of life, to draw us closer to Him, and mostly because He loves us. No one likes to stay in the fire. Even the evil one does not want to suffer. Look around you, get your mind off of your suffering, stop having a pity party, and ask God to show you, and to help you to learn the lesson He is teaching you. And then be patient until He delivers you. You can not get out of the fire until He says it is over anyway. So why fight, looking sad and down cast won't solve a thing, it will just add wrinkles to your face and bags under your eyes. Strokes, high blood pressure, meanness, irritability, obesity, and fast death, are sure to be your destiny. Help me to know why I am here and the lesson I should learn while I am here. If I learn the lesson well then I will not have to come back here again. And the greatest thing, I can help someone else to go through, to be able to wait on the Lord Jesus to deliver them from their suffering, because I have been there.

The Tuesday before David was to be admitted we had to carry him to the hospital for them to surgically install a center line into his heart through his chest. This line would be used for them to administer medicines to him; also it would be used to administer the bone marrow in a liquid form in to his heart. There would be two lines that were installed into the top of his heart. These lines were exposed out side of his chest. They did this so they would not have to keep sticking him with needles every time he was to receive medicines and the new bone marrow. I was wondering how they would administer the new bone marrow into his system. I was wondering if they would have to cut him open and insert the new marrow into one of his bones. I found out that the procedure was very simple. The only surgery he would have to have was to put the tubes into his body, and then surgery to remove the tubes.

They told us that once they collected the new bone marrow they would administer it to him through an IV into these tubes they had placed into his heart. They said that the new bone marrow would find its way through the body to where it was supposed to go.

How awesome is God? How wondrous is His creation? Each part of the body knows where it is supposed to be. Each part knows its specific function. Like a well oiled machine are the workings of the human body. The parts of our body know what they are supposed to do and when they are supposed to do their part. And look at the brain, all it does is send out electrical waves (impulses) controlling the whole body, a small mass controlling a larger mass.

I stand in awe of the Lord God and His creation. Can man duplicate what only God has made? Although man may try he can not make the perfect human being. He can not duplicate life. Look at a tree for instance, can man make a tree? He can transplant, graft, water and feed, but with all his knowledge he can not make a tree. And no matter how many his efforts he can not even make a tree grow. It is the Lord God who provides the elements (water, sunlight, earth) and all the other elements to make a tree grow. It is the Lord God who provides food for His creation. All things eatable comes from Him. Those things which sustain life are Gods creation. Even the medicines we use are made from Gods creations. How can we exist with out Him? It is God who provides food not only for human beings, but also for plants, animals, fish, and yes even for those pesky bugs that live on this earth with us. What can man do without the Lord God? Though some may not want to acknowledge Him as Lord and Master, all people acknowledge that there is a higher power at work in our universe. One day all will have to acknowledge that God and The Lord Jesus are Lord and Master of all creation. See Isaiah 45:23-24, Romans 14:11-12 for references.

The doctors told us that they would have to administer Chemotherapy to David to destroy the diseased bone marrow and blood cells in his body. They told us that one of the affects of the chemo was that David would loose all of his hair. But his hair would grow back once the chemo had been taken out of his body. They told us the benefits and the possible long term risk of performing this procedure. I was not interested in the long term risk. This had to be done to save my Childs life right now. I knew that God could and would handle the future; my concern was how were they going to sustain him after they had destroyed his bone marrow and all of his blood cells? They told us that they would give him blood transfusions if needed, and that they have certain medicines that would sustain him until the new bone marrow started to produce new blood cells that were needed. I understood, but I did not understand, but my faith was in God. I knew that the Lord My God was in control. I placed all of my trust in the lord God and Christ Jesus.

Isaiah 54:16 – "See it is I who created the blacksmith who fans the coals into flame, and forges a weapon fit for its work. And it is I who has created the destroyer to work havoc; No weapon forged against you will prevail, and you will refute every tongue that accuses you. This is the heritage of the servants of the Lord, and this is their vindication from me." Declares the Lord. NIV. This scripture came to me as I was thinking about them giving David chemotherapy. I thought about how they would administer this destroyer into his body to kill off not only the disease that was there, but to also destroy all of his blood cells. Isn't it awesome how God can make a destroyer to kill off a destroyer? For example,

God made Gabriel and Michael and called them His warring Angels. God has Angels whom He has created to be destroyers. Remember when the children of Israel were in Egypt, when God sent Moses to Pharaoh to tell him to let the Israelites go? Remember one of the plagues God sent among the Egyptians was a destroying Angel to destroy all of the first born children in Egypt. Exodus 11:1-15.

God can use a destroyer to bring about deliverance, to do His will. Also remember King Nebuchadnezzar, how God used him to punish His children? God used him to punish Israel and Judah. God also punished him and took his kingdom away from him. Second Kings 24: - Chronicles and Daniel. You can find other references in the Bible. All destroyers other than God's Angels have to pay for their destruction.

God used the destroyer call chemotherapy to kill the diseased bone marrow and blood cells in David's body. They would use water to flush the chemotherapy the destroyer out of David's body. Then his body would be used to repair the damage the chemotherapy did. **John 3:1-6 – (1) Now there was a man of the Pharisees named Nicodemus, a member of the Jewish ruling council. (2) He cam to Jesus at night and said, "Rabbi, we know you are a teacher who has come from God. For no one could perform the miraculous signs you are doing if God were not with him." In reply Jesus declared," I tell you the truth no one can see the kingdom of God unless he is born again." (4) "How can a man be born when he is old? Nicodemas asked, "Surely he cannot enter a second time into his mother's womb to** be born!" (5) Jesus answered." I tell you the truth; no one can enter the Kingdom of God unless he is born of <u>water and the Spirit</u>. (6) Flesh gives birth to flesh, but the spirit gives birth to Spirit. NIV

In the beginning of creation when the Lord God was in a creative mode **Genesis 1:-2:. In the beginning God created the Heavens and the Earth (2) Now the earth was formless and empty, darkness was over the surface of the deep, and the Spirit of God was hovering over the waters.**

David's body would become lifeless for a while. The old David would die. Now this statement would take some thinking and praying to understand. I ask that you would pray and seek God for understanding. Let me give you some help, passing on to you what God showed me. First Christ said "you must be born again." **<u>To be born again you must die</u>**. Some people, Pastors, Theologians, Professionals, and Doctors of Theology may theorize all sorts of explanations for this statement "you must die". Some will say "that this refers to a spiritual death". Some will say that "this is a death in the flesh (wants, desires which are contrary to the will of the Lord God)". Some will repeat the statement that Nicodemas made, **"How can a man be born again after he has left his mothers womb?" John 3:4-5.** In this passage the Lord God showed me **<u>Life</u>** and **<u>the Spirit.</u> Life – Leviticus 17:10-11 NIV. (10) Any Israelite or any alien living among them who eats blood, I will set my face against that person who eats blood and will cut him off from his people. (11) <u>For the life of a creature is in the blood. NIV.</u>** The life of all creatures is in the blood of that creature. It is the blood which sustains life. Without blood we can not exist. Blood has to flow to all parts of the body, without blood that part of the body which does not receive it will die. Our blood is made up of cells, or consists of cells and platelets (white, and red) this is the make up of all living creatures.

And the bone marrow produces all of these blood cells. So to destroy your bone marrow would result in destroying your blood cells, and this would mean that you would die. No bone marrow, no blood, no blood, no life, **THE END.** In order for you to continue to walk around, talk, and have the use of your organs on this earth, something has to happen. Something has to sustain your life during your transformation.

The Lord showed me David and the Holy Spirit. **"The earth was formless and <u>empty".</u> Genesis 1:1-2.** David's body would become empty of life (blood). **"The Spirit of God hovered over the waters."** They would use water to cleanse his body from the chemotherapy. It was only by the Spirit of God that his life would be sustained until the new bone marrow started to work, to begin producing new blood, (new blood cells and platelets). He had to be hooked to a monitor and given blood and plasma to sustain his life. Can't you see how we have to be hooked up to God, Christ Jesus and the Holy Spirit to sustain our lives? The Lord God, Christ Jesus and the Holy Spirit have to be hooked up to us to sustain our lives, for us to live, to be alive. I'll write more about this later. I don't want to take you to fast.

The day we took David to the hospital was January 3, 2008. He was admitted on a Thursday. We went to his room to where they said that he would spend four to six weeks. The Nursing staff was very friendly and the Doctors also. They explained everything to us and got us settled in. His room was in an isolation ward. They called it a critical word. The children in this area were not to leave the area. They were restricted to certain areas in this isolation ward. There were children there with very serious diseases. No child or parent was allowed to go into another Childs room. I kind of broke that rule. I will explain later. They kept the doors to every room closed. There were bottles of sterilized solutions at the doors out side and inside the rooms. You had to wash your hands with this solution before you entered the room and every time you gave David anything or touched him. Everything that touched him or came close to him had to be sterile.

They gave strict rules about clothing you ware when visiting him. He could not eat any outside foods. All of his food was specially made in the hospital. They monitored his diet closely. If you had any sort of cold they would not allow you to enter the ward where any of the children were kept. They had special computers for them, games, and they even had areas separated within this ward where children with certain diseases could not go. They were very serious about germs. They kept the area germ free. This was done because it was very important to keep him from getting sick when his blood counts were low. During this time he would not have any immune system. He would be acceptable to contract a disease and that would be very critical for him. At that time when his immune system was low we could loose him if he were to get sick. No one with a cold could enter his room, or even go into the ward where the special children were. Everything in David's room was sterile and they made sure they kept it that way. There were double doors that were kept closed at all times to the area where David was, and a door to his room. You had to touch a button and the doors would open automatically. We had to ware special hospital clothing over our clothes and those wraps over our feet. David had to ware gloves at all times and a mask. To get to the rooms in this ward you had to go pass the Nurses station. Someone in the Nurses area had their eyes on you when you entered and when you came out. They had a full kitchen for parents, and also a lounging area with television, computers and telephones for parents. The children admitted could not go into those areas. In the rooms they had beds for parents to stay with their children. His mother and I took turns staying with him. One of us would be there all night every night. I was there every day after I got off work. I did not miss a day.

His mother would stay home some weekends with his brother, but there was not a weekend that I was not there. I did not want my son to be there, or think he was going to be there without someone in his family present. Daniel, his brother would visit him on the weekends. He would call him just about every day.

When they started the chemotherapy on February 1, 2008 to destroy David's blood cells I began to pray very hard for him and for me. I did not want him to see how concerned I was. Sometimes I would have to leave the room to stop from crying. I knew that God had everything under control, but I am still human, and this is my child going through this. What parent would not get emotional at a time like this? I would not allow him to see me tearing up. I was always smiling and jovial around him. I wanted to keep his spirits up. I did not want him to think that something was going wrong. It was not easy. Sometimes I would have to go out of the room into the reception area and take a good long breath and then go back into his room. When his mother and Daniel were there I would walk down to the cafeteria, or around the lobby to keep myself together. It was especially hard for me when his hair started falling out. His hair would come out in lumps when he would take a bath. He wore a scarf so it would not be visible. It hurt worst when all of his hair fell out.

After all of David's blood cells had been destroyed they took Daniel to surgery to draw bone marrow from him. I went with Daniel while their mother stayed with David. I sat there when they put him to sleep. Then they came and got him and took him to the operating room. My heart was heavy. Both of my boys were lying in a hospital bed. I was so hurt that I became numb. When they drew the bone marrow from Daniel they brought it to me to let me see it. They had two bags about 11" tall and about 5" wide. They said that they could not draw too much because it would be harmful for Daniel. Once they had the bone marrow they said they had to take it to be processed before they would give it to David. I waited for Daniel to come out of the recovery room, and then rolled him in a wheel chair back to the room where David was. Daniel was very drowsy, and stiff, When we got back to the room he went back to sleep.

Later that evening the Doctors and Nurses that attended David came into the room with the bags of bone marrow.

It was like they were having a party. They came in taking pictures laughing and very happy. They hung the bone marrow onto David's IV stand and started administering the bone marrow. Everyone was exciting. They said that it would take a while to see if his body would accept or reject the bone marrow. Here I go again praying crying out to the Lord that David's body would accept the bone marrow. I did not want Daniel to go through that again, and I did not want them to have to find another donor. The wait was on. They said that his red blood cells would start to increase first, then his white, and last his platelets. Before they had administered the bone marrow they had to check him to see if the entire diseased cells and bone marrow had been destroyed, they did not want to give him new bone marrow and then it would become infected. Everything was going well. From the time they gave him the bone marrow until his body began to accept it seemed forever. It took about a week before all of his blood counts began to come back to normal. And the following week his platelets began to come back to normal. All of the doctors and Nurses were very surprised to see it happen so fast. They thought it would take longer. They had calculated four weeks, and it took only three. Look at the Lord God work. When I think about three, the first thing that came to my mind was the Father, Son and the Holy Spirit. I really saw God in action. You talk about someone rejoicing, happy and praising my Father God, The Lord Jesus, and the Holy Spirit, I was walking on cloud nine. I was so thankful, so happy, and so joyful, that I could have shouted it all over the hospital. The Lord God had heard the cries of His children and had healed my son. There was not a sign of the disease left in his body. I would laugh at him and say that there is no more David, now he is David Daniel. Truly you are one. Daniel is inside of you, you are a new creation.

Look at the Lord, He took my son and showed me what salvation in its natural form is all about. He showed me though suffering, healing, deliverance, and being born again. All these things he showed me by using my son David. David suffered in his body. David was healed and delivered from the diesels. David was born again. Te old David died, they took all of the old David's blood out of him. When the blood is gone we die, they drained his old blood, and Just as Christ did He put new blood into our bodies.

Daniel was a representative a symbol of Christ Jesus. It is the blood of Christ that saves us. It is the blood of Christ running through our bodies that preserves us. It is the power of the Holy Spirit in our bones making new bone marrow which in turn makes new blood that sustains us. And it too water washing all of our old selves away the disease (sin inside of us) that made all of this possible. The Lord God showed me real salvation. It is no longer a mystery to me. The Lord blessed my eyes and my mind to behold what many do not understand. I learned the hard way, through my suffering, and the suffering of my family.

Before I go I said that I would tell you how I got in trouble in the ward.

One day as I was in the lounge a lot of people began to come in. Most of them were young people. All of them had sad faces. I over heard what they were talking about.

They would be crying in the hallways and next to the elevators. There were a lot of them and they were coming in an out of the isolation ward where David was kept. I was very concerned for my child because some of them were lingering out side in the hallways next to David's room. I did not see any masks on them, nor did they have on any protective clothing. That bothered me. David was in a critical state. His counts had not completely come up. I talked to David's mother in disbelief. I wanted to know why the staff was allowing all of these people to venture in and out of the sterile area. I would always look first out of David's room to see if the hallways were clear before I would allow David to leave his room. I asked one of David's nurses what was going on across the hallway. She told that there was a young baby over there with a brain tumor that was expecting to die at anytime. I began to feel sorry for the child, and the family. My heart went out to them. One Saturday as I arrived back at the hospital the crowd was larger. They were in the lounging area, in the hallways, and in the room. The mother and dad of the baby would come in and out of the room. The mother and dad were young. This was their first child. God showed me their spirits. Then I began to cry out to him even more. I had already heard about one child that died while we were there with cancer. I had an opportunity to console and pray with his mother. I was at work when that child died. I would see his mother in the lounging area. We talked briefly. She told me that her child had cancer, and that she was holding on. They were from somewhere up north. I had made up my mind to go and pray for her and the child one day as I was returning, but I never got the chance. The Lord took the child the same day that

I was going to go and pray. That hurt me deeply. I was there and I did not take time to go and pray for a child in need of prayer. I said that will not happen again. I was so concerned about my child that I over looked work that needed to be done. I did not even have the opportunity to pray for the child's mother. I know that God honors our prayers, and sometimes God will put stumbling blocks in our way to keep us away from what He is going to do. That did not make me feel better though. I still carried that burden in my heart. I said the very next time I come across that situation I would put all aside and go and pray for the child and their parents.

When I learned about what was going on across the hall I began to ask God should I go and Pray. I did not want to go where I was not wanted. One day I was coming back to the room the dad and mother were standing in the hallway. I asked them about their child. They told me what the doctors had told them. They said that it would be just a matter of time before the child would pass. All of the family and friends were there in support of them. I asked them had a minister been there to pray with them. They told me no. I told them that I was a minister, and I asked them could I come in to pray for the child. They gladly accepted. As we went into the room it was full of people. There was hardly any room to walk. I looked around as the mother introduced me. The grandmother was holding the child. The child's head was an abnormal size because of the brain tumor. If you could see the child, it would tare your heart out. I felt so many different spirits in the room that was upsetting me. I had this uptight feeling in my stomach. I can always feel unfamiliar spirits. I know when a spirit is around that does not belong there.

I told the crow of people that were there that I wanted to pray for the child, his mother and dad. I asked everyone to leave except the child's mother, dad, grandmothers on both sides and one lady I felt good about her spirit, and the lady that was holding and rocking the baby. They grumbled and began to leave. I heard some of them say "who is he?" As they left I told them that I will seek the Lord and Pray the prayer He puts in my mouth. As I was talking to them, the Lord showed me that the parents were not married. I asked them was that right? They said yes. They said that they were planning to get married. I knew that the only reason they said that was for the sake of the child. I know in their hearts that they did not really want to get married. I did not reveal this to them though. Why should I? I was there to pray not to convict. They were going through enough why should I add to their misery. Sometimes when God shows us something, we have to be careful In the ways we use the message. It is not ours to destroy, but to build up. Sometimes God will make me speak bold and tough, but this was not the time. There is a time and a place for everything under the sun. God showed me a few things about those who were still left in the room. I began to minister His word accordingly, before I began to pray for the child. I guess God was setting the stage up for them to hear the pray that was about to be prayed. When I went to the child I anointed the grandmother that was holding the child, and then the child. I began to pray what was given to me. As I prayed tears began to flow heavily down my face until I could hardly talk. I knew that God was going to take the child away. I prayed heavily for the child and his parents, asking for the forgiveness of sins. I did not say their sin, but the forgiveness of sins. I prayed that the Lord's will would be done with the child. I do not usually pray that way when I am praying for someone sick. There have been occasion when the Lord has lead me to pray that way when the person is going to leave. This was one of those occasions. It is wrong to pray any other way giving false hope when God has already shown you what He is going to do. You will make people loose faith in God through your prayers. I know of only two times God changed His mind. One was when He was going to destroy the Children of Israel at Mount Sinai. The other was when Hezekiah turned his face to the wall and cried to the Lord and asked Him to let him live. Exodus 32:9-14, 2 Kings 20:1-11.

This was not the time though they had committed a sin and God showed me that he was going to take the child. I cried out harder for the child and his parents, until sweat and tears began to roll down my body. I did not let them know what God was going to do. They were going through enough. After the prayer was over I left the room. When I went out side, those I had asked to leave turned their backs to me and began to mummer about me under their tongs. I did not care though. I was not there to put on a show. I was there to do my Masters will. The next day as I was coming to David's room one of the ladies that I had asked to stay stopped me in the hallway and thanked me for praying for the child. She thanked me for my boldness in asking the others to leave. She said that she was a Christian and that she had also prayed for the child. We shared for a while about her experiences and thank each other. Two days later the child went back to God. I told the young man and lady that it was not over. I told them that they were young and can start a family, but they have to do it God's way His way is the only way it will work. Both of them said honestly this time that they were going to get married. I began to thank God. God moves in mysterious ways. He can take, and He can restore if we obey Him. There is no one who knows that better than me.

As I said earlier I got in trouble for being in the room. One of the nurses came into the room to check on the child, while I was praying. She did what she had to do and then left. Later as I was at the nurse's station she told me that I had no right to be in that room. I told her that I had the parent's permission so I went in. I felt her spirit also, and I did not stand there and argue with her I just turned and walked away. The next day the head nurse stopped me in the hallway and confronted me also. She told me that I should not have been in the room because I could have carried some foreign thing back into David's room endangering his life. I listened to her politely, and then I told her that I am a Minister and by law I can inter any room in this hospital if I am asked by the parents or patient. I thanked her for her concern though, and I told her that I would not do anything to endanger my son's life. If I had not been sent into that room by my God I never would have entered it. She had nothing else to say after that. From then on the other nurse would not enter David's room because of me. After that all the nurses and Doctors would look at me when I would walk pass the nurses station. One of David's nurses was a male; we had to have the same conversation. I stood my ground though. I was not going to let them stop me from doing my Masters will. I knew that God would protect my child. Even one of the ladies that clean up came to me and said that I had done the right thing. She said that she had been talking to the nurses and Doctors about to many people being in that room, and she was not able to do her work. No doctor confronted me about the incident though.

In the end God showed up and showed out. They had said that David would be in the hospital five to six weeks. David was there only three weeks. Look at my God work. Praises to His name, Amen

I pray that the things I have been allowed to see, to hear, to know, to suffer through will be a blessing to you. I have made a lot of mistakes in my life, but my life was destined to be this way. If it were not for my failures and successes I could not write these things down for you. My journey is not over yet, but I do not know what tomorrow will bring. I don't know if I will write a sequel, or if someone will write it for me. It took long enough for me to write these pages (January 20, 2009). I hope that what I have been allowed to write will bring you closer to the Lord God, Christ Jesus and the Holy Spirit. Let no one take your joy away, there is a better day coming just around the corner have faith.

May the Lord God's light shine all around you, May His love always be with you, May His blessings overshadow you, May His saving grace always protect you.

In the Name of the Father, the Son Christ Jesus, and the Sweet Holy Spirit

Amen